The Impact of Anti-Money Laundering Legislation on the Legal Profession in South Africa

ABRAHAM JOHN HAMMAN

The Impact of Anti-Money Laundering Legislation on the Legal Profession in South Africa

GALDA VERLAG 2018

Bibliografische Information der Deutschen Nationalbibliothek
Die Deutsche Nationalbibliothek verzeichnet diese Publikatioan in der Deutschen Nationalbibliografie; detaillierte bibliografische Daten sind im Internet über http://dnb.ddb.de abrufbar.

Originally presented as the authors' doctoral thesis:
University of the Western Cape, Republic of South Africa
June 2015

ISBN 978-3-96203-053-7 (Print)
ISBN 978-3-96203-054-4 (Ebook)

TABLE OF CONTENTS

SYNOPSIS

This work investigates the legislative measures employed in South Africa to combat the implication of lawyers in money laundering schemes. Criminals make use of sophisticated technological means to transfer money and launderers routinely approach lawyers to assist them in their illegal endeavours. The legal profession is almost tailor-made for abuse by launderers, because lawyers work with huge amounts of money, clients are entitled to legal professional privilege and the right to legal representation is guaranteed constitutionally.

The South African anti-money laundering regime, for the most part, is contained in two statutes, the Financial Intelligence Centre Act (FICA) and the Prevention of Organised Crime Act (POCA). Whilst FICA and POCA require the legal profession to be vigilant and accountable in the fight against money laundering, unfortunately they also infringe on hard-won rights, such as legal professional privilege, the right to legal representation and attorney-client confidentiality. The study considers South Africa's efforts to fulfil its international anti-money laundering obligations whilst upholding the criminal procedural rights guaranteed in the Constitution. It is suggested that certain sections of FICA and POCA fail to find the required balance between protecting citizens from the harms of money laundering and protecting the fundamental rights of attorneys and their clients.

Lawyers are in a unique position of trust and in some instances have access to information that may incriminate their clients. Unfortunately, in its quest to combat money laundering, Parliament did not consider seriously enough the position of lawyers and took the easy option of criminalising fees paid with tainted funds, as well as the non-submission of suspicious transaction reports (STRs) and cash transaction reports (CTRs). As a result, the South African legal profession is saddled with unacceptable constraints.

KEY TERMS

Money laundering control
Attorneys
Financial Intelligence Centre Act of 2001
Prevention of Organised Crime Act of 1998
Lawyer-facilitated money laundering
Attorney-client confidentiality
Legal professional privilege
Right to legal representation
Right to exercise a profession
Tainted fees
Independence of the legal profession
Suspicious transaction reports
Cash transaction reports
Exemption from prosecution

ACKNOWLEDGMENTS

I would like to thank various people who have been involved, in one way or another, in the preparation of this study. First and foremost, I would like to thank my Promoter, Professor Lovell Fernandez, Deputy Dean of the Faculty of Law, University of the Western Cape, to whom I am deeply indebted for his guidance during the writing of this research and for his useful, critical and always sagacious comments on my drafts. He suggested that the impact of money laundering legislation on the legal profession was a question worth investigating for a doctoral study.

In addition, I would like to express my sincere gratitude to Professor Raymond Koen, Deputy Dean and Head of the Department of Criminal Justice and Procedure at the University of the Western Cape, for his guidance, assistance and insights. His attention to detail, reviews, and comments on the drafts of this study were invaluable. I am indebted also to Professor Julia Sloth-Nielsen, former Dean of the Faculty of Law, University of the Western Cape, who was instrumental in my procuring the NRF funding that allowed me a sabbatical to finalise this study. Thanks to the NRF for making funds as a sabbatical grant available to enable me complete this study.

I am grateful also to Professor Bernard Martin, Dean of the Faculty of Law, for his encouragement, support and advice during the writing of this work. I am appreciative also to my colleagues in the Department of Criminal Justice and Procedure for all their support during our departmental research seminars, where I presented parts of this study.

My family always took a keen interest in and supported my work. I would like to say thank you. In this respect, a very special thanks must go to my wife, Merle, for her assistance, enthusiasm and sound advice. To my children, Adrian and Nicole thanks for your input, thoughts an unwavering encouragement.

LIST OF ACRONYMS

ABA	American Bar Association
ACTEC	American College of Trust and Estate Counsel
AFF	Attorneys Fidelity Fund
AML	Anti-Money Laundering
AU	African Union
BIS	Bank for International Settlements
BSA	Bank Secrecy Act (USA)
CBA	Canadian Bar Association
CCE	Continuing Criminal Enterprise Statute (USA)
CDD	Customer Due Diligence
CFA	Comprehensive Forfeiture Act (USA)
CFT	Combating the Financing of Terrorism
CoE	Council of Europe
CTR	Currency Transaction Report/Reporting
DNFBPs	Designated Non-Financial Business Professionals
EAAA	Estate Agency Affairs Act (South Africa)
EU	Countries on the European Continent subject to EU Law
FATF	Financial Action Task Force on Money Laundering
FFC	Fidelity Fund Certificate
FLSC	Federation of Law Societies (Canada)
FICAA	Financial Intelligence Centre Amendment Act (South Africa)
FICA	Financial Intelligence Centre Act (South Africa)
FIC	Financial Intelligence Centre (South Africa)
FinCen	Financial Crimes Enforcement Network (USA)

FINTRAC	Financial Transactions and Reports Analysis Centre of Canada
FIU	Financial Intelligence Unit
IMF	International Monetary Fund
IRC	Internal Revenue Code (USA)
KYC	Know Your Customer/Know Your Client
LSSA	Law Societies of South Africa
MLCA	Money Laundering Control Act (USA)
NDPP	National Director of Public Prosecutions
NTO	No Tipping Off
PCMLTFA	Proceeds of Crime (Money Laundering) and Terrorist Financing Act (Canada)
POCA	Prevention of Organised Crime Act (South Africa)
POCDATARA	Protection of Constitutional Democracy against Terrorism and Related Activities Act (South Africa)
RBA	Risk-Based Approach
RICO	Racketeer Influenced and Corrupt Organizations Act (USA)
STR	Suspicious Transaction Report/Reporting
UN	United Nations
UNCAC	United Nations Convention against Corruption
UNCTOC	UN Convention against Transnational Organised Crime
US	United States of America
USA PATRIOT ACT	Uniting and Strengthening America by Providing Appropriate Tools Required to Intercept and Obstruct Terrorism Act
USC	United States Code
$	United States Dollar & Canadian Dollar
R	South African Rand
€	Euro

1

SETTING THE SCENE

1.1 Introduction

According to the various Typologies Reports of the Financial Action Task Force (FATF), lawyers, accountants and other professionals who offer legal and financial advice have become the common element in complex money laundering schemes.[1] As a result of the growth of organised crime internationally, South Africa, too, has been targeted by organised criminal syndicates.[2] The country has become a destination for launderers who attempt to retain the benefits of their criminal activity without being detected.[3]

The FATF was established specifically to combat money laundering. South Africa is a member and has enacted laws to combat money laundering and the financing of terrorism to give effect to the FATF's Recommendations.[4] South Africa's anti-money laundering laws also compel the legal profession to combat money laundering.[5] Lawyers carry onerous reporting duties to prevent them from being used by money launderers as conduits for laundering the proceeds of crime.[6]

---

[1]FATF Report (2000-2001: 1, 2 & 14), FATF Report (2003-2004: 24) and FATF Report (2013:13).

[2]*Roestof v Cliffe Dekker Hofmeyr Inc* ZAGPPHC 219 (2012).

[3]*S v Hattingh*, Unreported, Bloemfontein Regional Court, Case Number 17/518/10. *S v Price* 2003 2 SACR 551 (SCA), *Roestof v Cliffe Dekker Hofmeyr Inc* ZAGPPHC 219 (2012).

[4]The FATF, established in 1989, is an inter-governmental body whose purpose is the development and promotion of national and international policies to combat money laundering and terrorist financing.

[5]Sections 28 and 29 of FICA 38 of 2001.

[6]Schedule 1 of FICA 38 of 2001 includes attorneys in its list of accountable institutions.

This study explores national and international measures that are in place to prevent lawyers from being used as money laundering channels. It studies the constraints placed on the profession by these measures and the effects they have for lawyers in the exercise of their profession.

1.2 Background to Study

During the 1980s there was a growth in organised crime internationally. In response, the international community launched a new anti-crime initiative targeting the proceeds of crime, specifically money laundering .[7] The FATF formulated international anti-money laundering (AML) standards in 1990. The 40 + 9 recommendations were published and a number of issues pertaining to money laundering were addressed.[8] These include customer identification and national and international information sharing. Most countries subscribe to these standards and a number of UN conventions and directives emanating particularly from the European Commission also require compliance with them.[9]

In 2000, South Africa signed the UN Convention against Transnational Organised Crime, which came into effect on 29 September 2003. By ratifying this instrument, South Africa agreed to incorporate its provisions into domestic law, thereby committing itself to criminalising both corruption and money laundering. In June 2003, the Paris-based FATF accepted South Africa as its thirtieth member.[10] South Africa since has developed a comprehensive set of overlapping laws to combat money laundering. The main anti-money laundering laws are the Prevention of Organised Crime Act (POCA),[11] the

[7]See Van Jaarsveld (2011: 2) and Burdette (2010: 2).

[8]These consist of the previously forty FATF recommendations pertaining to international standards on combating money laundering and the financing of terrorism and proliferation, and the nine special FATF recommendations on terrorist financing. They are now known as the FATF Recommendations or FATF Standards (2012).

[9]The Vienna Convention was adopted on 20 December 1988 and entered into force on 11 November 1990, UNCTOC was adopted on 15 November 2000. As regards the European Council Directives, see Council Directive 91/308/EEC (1991 EU ML Directive); Council Directive 2001/97/EC (2001 EU ML Directive); and Council Directive 2005/97/EC (2005 EM ML Directive).

10SA joins anti-dirty money body. http://www.southafrica.info.

[11]Act 121 of 1998. See also Van Jaarsveld (2011: 461) and Burdette (2010: 4).

Financial Intelligence Centre Act (FICA),[12] and the Protection of Constitutional Democracy against Terrorism and Related Activities Act (POCDATARA).[13]

Part of the study is aimed at determining whether POCA and FICA have been effective in curbing the recruitment of lawyers for money laundering purposes. It also investigates whether the obligations placed on lawyers by legislation complies with the South African constitution. In terms of FICA, legal practitioners, as designated non-financial businesses and professions (DNFBPs), have certain obligations that compel them, in addition to identifying and verifying the personal particulars of each client, to keep updated client profiles and records and report all suspicious and unusual transactions to the FIC. Practitioners also are prohibited in terms of FICA from informing clients that a report has been filed. This is the so-called no-tipping-off (NTO) clause. There is also the real possibility that a lawyer could be prosecuted and convicted for being paid a fee with the proceeds of crime.[14] This could have consequences for the right to counsel and a lawyer's right to exercise his profession. These constraints on the legal profession and their effects on attorney-client confidentiality, legal professional privilege, and the right to legal representation are examined in this study. Failure to file a Section 28 cash threshold report (CTR) or a Section 29 suspicious transaction report (STR) in terms of FICA could result in the prosecution of lawyers and the imposition of fines of up to R10 million or a term of imprisonment of up to 15 years. This research evaluates the way in which effect is given to the obligations imposed on lawyers by South Africa's AML legislation. These obligations are analysed against Section 35 of the Constitution[15] to determine whether they are compatible with the Constitution.

There is no doubt a need for laws to eradicate crime, and the AML legislation attempts to do precisely this. However, it also places serious impediments on the legal profession. These affect attorney-client confidentiality, legal professional privilege, and the right to legal representation. To what extent do these legislative measures compromise the independence of the legal profession? Combating the use of lawyers in money laundering schemes is essential in the fight against money laundering, but it should not be pursued

[12]Act 38 of 2001. See also Van Jaarsveld (2011: 461) and Burdette (2010: 4).

[13]Act 33 of 2004. See also Van Jaarsveld (2011: 461) and Burdette (2010: 4).

[14]Jacobs (1989: 309).

[15]Sections 35(2)(b), 35(2)(c), 35(3)(f) and 35(3)(g) of the Constitution of 1996 (and Section 73 of the Criminal Procedure Act (CPA) 51 of 1977).

at the expense of constitutionally entrenched rights and freedoms. The challenge is to strike a balance between protecting the economy from the deleterious effects of money laundering, on the one hand, and giving effect to constitutionally guaranteed rights, on the other.

1.3 Why Combat Money Laundering?

"Money laundering threatens to undermine the principles associated with a free, fair and transparent democratic society because it allows criminals to operate with impunity."[16] It allows criminals to accumulate capital on a huge scale without paying tax. Tax-free income for money launderers means that the government has less money to spend on welfare programmes and other fiscal and social policies. A country notorious for money laundering also deters investors as they cannot be sure whether or not they will fall victim to the crime. This means that money laundering also has a negative impact on international financial markets.[17]

Rampant crime is a huge problem worldwide, not least in South Africa, and the South African courts have singled out crime as a phenomenon of great public concern.[18] The former Chief Justice of South Africa, Chaskalson J, stated that the level of crime in South Africa has reached such alarming proportions that it poses a great threat to the transition to democracy, and the creation of development opportunities for all, which are the primary goals of the Constitution.[19] In *Ferreira v Levin,*[20] it was held that judicial notice should be taken of the particularly high crime rate in South Africa.

According to Cameron, crime denudes the right to freedom and security and deprives the right to property of meaning.[21] In the matrix of South African crime, it is drug trafficking which provides the main predicate offences for

[16]Hinterseer (2000: 23). See also Durrieu (2013:225).

[17]See Hinterseer (2000: 23) and Durrieu (2013:82).

[18]*S v Makwanyane* 1995 6 BCLR CC P 152. Madala J "From the statistics supplied by the Attorney General and what one gleans daily from the newspapers and other media, we live at a time when the crime rate is unprecedented, when the streets of our cities and towns rouse fear and despair in the heart, rather than pride and hope, and this in turn robs us of objectivity and personal concern for our brethren."

[19]*S v Makwanyane* 1995 6 BCLR 665 CC.

[20]*Ferreira v Levin No* 1996 1 BCLR CC 152.

[21]Cameron (1997: 504).

money laundering. Huge amounts of money are usually involved in the illegal drug trade and the police services initially focused their efforts on disrupting the supply of certain narcotic products and then on arresting the leaders or kingpins in the drug business.[22] From the mid – to late 1980s, the focus shifted to targeting the profits of the crime. The logic behind the shift in focus was that seizure or forfeiture of criminal profits would remove the incentive to make money which motivates criminals to continue with their illicit business.[23]

Criminals, obviously, did not want the proceeds of their illegal activity to be seized and/or forfeited, and turned to laundering them. What is more, the criminals are becoming very sophisticated, using banks, other financial institutions, securities brokers, wire-transfer businesses, money remitters and casinos to ply their trade and to launder their money.[24] Attorneys' accounts, which are protected by the legal professional privilege, also provide a vehicle for money launderers to hide their money and to clean it.[25] If a scheme is devised whereby gang members instruct a number of attorneys to represent them, and separate deposits are made into the various attorneys' accounts, it is possible that the origin of the money is not revealed. Criminals utilise the services of legal practitioners in various ways.[26] Lawyers often are consulted for advice on how to establish and register financial or commercial entities, such as companies and trusts.[27] The drafting and execution of various forms of contracts, such as leases, deeds of sale, mortgages and loan agreements, are also part of the daily services rendered by attorneys.[28] Practitioners can represent clients in civil as well as in criminal matters and can be requested by clients to give them advice on how to launder money.[29] The expertise of lawyers, especially conveyancers, can be used in property matters, and that of

[22]See Richards (1999: 45) and Durrieu (2013:86).

[23]See Richards (1999: 45) and Durrieu (2013:199).

[24]See Richards (1999: 45).

[25]FATF Report (2013: 20). See also Allen (1997: 802), Bell (2002: 20), Schneider (2006: 28) and Shepherd (2002: 26).

[26]See Itsikowitz (2006: 78-79), Burdette (2010: 36), Schneider (2006: 27), Hamman & Koen (2012: 73) and Bell (2002: 19).

[27]See Itsikowitz (2006: 78-79), Hamman & Koen (2012: 73), Bell (1999: 105), Bell (2002: 20), Shepherd (2002: 26) and Schneider (2006: 200).

[28]See Itsikowitz (2006: 78-79), Hamman & Koen (2012: 81), Bell (2002: 20), Schneider (2006:32) and Shepherd (2002: 26).

[29]See Schneider (2006: 32), United States v Mcquire 79 F 3d 1396 (5th Cir.1996) and United States v Arditti, 955F, 2d331 (5th Cir.1992).

commercial lawyers can be used to establish separate legal entities.[30] Attorneys and other personnel in a legal practice can become involved, knowingly or unknowingly, in money laundering schemes, where their fees for rendering an array of professional services are paid with tainted money.[31]

Money laundering can have positive elements.[32] The existence of off-shore banking industries has transformed the otherwise dormant economies of many Caribbean nations, such as Aruba and the Netherlands Antilles, and promoted the tourism industry.[33] There are clearly some beneficial spin-offs from having large amounts of money moving in and through a nation's financial sector. However, the negative impact flowing from money laundering practices, such as the corruption of the financial system and all arms of the government of a country, far outweigh whatever gains money laundering can bring to a country.[34]

The real danger of money laundering is that it can destroy the entire global economy and the fact of the matter is that it affects the entire world's financial industry in a catastrophic way.[35] It can result also in the public losing confidence in the integrity of the legal profession, if lawyers are party to money laundering wittingly or unwittingly. This can happen easily, because it is in the nature of legal practice to defend criminals, to incorporate companies, to give advice, to draft agreements, to attend to transferring property and the like. The legal profession is exposed naturally to money launderers who require legal assistance. Lawyers thus need to be on their guard against the possible illegalities of such exposure.

1.4 What is Money Laundering?

The term "money laundering" is relatively new.[36] Initially, the view was held that the term derived from the practice of the Chicago mobsters, such as Al

---

[30]See Schneider (2006: 32), *United States v Foster* 835 F. Supp.360 (1993), *R v Griffiths* [2006] All ER (D) 19 and *S v Hattingh*, Unreported, Bloemfontein Regional Court, Case Number 17/518/10.

[31]See Bell (2002: 19), Bussenius (2004: 1045), Schneider (2006: 28), Irvine & King (1988: 185) and *USA v Velez, Kuehne and Ochoa* US District Court, Southern District of Florida Miami Division, Case No. 05-2-770-CR-COOKE.

[32]See Richards (1999: 45) and Durrieu (2013: 84).

[33]See Richards (1999: 44).

[34]See Richards (1999: 44) and Durrieu (2013: 189).

[35]See Moodley (2008: 68).

[36]See Mugarura (2012: 1), Richards (1999: 43), Shams (2004: 17), Gilmore (2011: 22) and Madinger (2012: 11 & 91).

Capone and his followers in the 1920s,[37] because they bought and operated laundries as fronts to conceal the illegal profits they made from gambling and the illicit sale of liquor. However, the term was first used in a newspaper article on the 1973 Watergate Scandal.[38] In June 1972, five employees of President Nixon's re-election campaign were caught breaking into rival Democratic Party offices at the Watergate complex in Washington DC. They were convicted of burglary and wiretapping. During congressional hearings which followed, it emerged that Nixon had recorded conversations and telephone calls in his office which revealed his role in the cover-up of the burglary and other crimes. The Watergate Scandal led to Nixon's resignation in 1974. It was disclosed later that Nixon had been involved in campaign fraud, political espionage, sabotage, illegal break-ins, improper tax audits and illegal wiretapping on a massive scale. Money obtained from illegal party financing had been deposited into a secret slush fund and then "laundered" in Mexico and repatriated to the US to pay those conducting the operations.[39]

The term was used first in a legal context in the case of *United States v $4,255,625.39. et seq.*[40] This matter was a case of civil forfeiture filed by the government against amounts of money to the tune of $4 255 625 39 and $3 668 639 held in an account at AR Capital Bank in the name of a certain Sonal of Miami Florida. The money had been paid into the account by one Molina. The court stated that the process according to which the money was transferred by Molina to Sonal to Capital Bank, more likely than not, was a money laundering process.[41]

1.4.1 Money Laundering Defined

Money laundering is defined variously. The FATF defines it as "the processing of … criminal proceeds to disguise their illegal origin".[42] The International Monetary Fund (IMF) defines it as a process by which the illicit source of assets obtained or generated by criminal activity is concealed to

---

[37]See Richards (1999: 43), Van Jaarsveld (2011: 161) and Madinger (2012: 11 & 91).

[38]See Mugarura (2012: 1 & 35), Richards (1999: 43), Shams (2004: 17), Gilmore (2011: 22), Madinger (2012: 14) and Leslie (2014: 11).

[39]Richard Nixon http://conservapedia.com. See also Madinger (2012: 14 & 15).

[40]*United States v $4,255,625.39.et seq*, 551 F.Supp.314, SD Fla 1982. See also Richards (1999:43), Shams (2004: 26), Gilmore (2011: 22) and Leslie (2014: 11).

[41]*United States v $4,255,625.39.et seq* 325.

[42]FATF "What is money laundering" http://www.fatf-gafi.org. See also Shams (2004: 44).

obscure the link between the funds and the original criminal activity.[43] Some authors define it as a process of making dirty money appear clean, or as a process of disguising the unlawful source of criminally-derived proceeds to make them appear legal, or as the disguise or concealing of illicit income to make it appear legitimate.[44]

The Financial Intelligence Centre Act of South Africa defines money laundering as:

> "[A]n activity which has or is likely to have the effect of concealing or disguising the nature, source, location, disposition or movement of the proceeds of unlawful activities or any interest which anyone has in such proceeds, and includes any activity which constitutes an offence in terms of Section 64 of this Act or Section 4, 5 or 6 of the Prevention of Organised Crime Act."[45]

From the above definitions it is clear that money laundering can be described as a process designed to legalise illegal income or assets.[46] This process, relatively easy or very complicated, can involve a number of transactions and a number of participants. It includes committing crime(s) to acquire the dirty money or assets,[47] intermingling them with legitimate funds,[48] concealing the origin of the money,[49] and creating the appearance of legitimacy of the

[43]Money laundering http://www.imf.org. See also the definition in Hinterseer (1997: 54).

[44]See Unger (2007: 15), Mugarura (2012: 9), Madinger 2012: 6), Woods (1998: 56) and Richards (1999: 44).

[45]Section 1 of FICA. See also Van Jaarsveld (2011: 29 & 474).

[46]See Shams (2004: 45) and Gilmore (2011: 35).

[47]The proceeds need not always be cash: they can assume whatever form in assets such as diamonds, gold, credit cards slips, stocks and bonds, cashier cheques, airplanes, rare coins, livestock, postal money orders, airline tickets, and wire transfers. Other synonyms, such as, "tainted money", "illegal money", "hot money", or "black money", are all used to describe the proceeds of crime. See also Shams (2004: 49), Madinger (2012: 5), Richards (1999: 44), Hamman & Koen (2012: 69), Rider (1999: 212) and Van Jaarsveld (2011: 575).

[48]During this process the illicit proceeds of the criminal activities are intermingled with legitimate funds, which means that the "dirty money" is mixed with the "clean money". This can occur when criminals deposit money into their bank accounts or into the bank accounts of their lawyers.

[49]The main aim of the money launderer is to hide or disguise the fact that the money that is finally merged into the legal financial system derives from illegal activity.

money at the end of the process.[50] Although some commentators hold that the money ought to have been shifted through other jurisdictions,[51] it is submitted that this is not an essential requirement for money laundering.[52] Large cash amounts obtained illegally constitute "dirty" money[53] which needs to be "cleaned" before it can be injected into the legitimate economy and permit whoever has access to it, to use it freely and without any fear of prosecution. In essence, no matter what definition is used, the main aim of a money launderer is to reduce or eliminate the risk that the money can be seized or forfeited. For the money launderer, the ultimate goal of the underlying criminal activity is to spend and enjoy its fruits.

Money laundering is a global phenomenon and launderers are always on the look-out for avenues to clean their ill-gotten gains.[54] Lawyers, because of their unique position of trust they have in society, are vulnerable to being abused by launderers.[55] Whilst it must be accepted that there are some bad apples who choose to launder money themselves,[56] there are a number of other ways in which lawyers can become involved in money laundering schemes. It may be a request from a client that a lawyer assist him in devising a scheme to launder the money or a request for advice on how to launder money. Lawyers can be requested to collect money from debtors which could be the proceeds of a laundering scheme. Then there are the trust accounts of lawyers and the many ways in which they may be transformed into money laundering channels.[57] Launderers are also aware that should clients approach lawyers for advice on pending litigation or contemplated litigation, the communication between the attorney and the client is confidential, and a legal professional privilege attaches to such communication, which can be waived only by the client.[58] The possibilities of utilising the services of lawyers in money laundering schemes

---

[50]See Richards (1999: 48) and Durrieu (2013: 245).

[51]See Richards (1999: 49).

[52]*Pillay & others v S* 2004 (1) All SA 61 (SCA), *S v Hattingh*, Unreported, Bloemfontein Regional Court, Case Number 17/518/10 and *Roestof v Cliffe Dekker Hofmeyr Inc* ZAGPPHC 219 (2012).

[53]See Gilmore (2011: 35) and Mugarura (2012: 9).

[54]See Hamman & Koen (2012: 98).

[55]The FATF Recommendations, February 2012.

[56]*S v Hattingh*, Unreported, Bloemfontein Regional Court, Case Number 17/518/10. *S v Price* 2003 2 SACR 551 (SCA), *Pillay & others v S* 2004 (1) All SA 61 (SCA).

[57]See Hamman and Koen (2012: 69).

[58]Schwikkard & van der Merwe (2009: 151). *S v Boesman* 1990 (2) SACR 389 (E). *S v Safatsa* 1988 (1) SA 868 (A).

are endless and it is therefore essential that such schemes be combated. Criminals may utilise the various services of legal practitioners as part of their efforts to clean dirty money.[59] Money, in whichever form, is intermingled with legitimate funds when deposited into an attorney's trust or business account. Such deposits conceal the origin of the money and when the lawyer passes the money as a fee or furnishes the client with a refund at the end of the mandate, the money acquires the appearance of legitimacy.[60] Indeed, it is legitimate!

1.4.2 Stages of Money Laundering

Criminals often have large amounts of money, stemming from their criminal activities,[61] and they are confronted with the challenge of converting the money into a legitimate usable form without leaving a trace as to its criminal provenance.[62] In other words, they have to launder the dirty money. From the definitions given above, the money laundering process involves three distinct phases, namely, the placement of the money, followed by its layering, and then its integration into the legal economy. [63] These phases are discussed below, in the order in which each follows the other in practice. The money laundering process is a triadic one, commencing with placement, proceeding through layering, and terminating with integration.[64] Lawyers can become involved, wittingly and unwittingly, in all three stages simultaneously.[65]

1.4.2.1 Placement

The first step in the money laundering process is called the placement stage.[66] This stage involves changing the bulk of the money derived from the crime into a more portable and less suspicious form[67] in order for it to be

[59]FATF Report (2013).

[60]See Hamman and Koen (2012: 69).

[61]See Van Jaarsveld (2004: 694), Richards (1999: 46), Mugarura (2012: 10) and Madinger (2012: 259).

[62]See Van Jaarsveld (2004: 687), Mugarura (2012: 9) and Madinger (2012: 259).

[63]See Richards (1999: 47-49), Madinger (2012: 7& 259), Gilmore (2011: 34) and Leslie (2014: 16).

[64]See Richards (1999: 11) and Madinger (2012: 7).

[65]FATF Report (2013).

[66]See Hinterseer (1997: 155), Moodley (2008: 66), Madinger (2012: 6 & 259), Mugarura (2012: 10) and Gilmore (2011: 34).

[67]See Richards (1999: 48), Mugarura (2012: 10) and Madinger (2012: 259).

injected into the lawful economy later.[68] The problem that the money launderer is faced with is that large amounts of cash are bulky and difficult to conceal.[69] What is more, bank tellers, casino employees, and cashiers at any reputable currency exchange bureau are trained to detect sums of money with a possible illegal provenance.[70]

The money launderer therefore first has to devise a means to transform the money into a form that will not evoke suspicion as to its origin.[71] This can be done, for example, by simply depositing the money into the accounts of front businesses known for their high cash turnover, such as jewellery stores or cheque cashing businesses.[72] Alternatively, the cash can be converted into negotiable instruments, such as cashiers' cheques, money orders or travellers' cheques. At this stage, smuggling is a way to move huge amounts of cash out of countries with strict bank reporting laws into countries with strict bank secrecy laws.[73] The money then is returned from these offshore banking havens to be used further in the criminal process.

Launderers also use a process which is referred to as "smurfing"[74] or "structuring" to place smaller amounts of money, below the reporting threshold, into bank accounts. The term is said to have originated from the animated fantasy-comedy television series, The Smurfs, and indicates how drug dealers launder money undetected, trickling it out in small amounts, just like little smurfs running around.[75] The term is in widespread use in the context of money laundering. Smurfing consists in the breaking down of large sums of cash into multiple smaller amounts that can be deposited into bank accounts without the fear that the bank will have to make a suspicious transaction report.[76] Money launderers could use, for example, 10 smurfs,

---

[68]See Van Jaarsveld (2011: 33) and Mugarura (2012: 10).

[69]See Richards (1999: 48) and Mugarura (2012: 10).

[70]See Richards (1999: 48).

[71]See Van Jaarsveld (2004: 687) and Madinger (2012: 259).

[72]See De Koker (2004: 92), Mugarura (2012: 10) and Madinger (2012: 243).

[73]See Richards (1999: 51), Mugarura (2012: 10) and Moodley (2008: 68).

[74]See Welling (1989: 14), Mugarura (2012: 9) and Madinger (2012: 243). It refers to the practice of dividing up large illicit bank deposits into smaller individual transactions, each below the limit beyond which a bank must identify or report the transaction.

[75]See Madinger (2012: 243).

[76]Reporting threshold in USA is $10 000. In South Africa the threshold is R25 000,00. Section 28 of FICA.

each of whom would deposit, say, $ 9,900 in 10 banks per day for one week. It is thus possible to deposit as much as $4.5 million in this way in one week.[77]

Businesses such as jewellery stores, travel agencies, import-export agencies, insurance companies, liquor stores, restaurants, or any other businesses with a high daily cash turnover, can serve as placement points of the proceeds of crime. [78] The placement sites also could be businesses dealing with goods, the value of which is hard to tell, such as dealers in precious metals, antique furniture, works of art, and so forth. The trust and business accounts of lawyers also can be used by criminals as a placement destination.[79] These accounts provide such opportunities for launderers because they can conceal and move plenty of cash via law offices without arousing suspicion.[80] Money launderers, in their efforts to search for alternative placement sites, therefore have turned to the legal profession.[81]

Criminals can pose as clients by engaging the services of a legal practitioner and then using the access thus obtained for the placement of funds, either directly or indirectly. Direct placement usually takes the form of deposits into the attorney's accounts, as fee payments for fictitious services to be rendered by the attorney. Property transfers can be a very useful direct placement mechanism also, since they invariably involve huge amounts of money being deposited with conveyancing attorneys for seemingly standard legal transactions. Indirect placement refers to the use by criminals of the services of legal practitioners to establish and register financial or commercial entities, such as companies, close corporations and trusts, which will be used as placement vehicles for illegally-obtained assets. The same would apply to the drafting and execution by attorneys of various forms of contracts such as leases, deeds of sale, mortgages and loan agreements. The point is that there is no shortage of ways in which a legal practice can be used as a placement tool and ways in which lawyers can become, knowing or unknowingly, parties to a money laundering scheme.[82]

---

[77] *Ratzlaf v United States*, 510 US 135 (1994).

[78] See Madinger (2012: 259 & 319) and Richards (1999: 53).

[79] *Roestof v Cliffe Dekker Hofmeyr Inc* ZAGPPHC 219 (2012).

[80] See Van Jaarsveld (2004: 694), Hamman & Koen (2012: 69) and *Roestof v Cliffe Dekker Hofmeyr Inc.*

[81] LAWPRO (2003: 21).

[82] See Richards (1999: 11), Bell (2002: 22), Schneider (2006: 27) and Hamman & Koen (2012:69).

1.4.2.2 Layering

The second stage in the money laundering process is referred to as layering.[83] This stage focuses upon the creation of false paper trails by means of multitudinous transactions occurring across several locations and even jurisdictions.[84] All of these have as their main aim to create smokescreens by generating complex financial structures to hide the origin of the money. It is a form of sleight of hand which relies upon the rapid and frequent movement of the funds in question in order to make them indistinguishable from legitimate funds.[85] A common method of layering is to wire-transfer funds through offshore banking havens, such as the Cayman Islands, Panama, the Bahamas, the Netherlands Antilles, and, increasingly, Pakistan and Chile.[86] Countries with strong bank secrecy laws make it difficult to trace the origin of the money.[87] The masses of transactions that go through the banks daily also contribute to the problem of tracking their origins. One of the key components of successful layering is to ensure that the layering transactions cross several borders, either physically or electronically.[88] This can take place through corporate entities in a number of countries, for the more the number of jurisdictions through which the money passes the better for the money launderer. The accounts of lawyers can be utilised in this process in order to layer the money.[89]

Lawyers participate in layering when they shift dirty money deposited with them by a client or when a business form which they have created for a client is deployed for this purpose. In either case, their expertise is harnessed into the service of a criminal design to legalise the illegal. Typically, the client would have deposited an amount into the attorney's trust account for services to be rendered in future, allowing the money to remain in the account for some time, even allowing the attorney, say in South Africa, to use some or all of it to make a trust investment in terms of either Section 78(2)(a)[90] or

---

[83]See Hinterseer (1997: 155), Moodley (2008: 67), Gilmore (2011: 34) and Mugarura (2012:10).

[84]See Richards (1999: 49) and Madinger (2012: 260).

[85]See Van Jaarsveld (2004: 694) and Mugarura (2012: 11).

[86]See Richards (1999: 49). *In United States v Foster* 835 F.Supp. 360 (1993).

[87]See Bell (1999: 105).

[88]See Richards (1999: 49).

[89]*Pillay & others v S* 2004 (1) All SA 61 (SCA). *Roestof v Cliffe Dekker Hofmeyr Inc* ZAGPPHC 219 (2012).

[90]Attorneys Act 53 of 1979. See also Palmer & Crocker (2012: 345).

Section 78(2A)[91] of the Attorneys Act 53 of 1979. Alternatively, the client may instruct the attorney to transfer the money, in whole or in part, to third parties, which may include business entities created by the attorney for the client, as payment for services supposedly rendered or goods supposedly supplied by such parties.[92] Of course, money being dispensed from the trust account of an attorney is legitimate. And, willy-nilly, the attorney thus becomes a party to the process of layering the proceeds of crime.[93]

The formal process of conveyancing is prone to being diverted as a layering mechanism. It is possible for a property which has been sold to be resold again and again before registration in the name of the original purchaser takes place. In a South African Deeds Office, for example, it is not uncommon for simultaneous transactions to take place, where one property is registered in the name of a number of people on the same day.[94] If the original purchase was made with dirty money, such serial registrations amount to layering the money through a number of transactions in order to conceal its odious provenance. Attorneys can assist launderers also in the flipping of properties, the so-called reverse flip, which is prevalent in the real estate business.[95] The money launderer will find a willing seller, from whom the property is bought at a price well below its market value, paying the balance under the table to the seller, who thereby receives value for his property. After taking transfer of the property, the launderer then resells the property for its real value, realising a profit in the process. For example, the launderer and willing seller agree that the former buy a property worth R1 million for R 500 000,00. He pays a deposit of R100 000,00 and arranges a mortgage bond of R400 000,00. He pays the balance of R500 000,00 to the seller covertly, using his illegal funds. He takes transfer of the property. After a while, he puts the property on the market and sells it for its true value of R1 million. He thus has flipped the property for a profit of R500 000,00. This is layering *par excellence*: everything (bar the under-the-table payment) was done through the good offices of a conveyancer and a paper trail of legitimate transactions has been created and a seemingly honest profit has been made.[96]

---

[91] Attorneys Act 53 of 1979. See also Palmer & Crocker (2012: 345).

[92] *Roestof v Cliffe Dekker Hofmeyr Inc* ZAGPPHC 219 (2012).

[93] See Hamman & Koen (2012: 82), Hamman (2013: 50) and *Roestof v Cliffe Dekker Hofmeyr Inc.*

[94] See Section 14 of the Deeds Registries Act 47 of 1937. See also Nel (1991: 12).

[95] See Richards (1999: 58).

[96] *Pillay and others* v S [2004] 1 All SA 61 (SCA).

1.4.2.3 Integration

Integration is the final stage of the money laundering triad.[97] This is the stage at which the laundered money, its links to illegality now sundered, is reintroduced into the mainstream economy. After all, the launderer is not placing the money into the financial or electronic systems only for it to be hidden through certain elaborate schemes. It is about manoeuvring the laundered money through a circuit of transactions at the end of which it can be invested freely and spent with impunity. Integration occurs by means of financial instruments, such as cheques, letters of credit, securities, banknotes, bills of lading and guarantees.[98] These instruments constitute so many routes for the money to be blended back into the financial system and to be made available as legitimate earnings.[99] Such perambulation makes it virtually impossible to discern the illegal lineage of the money because it would have passed through various bank accounts, a number of businesses, or different jurisdictions in order to remove the last whiff of its sordid derivation.

The accounts of lawyers also are ideally suited to the process of integration.[100] In South Africa, for example, if a client has made a tainted fee deposit into an attorney's trust account and the attorney has rendered the services as instructed by the client, he is entitled to transfer the fees from his trust account into his business account. Once so transferred, the fees become part of the attorney's legitimate income and can be utilised by him for such items as salaries, rental and telecommunications, and for his own subsistence. Here the attorney himself is the beneficiary of the integration process. A crooked client can benefit in various ways as well, in that any dodgy deposit into an attorney's trust account by such a client stands to emerge free of any criminal blemish.

Characteristically, after a period of time has elapsed, and with no or minimal services having been rendered, the client terminates the mandate of the attorney, who then refunds the money or the bulk of it. Such a deposit may be part of a smurfing-type scheme devised by a crime syndicate in terms of which various attorneys are furnished with identical instructions in respect

---

[97]See Hinterseer (1997: 155), Moodley (2008 : 67), Richards (1999: 49), Gilmore (2011: 34) and Madinger (2012: 260).

[98]See Richards (1999: 50), Mugarura (2012: 12 & 13) and Madinger (2012: 260).

[99]See Van Jaarsveld (2004: 694), Madinger (2012: 260) and Mugarura (2012: 14).

[100]*Pillay & others v S* 2004 (1) All SA 61 (SCA). *Roestof v Cliffe Dekker Hofmeyr Inc* (34306/2010) [2011] ZAGPPHC 219 (2012).

of fictitious transactions to be performed sometime in the future and separate deposits are made into each attorney's trusts account, for later refunding. Any deposit so refunded from an attorney's trust account is decontaminated and may be used by the erstwhile client with complete licence. And if the money was invested by the attorney in terms of Section 78(2A) of the Attorneys Act, the client will enjoy a double benefit, in the sense that his money has been cleaned and it has increased.[101] Once the proceeds are received from the offices of a lawyer or via payment of a trust cheque, they are integrated fully into the legitimate economy.

Again, conveyancing transactions lend themselves readily to integration schemes. The serial registration of one property in the names of a number of different purchasers in a composite conveyancing transaction[102] has the effect that, once registration in the name of the last purchaser has been executed, the dirty money with which the scheme commenced is clean and ready to be used in the mainstream economy. The same applies to the flipping of a property, which results in the purchaser making a hefty profit. The profit in question, albeit generated by unconscionable manipulation, is perfectly legal for having passed through an attorney's trust account and the profiteer is at liberty to transact with it as he pleases. The success of both serial registrations and reverse flips depends crucially upon the trust account of the attorney being available as a conduit of integration.

The tarnished property transaction is in many ways a money laundering archetype. Usually it telescopes the stages of the money laundering process: placement is achieved by the dirty money being deposited into the attorney's trust account; layering occurs when the attorney disburses the dirty money to fund the various aspects of the property transaction; and integration is effected when the property has been transferred from seller to purchaser and becomes a legitimate asset at the disposal of the money launderer. It would appear that money launderers are rather partial to the material facticity of property and routinely rely upon the skills of lawyers to devise property transactions through which to launder criminal proceeds.[103] Property transactions are attractive to money launderers because they invariably involve the movement of large amounts of money, from a few hundred thousand to millions of rand. Property transfers are staples for conveyancers who attend to thousands of

[101] Act 53 of 1979. See also Palmer & Crocker (2012: 345).

[102] See Section 14 of the Deeds Registries Act 47 of 1937. See also Nel (1991: 12).

[103] *S v Hattingh*, Unreported, Bloemfontein Regional Court, Case Number 17/518/10.

registrations of properties and mortgage bonds in the various Deeds Offices across South Africa on a daily basis. Such transfers are regulated minutely and seldom attract attention for being suspicious, making them a typology of choice for money launderers.[104] A lawyer who is willing to use property transactions as a façade for channelling huge amounts of illegally obtained money through his trust account does much to advance the cause of the money launderer. The truth of this classification is self-evident. Lawyers can become complicit in money laundering in all its stages.

Legal practitioners typically can become involved, advertently or inadvertently, in money laundering activities via the attorney-client relationship. Economic crimes are committed for the primary purpose of enriching the perpetrators and their families and associates. Money laundering is a way of their severing the nexus between the crime and its proceeds, and to their enjoying the latter openly and even conspicuously. It is a process of criminal legitimation which the perpetrators will seek to facilitate and expedite in every which way, including enlisting the skills and resources of legal professionals, with or without their assent.

The advocates' profession in South Africa generally specialises in forensic skills, gives advice or opinions, and focuses on litigation, especially high court litigation.[105] The attorneys' profession focuses on general skills of practice and many of its members are qualified as conveyancers and notaries.[106] Advocates presently are not required to have a trust account.[107] An attorney's trust account is required by law; any attorney who wants to commence his own practice must open, in addition to his business account, a separate trust account.[108] The trust account is also the account in respect of which the Attorneys Fidelity Fund (AFF)[109] requires an annual audit to determine whether an attorney is to be granted a Fidelity Fund Certificate (FFC) which he requires in order to practise.[110]

This examination is concerned with the South African attorneys' profession

---

[104]Middleton & Levi (2005: 130).

[105]See De Klerk (2006: 11), McQuoid Mason (2013: 566) and Meintjies Van der Walt (2011: 70).

[106]See De Klerk (2006: 11) and McQuoid Mason (2013: 566).

[107]Advocates may be required to have a trust account in future. See Sections 1, 24 and 30 of the Legal Practice Act 28 of 2014.

[108]Section 78 of the Attorneys Act 53 of 1979. See also Palmer & Crocker (2012: 345).

[109]Section 25 of the Attorneys Act 53 of 1979.

[110]See Sections 41 and 42 of the Attorneys Act 53 of 1979. See also Hamman & Koen (2012:69); Maisel (2010: 21).

and monies paid into the accounts of attorneys. Where reference is made to legal practitioners or lawyers it should be read as a reference to attorneys, unless the advocates' profession is identified explicitly.

1.5 Attraction of Attorneys' Trust Accounts

Attorneys and their trust accounts have become attractive destinations for launderers to clean their ill-gotten gains.[111] In South Africa, an attorney's trust account is regarded as sacrosanct.[112] All funds paid in trust by a client to an attorney should be deposited into this account and clients tend to have complete confidence in the fact that their money is entrusted to an attorney. Its very designation as "trust money" encourages such confidence.[113] The trust account is the barometer of the good standing of a law practice, and the index of its trustworthiness.[114] Even if misappropriation of funds takes place by practitioners, clients will be compensated by the AFF.

However, the trust account is also vulnerable. Because of the high level of trustworthiness it enjoys, an attorney's trust account can be transformed easily into a vehicle of crime. A launderer who has access to the trust account could manipulate it easily for a criminal purpose. Furthermore, such violation likely would be concealed because of the credibility of the trust account, making it especially attractive to persons or organisations that seek to launder money.[115] It is similar to a one-stop laundromat: the money enters dirty on one side, makes its way through a cleaning cycle, and exits clean on the other side.[116]

There are various ways in which an attorney's trust account may be transformed into a money laundering device. The attorney himself may use his trust account to wash the proceeds of his own criminal activities.[117] The attorney may be recruited and remunerated, for example, by a crime syndicate to make his trust account available to it as a laundering tool. Criminal clients may deposit criminal proceeds into an attorney's trust account as payment

---

[111]FATF Report (2013: 4). See also Schneider (2006: 270).

[112]See Hamman & Koen (2012: 69).

[113]See Lewis (1982: 269) and LAWPRO (2003: 21).

[114]See *Hirschowitz Flionis v Bartlett* 2006 (3) SA 575 (SCA) Para 30.

[115]See Shepherd (2002: 26).

[116]See Hamman & Koen (2012: 69).

[117]*United States v Foster* 835 F. Supp.360 (1993). *S v Hattingh*, Unreported, Bloemfontein Regional Court, Case Number 17/518/10.

for fake transactions and then receive back clean money as a refund when the transactions supposedly fall through or the attorney's mandate is terminated. Criminal clients may use the attorney's trust account as a bank account into which to deposit criminal proceeds for onward transmission to various payees on the instructions of the clients. In this manner the attorney's trust account, which is supposed to be a safe haven for clients' money, becomes a vehicle in the money laundering process.

Legal practitioners thus always are exposed to the possibility that payment of their fees is effected with dirty money. Criminal defence practitioners, especially, retain the receipts for the bail, which their clients have paid in cash into court before being released, as part of their fees. This money could be the proceeds of the criminal activity of their clients.

It is a common occurrence that clients pay certain amounts in trust to attorneys and that the money remains in the attorney's trust account for a considerable period of time. Attorneys and their clients have a confidential relationship and the attorney may invoke attorney-client confidentiality or legal professional privilege in order not to divulge details of illicit transactions of clients.

The attorney's trust account has proved to be an excellent haven for hiding illicit gains from the prying eyes of law enforcement officials. A chartered accountant must do an annual audit of an attorney's trust account and the report must be submitted to the relevant law society.[118] However, the audit is concerned with assessing the practitioner's level of compliance with the requirements stipulated for the conduct of the trust account. It is not a reporting requirement for the practitioner to divulge the origin of monies in his trust account. It is precisely this lack of transparency which makes the attorney's trust account a target of choice for money launderers, and which can inculpate the attorney in any or all of the stages of the money laundering process.

The internet has become an essential part of our daily lives,[119] and has made it possible to shift money almost instantaneously through cyberspace.[120] The

[118]The various law societies have rules which require their members to undergo an annual audit in order to apply for a Fidelity Fund Certificate. See, for example, Rule13 of the Rules of the Cape Law Society and Rule 70 of the Rules of the Law Society of the Northern Provinces.

[119]See Richards (1999: 69), Van Jaarsveld (2004: 694), Ping (2004:50), Phillipsohn (2001: 87) and Hamman (2013: 50).

[120]See Weatherford (1997: 248) and Hamman (2013: 51).

movement of money via the internet has become very effective and enables individuals to execute their financial transactions on-line, thereby making visits to a bank almost totally redundant.[121] Today private individuals and companies are able to conduct much of their business through the internet.[122] Law offices also utilise this technology to transfer their clients' money by electronic means via their trust accounts. This occurs regularly in conveyancing and commercial transactions. Regrettably, this has also provided money launderers with an opportunity to perpetrate crime via the trust accounts of legal practitioners.

Money can be routed anywhere with the stroke of a few computer keys, almost risk free.[123] As regards attorneys' trust accounts, cyberlaundering is ideal from a launderer's point of view, because of the potential anonymity and because the financial crimes committed in cyberspace are almost undetectable. As the anti-money laundering campaign gathers momentum, so, too, are money launderers forced to rummage for alternative placement sites. One such site upon which they have alighted is the attorney's trust account, and lawyers should be aware of this.[124]

1.6 Attorney-Client Confidentiality and Legal Professional Privilege

Lawyers are in the unique position that they have access to information which can be detrimental to their clients. Attorney-client confidentiality and legal professional privilege prohibit them from disclosing such information without the client's consent.[125] To be sure, not all communications between attorney and client qualify for protection on the basis of legal professional

---

[121]See Richards (1999: 69) and Phillipsohn (2001: 87).

[122]See Ping (2004: 51), Joyce (2001: 146), Hugel and Kelly (2002: 57) and Richards (1999: 69).

[123]See Van Jaarsveld (2004: 685).

[124]See LAWPRO (2003: 21): "For those who prefer not to leave a paper trail, lawyers' trust accounts are an attractive alternative to traditional financial institutions." See also *Roestof v Cliffe Dekker Hofmeyr Inc.* 34306/2010) [2011] ZAGPPHC 219 (2012.

[125]FATF Report (2013: 16). See also Schwikkard & Van der Merwe (2009: 145), Burdette (2010:24) and Yasin (2004: 364). See further *Thint Pty Ltd v National Director of Public Prosecutions and Others, Zuma and Another v National Director of Public Prosecutions and Others* [2008] ZACC 13 and *A Company and Two Others v The Commissioner for the South African Revenue Services* Western Cape High Court, Case No 16360/2013 [2014] ZAWCHC 33.

privilege.[126] Be that as it may, lawyers are attractive to money launderers because they know that certain communications between attorney and client are subject to privilege. [127] Although legal professional privilege may be significant, the attorney-client relationship transcends it, comprehending also such crucial ethical matters as trust, confidence, security and reliability. In the day-to-day world of legal practice, the distinction between legal professional privilege and attorney-client confidentiality is a purely formal one.[128] Clients tend to expect that all communications with attorneys will be confidential and hence privileged; they confuse confidentiality and privilege.

One of the main reasons why privilege attaches to certain communications is to allow clients to provide lawyers with all the relevant information and not only the facts that a client may think favour his case.[129] If a lawyer does not know all the facts, a client could be advised that his case is stronger than it actually is, making him believe that it would be better for him to litigate than settle the matter. The lawyer-client relationship should not be characterised by tension, suspicion, fear and distrust.[130] It was confirmed in *S v Safatsa*[131] that confidentiality is necessary for the proper functioning of the legal system[132] and should create an open line of communication between the lawyer and client.

In *Minister of Safety and Security v Bennet and Others*, the court held that legal professional privilege is a fundamental right.[133] The privilege extends not only to communications in respect of litigation that is pending or underway, but to all communication made for purposes giving or seeking legal advice.[134] However, as noted earlier, launderers who pose as clients cannot bank on all communications between attorney and client being privileged.

The communication must have been made to a legal adviser acting in a professional capacity, in confidence, for the purpose of pending litigation or

---

[126]See Schwikkard & Van der Merwe (2009: 147).

[127]FATF Report (2013: 17). See also Burdette (2010: 37).

[128]For a useful discussion of this distinction, see Itsikowitz (2006: 73-75).

[129]See Bellengere *et al* (2013: 308), Zeffert & Paizes (2009: 561) and Zeffert & Paizes (2010:197).

[130]See Zeffert & Paizes (2009: 562) and Rudowski (1988: 1970).

[131]*S v Safatsa and Others* 1988 (1) SA 868 (A) at 885-6.

[132]See Bellengere *et al* (2013: 308).

[133]*Minister of Safety and Security v Bennet and Others* 2009(2) SACR 17 (SCA). See also *Euroshipping of Monrovia v Minister of Agricultural Economics and Marketing and Others* 1979 (1) SA 637(C). See further Schwikkard & Van der Merwe (2009: 146) and Bellengere *et al* (2013: 308).

[134]See Bellengere *et al* (2013: 308).

for the purpose of obtaining professional advice.[135] This common law privilege has been confirmed by statute.[136] The privilege is that of the client and not the lawyer, although the lawyer can claim the privilege on behalf of the client, if instructed to do so. Whether or not a lawyer acted in a professional capacity will depend on the facts of each case.[137] Confidentiality could be inferred if it is proved that the consultation was with an attorney acting in a professional capacity for the purpose obtaining legal advice.[138]

Lawyers should acquaint themselves with the circumstances when communications between attorney and client are subject to legal professional privilege. If lawyes are not aware of these, they could be exploited easily by launderers who provide them with information, and then want and expect their lawyers to withhold facts from police and the courts.[139] Lawyers should be aware also that not all legislation trumps legal professional privilege[140] and that a law that infringes legal professional privilege can be challenged.[141]

1.7 Right to Legal Representation

Another factor that attracts launderers to lawyers is the fact that an accused has a right to legal representation. Although lawyers have a role to play in combating money laundering and should be alert to the fact they can facilitate money laundering, the person who is charged with the offence of money laundering, as any other accused, is entitled to legal representation. It is easy to say to lawyers that they should not represent accused charged with money laundering and to leave them to defend themselves in court without legal representation. However, the right to legal representation is a universally

---

[135]See Bellengere *et al* (2013: 308), Schwikkard & Van der Merwe (2009: 147) and Zeffert & Paizes (2009: 579).

[136]Section 37(2)(a)(b) of FICA. See also Burdette (2010: 30).

[137]See Burdette (2010: 30), Schwikkard & Van der Merwe (2009: 148) and Zeffert & Paizes (2009: 579).

[138]*S v Zimu and Others* case No CC 106/1977 and *Giovagnoli v Di Meo* 1960 (3) SA 393 (D). See also Schwikkard & Van der Merwe (2009: 148) and Bellengere *et al* (2013: 308).

[139]See Burdette (2010: 33).

[140]Section 37 of FICA. See also Van der Westhuizen (2004b: 37).

[141]See *Law Society of British Columbia v Canada* 2001 (BCSC) 1593, *Federation of Law Societies of Canada v Canada* 2011 (BCSC) 1270 and *Federation of Law Societies of Canada v Canada* 2013 (BCCA) 147.

guaranteed right.[142] Also, the right to legal representation is entrenched in the South African Constitution.[143] The right to counsel gives effect to the privilege against self-incrimination.[144] It may be presumed that lawyers will play a significant role in representing money launderers during pre-trial, trial, sentencing and appeal proceedings.[145]

During the apartheid era, emergency laws were passed which militated against the right to legal representation in criminal proceedings.[146] Some people were detained without trial and without access to lawyers despite the fact that the right to legal representation is a common law right which was confirmed by statute.[147] Before the decision of *S v Radebe, S v Mbonani,*[148] judicial officers were under no obligation to inform unrepresented accused of their right to legal representation or of the availability of legal aid. This situation changed with *S v Radebe, S v Mbonani,*[149] and the right was then emphasised in a number of subsequent decisions.[150] The right to legal representation is now entrenched in the Constitution, as part of the fair trial rights of every accused person. This includes the right to a legal representative of one's choice or the right to be provided with a representative at the state's expense where the absence of a legal representative would result in a substantive injustice. A "substantive injustice" has been interpreted to mean a prison sentence of more than three months.[151]

---

[142]Article 14(3)(d) The International Covenant on Civil and Political Rights (1966), Article 6(3) The European Convention on Human Rights, Article 8(2) of the American Convention on Human Rights(1969) and Article 7 of the African Charter on Human and People's Rights. See also Steytler (1998: 157).

[143]Section 35(3) of the Constitution of 1996. See also Schwikkard & Van der Merwe (2009:129), Steytler (1998: 299) and Currie & De Waal (2013: 769).

[144]*Miranda v Arizona* 384 US 436 (1966) and *S v Lwane* 1966 (2) SA 433 (A). Section 203 of the Criminal Procedure Act 51 of 1977; Section 35(3)(j) of the Constitution of 1996. Steytler (1998: 335).

[145]See Steytler (1998: 157) and Currie & De Waal (2013: 769).

[146]See Steytler (1998: 159).

[147]Section 73(2) of the Criminal Procedure Act 51 of 1977 and Section 35(2) and 35 (3) of the Constitution of 1996 See also *S v Lwane* 1966 (2) SA 433 (A). See further Schwikkard & van der Merwe (2009: 129) and Steytler (1998: 299).

[148]*S v Radebe, S v Mbonanai* 1988 (1) SA 191 (T).

[149]*S v Radebe, S v Mbonanai* 1988 (1) SA 191 (T).

[150]*S v Khanyile* 1988 (3) SA 795 (N), *S v Rudman; S v Johnson; S v Xaso; Xaso v Van Wyk* 1989 (3) SA 368 (E) and *S v Mabaso and Another* 1990(3) SA 185 (A).

[151]Section 35(3)(g) of the Constitution of 1996. See also Schwikkard van der Merwe (2009:140).

The right to legal representation is significant because the South African criminal justice system has a history of police violence, deaths in detention, suicides, coerced confessions, and torture. It must be accepted that rights such as the right to remain silent, to be presumed innocent, not to be compelled to give self-incriminating evidence and not to be compelled to make a confession or an admission will be worthless without the intervention of a lawyer.[152] The intervention of lawyers is essential. Police have proved not to be the best and most reliable agents for conveying this message.[153] With the assistance of a defence attorney, an accused can make an informed decision as to whether or not to invoke the right to remain silent or to co-operate with police. These rights form a safety net, protecting the accused against self-incrimination.[154] Even a lawyer facing criminal charges has a right to a legal representation and a right to be informed about it, despite his being aware of them.[155]

1.8 Research Questions and Aims of Study

Lawyers, by virtue of the nature of their work, are suited to serve as a medium for money laundering. They offer a wide variety of legal services and work with large amounts of money on a daily basis. They are independent professionals who enjoy a respectable social status and are subject to codes of professional ethics and discipline. Confidentiality is a hallmark of interactions with lawyers acting in a professional capacity. Attorney-client confidentiality attaches to certain communications between them and their clients. Section 35 of the South African Constitution guarantees the right to legal representation, [156] and clients are entitled to legal professional privilege in their communications with lawyers. The trust accounts of attorneys in South Africa are almost sacrosanct, and money paid out of a lawyer's trust account has all the trappings of legality. All these professional attributes combine to make lawyers especially attractive as a medium to originate and advance the money laundering process.

[152]*Miranda v Arizona* 384 US 436 (1966). See also Steytler (1998: 160, 314) and Schwikkard van der Merwe (2009: 133).

[153]See Steytler (1998: 113 & 160).

[154]See Steytler (1998: 338).

[155]*S v McKenna* 1998 (1) SACR 106 (C).

[156]This is a qualified right in terms of Sections 35(2)(b), 35(2)(c), 35(3)(f) and 35(3)(g) of the Constitution of 1996.

This study investigates whether South Africa's AML legislation fulfils its goal of making lawyers accountable in the fight against economic criminality. However, it also examines whether the AML enactments provide safeguards which uphold the constitutional right of lawyers to practise their profession freely and the right of the individual to legal representation. Both these rights are entrenched in the Bill of Rights in the Constitution. The legislature has an obligation not to limit these rights, except according to Section 36 of the Constitution.[157]

Lawyers are accountable not only to their clients, but also to society as a whole. They, too, have a role to play in combating crime and, therefore, are required to resist attempts by criminals to make use of their services in the furtherance of crime. They are in a unique position of trust and in some instances have access to information that may incriminate their clients. The AML legislation must be welcomed, but such legislation must not infringe upon hard-won rights, such as legal professional privilege, the right to legal representation, attorney-client confidentiality and the independence of the legal profession.

1.9 Research Agenda

This study begins with a description of the phenomenon of money laundering and an explanation of why it needs to be combated. It then scrutinises the international and South African source documents that have been adopted and institutions that have been established to fight money laundering and the financing of terrorism. This survey includes Resolutions of the UN Security Council and the AML Directives of the European Union (EU). The EU and its member states played a pivotal role in developing both international and regional AML measures.[158] The European community participated in the drafting of a number of conventions.[159] The Council of Europe has issued several directives with respect to the combating of money

[157]Section 36(1) of the Constitution of 1996.

[158]See Gilmore (2011: 222), Mitsilegas & Gilmore (2007: 119), Mugarura (2012: 71) and Kirby (2008: 268).

[159]The Vienna Convention, the 1990 Council of Europe Convention against Money Laundering and the 2005 Convention against Money Laundering. Member States also participated in the establishment of the FATF and took part in the development of the 40 Recommendations.

laundering and terrorist financing. These have a considerable bearing on the legal profession,[160] and therefore are invaluable for a discussion of the South African AML laws and their impact on the legal profession. Besides appraising the international AML instruments, the study examines the relevant soft law AML standards as enunciated in the Recommendations of the FATF. These Recommendations also have important implications for lawyers around the world, including South Africa. Also of significance for this study is the Egmont Group, an informal, international network of national FIUs, whose members play a valuable role in supporting their respective governments in the fight against money laundering, terrorist financing and other financial crimes. Importantly, it is in relation to FIUs that lawyers incur the onerous reporting obligations that are the main focus of this study.

The main South African AML statutes, namely, POCA and FICA are analysed to determine whether they successfully combat the involvement of lawyers in money laundering schemes, to assess their consequences for the legal profession and to consider whether comply with the South African constitutional framework. The South African AML legislation incorporates some of the main provisions of international AML legislation. Unfortunately, in its quest to combat money laundering, the South African Parliament did not consider seriously the position of lawyers regarding such crucial issues as attorney-client confidentiality, legal professional privilege, the right to legal representation and the independence of the profession. As a result, certain constraints were put on the profession and it is not protected sufficiently against the unintended consequences of the AML legislation.

Since South Africa is affected by globalisation and money laundering control is still in a relatively infant stage in relation to other jurisdictions, the approach of this study is comparative and the South African AML regime is compared to that in the US and Canada and, to some extent, Western Europe. It is useful to study how other jurisdictions with more advanced AML regimes have gone about attempting to balance the need to fight money laundering and terrorist financing with the need to safeguard the independence of the legal profession and the right to legal representation. For this reason, the US and Canada serve as comparators. Like South Africa, both these countries are constitutional democracies with a common law tradition and a legal profession with a shared heritage. The principle objective of the comparison is

[160]See Gilmore (2011: 222), Mugarura (2012: 71), Mitsilegas & Gilmore (2007: 119) and Shaughnessy (2002: 25).

to ascertain whether the AML regimes of these jurisdictions can offer possible solutions to shortcomings in the South African AML regime.

The United States, in particular, whose fight against money laundering dates back to the early 1970s, has accumulated a wealth of experience with regard to curbing money laundering. America has one of the most comprehensive AML regimes. The know-your-customer (KYC) requirement was initiated with the enactment of the Bank Secrecy Act in 1970.[161] The civil forfeiture of the proceeds of crime came with the enactment of the Racketeer Influenced and Corrupt Organizations Act (RICO)[162] and the Continuing Criminal Enterprise Statute (CCE).[163] The US Money Laundering Control Act of 1986[164] was the first piece of AML legislation in the world. Also, in response to the attacks of 11 September 2001, the Uniting and Strengthening America by Providing Appropriate Tools Required to Intercept and Obstruct Terrorism Act (USA PATRIOT Act) was passed, as a novel legal tool against the financing of terrorism. Notably, the US courts, on a number of occasions, have been called upon to adjudicate issues in which the legal profession challenged legislation dealing with the forfeiture of lawyers' fees.[165] The result of these challenges is that, at present, lawyers are exempt from the operation of money laundering statutes where the right to counsel is at issue.[166] American lawyers have been involved actively also in the FATF and in developing the 2008 risk-based customer due diligence standards for lawyers.[167] The US AML measures can provide valuable insights in relation to money laundering control and guidance to determine which measures should be excluded from, and which measures should be added to, the South African AML model.

---

[161]The Currency and Foreign Transactions Reporting Act of 1970 (BSA) 31 USC Sections 5311-5322.

[162]Racketeering Influenced and Corrupt Organizations Act (RICO), 18 USC. Sections 1971-1968.

[163]Continuing Criminal Enterprise Statute (CCE), 21 USC. Sections 848 *et seq.*, as part of the Control Substances Act of 1970.

[164]Money laundering Control Act (MLCA) was enacted as part of the Anti-Drug Abuse Act of 1986 Subtitle H of Title I, known as the Money Laundering Control Act of 1986.

[165]See *Caplin & Drysdale, Chartered, Petitioner v United States* 491 US 617 (1989), *United States v Monsanto*, 491 US 600 (1989) and *United States v Goldberger & Dubin PC* 935 F2d 501 (2d Cir 1991)at 501 & 504.

[166]Section 1957 of the Money Laundering Control Act 1986. See also *USA v Velez, Kuehne and Ochoa* US District Court, Southern District of Florida, Miami Division, Case No. 05-2-770-CR-COOKE.

[167]See Shepherd (2009: 609) and Terry (2010: 5).

Although the South African and US legal traditions have developed along different contours, making American law not directly transplantable to South Africa, both legal cultures place a high premium on an independent legal profession. The US experience in respect of how the legal profession has confronted the AML laws[168] holds important lessons for South Africa. Significantly, the South African Constitution authorises national courts, when interpreting the Bill of Rights, to consider foreign law.[169] In *National Director of Public Prosecutions v Cole and others* it was held that it is essential to examine foreign cases if they have dealt with issues with which South African courts must grapple.[170] Reference to the US AML jurisprudence thus is consonant with the South African Constitution.

Canada has been chosen as a comparator because the various issues discussed in this investigation have been considered by its courts.[171] It is one of the few countries where lawyers have challenged money laundering legislation successfully insofar as it affects the legal profession.[172] When the Proceeds of Crime (Money Laundering) Act and the Regulations implementing certain provisions of the Act came into force in November 2001, Canadian law societies instituted proceedings seeking to exempt lawyers from the force of the AML enactments and their associated regulations. The law societies challenged in particular the duty of lawyers to keep client records, to report suspicious transactions and the extent to which the anti-money laundering legal regime affected the independence of the profession and threatened attorney-client confidentiality.[173] Initially lawyers were exempted only from suspicious transaction reporting, which necessarily meant that the AML legislation had to be amended. The other exemptions followed later. The

---

[168]See, for example, *Caplin & Drysdale, Chartered, Petitioner v United States* 491 US 617 (1989), *United States v Monsanto*, 491 US 600 (1989) and *United States v Goldberger & Dubin PC* 935 F2d 501 (2d Cir 1991) at 501 & 504.

[169]Section 39(1) of the Constitution of 1996.

[170]*National Director of Public Prosecutions v Cole and others* 2004 (3) ALL SA 765 (W).

[171]*Law Society of British Columbia v Canada* 2001 (BCSC) 1593, *Federation of Law Societies of Canada v Canada* 2011 (BCSC) 1270 and *Federation of Law Societies of Canada v. Canada* 2013 (BCCA) 147.

[172]*Law Society of British Columbia v Canada* 2001 (BCSC) 1593, *Federation of Law Societies of Canada v Canada* 2011 (BCSC) 1270 and *Federation of Law Societies of Canada v Canada* 2013 (BCCA) 147.

[173]Gardiner http://www.canadianlawyermag.com.

Canadian Supreme Court just recently has considered the situation of lawyers in relation to the AML legislation.[174]

After the examination of the US, Canada and the European Directives, a comparison is drawn with the South African legislative framework which was enacted in response to the country's international obligations to combat money laundering. The comparison highlights the shortcomings of the South African AML legal regime. Recommendations as how to rectify them are offered.

1.10 Chapter Outline

Chapter Two considers the international legal framework relevant to the accountability and obligations of the legal profession in combating money laundering. It examines the main international source documents on AML and combating of the financing of terrorism (CFT). It also looks into standards and best practices developed by bodies such as the FATF[175] and the Egmont Group of Financial Intelligence Units.

Chapter Three studies the South African AML laws referred to above. These laws are assessed critically from the point of view of the right to legal representation, the requirement to file STRs and CTRs and the impact of the laws on attorney-client confidentiality and legal professional privilege. This chapter also investigates the impact of the South African AML legislation on the receipt of tainted fees.[176] In addition, this chapter deals with South African cases in which lawyers have been prosecuted as launderers. [177]

Chapter Four contains a comparative study of US, Canadian and South African jurisprudence pertaining to the payment of legal fees with suspected tainted funds. The tainted-fee-as-a-crime issue is analysed with reference to its effect on the right to legal representation and the right to exercise a profession. It also discusses case law in which the US and Canadian legal profession have challenged legislation dealing with the forfeiture and releasing of attorneys' fees.

---

[174] *Canada (Attorney General) v Federation of Law Societies of Canada* 2015 SCC 7.

[175] FATF Recommendations 1990, 1996, 2003, 2012 and its interpretive notes. FATF (2008) *Lawyer Guidance.*

[176] Tainted fees is shorthand for legal fees paid with dirty money.

[177] *S v Hattingh*, 2010; *S v Price* 2003 2 SACR 551 (SCA) and *Roestof v Cliffe Dekker Hofmeyr Inc* ZAGPPHC 219 (2012).

Chapter Five continues the comparison of the legislative regimes of South Africa, the US and Canada. The compulsory filing of STRs and CTRs is analysed and third party access to client records is scrutinised. The criminalisation of the non-submission of STRs and CTRs in South Africa is compared to the situation in the US and in Canada.

Chapter Six, by way of conclusion, considers whether the South African AML legislation, insofar as it seeks to combat lawyer-facilitated money laundering, infringes on the rights of accused persons and lawyers. This chapter ends with recommendations to align South Africa's AML regime with international trends.

2

THE INTERNATIONAL ANTI-MONEY LAUNDERING FRAMEWORK

2.1 Introduction

This chapter analyses the international AML legal framework with a focus on those aspects relevant to the legal profession. It studies the main source documents on AML and CFT. It also examines certain international legal instruments, such as the UN conventions and UN Security Council resolutions and the EU directives, in order to evaluate the measures envisaged to combat the implication of lawyers in money laundering schemes. The standards and best practices developed by bodies such as the FATF and the Egmont Group are discussed also.

2.2 International Instruments

The globalisation of money laundering since the 1980s elicited a concerted response from the international community and a new anti-crime initiative targeting the proceeds of crime, explicitly money laundering, was launched.[178] On 20 February 2004, South Africa ratified the UN Convention against Transnational Organised Crime (UNCTOC or the Palermo Convention),[179]

[178]See Hamman & Koen (2012: 71), Gilmore (2011: 55), Mugarura (2012: 64) and Richards (1999: 233).

[179]UNCTOC was adopted by General Assembly Resolution 55/25 on 15 November 2000 and entered into force on 29 September 2003. See also Burdette (2010:1) and Skinnider (2006:5).

thereby agreeing to be bound by its AML provisions.[180] South Africa also ratified the United Nations Convention against Illicit Traffic in Narcotic Drugs and Psychotropic Substances (the Vienna Convention),[181] the United Nations Convention against Corruption (UNCAC or the Merida Convention)[182] and the African Union Convention on Preventing and Combating Corruption (the AU Convention)[183] on 14 December 1998, 22 November 2004 and 11 November 2005 respectively. South Africa therefore is required to implement the AML aspects of these instruments as well.[184] Not all of these instruments unambiguously refer to the legal profession, but an analysis of how they deal with the topic of money laundering is essential for this study.

2.2.1 United Nations Convention against Illicit Traffic in Narcotic Drugs and Psychotropic Substances

The United Nations received a request from the Venezuelan government during the 1980s to assist it in tackling its drug problem.[185] As a result of this request, the UN commenced research with a view to establishing a convention to combat the escalating drug problem.[186] The research resulted in a 34-article convention which was presented and adopted by 106 countries at the Vienna Conference in 1988.[187] This Convention is regarded as the first internationally acknowledged instrument to deal with the problem of the illicit drug trade.[188] It is regarded also as the beginning of the internationalisation of money laundering prevention and control.[189] Article 3 deals with drug trafficking and money laundering. Each party is required to establish a criminal offence,

---

[180] See especially Articles 6 and 7 of UNTOC.

[181] The Vienna Convention was adopted on 20 December 1988 and entered into force on 11 November 1990. See also Ryder (2012: 12) and Leslie (2014: 9).

[182] UNCAC was adopted on 31 October 2003 and entered into force on 14 December 2005.

[183] The AU Convention was adopted on 11 July 2003 and entered into force on 5 August 2006.

[184] See Article 3 of the Vienna Convention, Articles 14, 23, 52, 54 and 57 of UNCAC and Article 6 of the AU Convention.

[185] UN Comprehensive Outline in UN International Conference on Drug Abuse and Illicit Drug Trafficking of 1987 Recital III. Van Jaarsveld (2011: 238) and Gilmore (2011: 54).

[186] See Van Jaarsveld (2011: 265), Shams (2004: 28), Richards (1999: 224) and Mugarura (2012:64).

[187] See Van Jaarsveld (2011: 238), Gilmore (2011: 54) and Kirby (2008: 274).

[188] Article 3(1)(a)(i-v) of the Vienna Convention. See also Van Jaarsveld (2011: 238), Richards (1999: 224), Mugarura (2012: 64), Shams (2004: 28) and Gilmore (2011: 56).

[189] See Shams (2004: 28), Richards (1999: 225) and Mugarura (2012: 64).

which in essence amounts to money laundering, under its domestic law. It is described in Article 3(1)(b)(i) as follows:

> "The conversion or transfer of property, knowing that such property is derived from any offence or offences established in accordance with subparagraph (a) of this paragraph, or from an act of participation in such offence or offences, for the purpose of concealing or disguising the illicit origin of the property or of assisting any person who is involved in the commission of such an offence or offences to evade the legal consequence of his actions."[190]

An obligation is imposed, therefore, on all state parties to criminalise the laundering of the proceeds of the illegal trade in narcotics.[191] Knowledge is a requirement for this offence in that the accused person must know that the property in question is derived from an offence. The main issue addressed in this convention is the regulation and criminalisation of illegal drug trafficking worldwide. If a person disguises or hides the illegal origin of the property in an attempt to evade the law, and is assisted by someone else to do so, this amounts to an offence.[192] Therefore, it is not only the conversion of the property that is criminalised, but also the concealment of the fact that the property is derived from an offence. Thus, Article 3(1)(b)(ii) criminalises:

> "The concealment or the disguise of the true nature, source, location, disposition, movement, rights with respect to, or ownership of property, knowing that such property is derived from an offence or offences established in accordance with subparagraph (a) of this paragraph or from an act of participation in such an offence or offences."[193]

Although the phrase money laundering is not mentioned expressly in the Vienna Convention, the effect of the cited provisions is that money laundering

[190] Article 3(b)(i) of the Vienna Convention. See also Mugarura (2012: 62), Bell (1999: 106), Gilmore (2011: 56) and Ryder (2012: 25).
[191] See Shams (2004: 28), Mugarura (2012: 65) and Gilmore (2011: 55).
[192] Article 3(b)(i) of the Vienna Convention. See also Shams (2004: 29), Richards (1999: 225), Mugarura (2012: 65) and Gilmore (2011: 56).
[193] See also Mugarura (2012: 65-66) and Gilmore (2011: 56).

is being criminalised.[194] It is a requirement that parties to this Convention criminalise the conversion or transfer of property known to be derived from criminal activity or which has the effect of concealing the property's true nature and/or source.[195] What is more, the Convention has established certain AML policies. It regulates mutual legal assistance,[196] covers other forms of co-operation and tracing of the proceeds of crime,[197] and encourages international co-operation among signatory states. It also allows for information to be distributed across international borders when requests for mutual legal assistance are made.[198] The Vienna Convention is regarded as one of the most detailed and far-reaching instruments ever adopted in international criminal law[199] and provides a foundation for the international enforcement of standard AML measures. [200] Indeed, it provided the impetus for the internationalisation of money laundering law.[201] The definition of money laundering contained in Article 3 has been repeated almost verbatim in other UN conventions and legal instruments adopted subsequently.[202]

Although the Vienna Convention does not expressly refer to legal practitioners, it initiated the notion that client confidentiality could be eroded, a possibility which subsequently was extended to the legal profession.[203] It challenged the agreements between financial institutions and their clients which stipulated that certain confidential information should not be disclosed to third parties, and provided that confidential information should be disclosed by financial institutions in order to fight crime.[204] Banks could no longer use confidentiality as an excuse not to divulge certain information. Article 5(3) strictly prohibits countries from invoking bank secrecy provisions.

---

[194]Shams (2004: 36). See Commentary on the United Nations Convention against Illicit Traffic in Narcotic Drugs and Psychotropic Substances 1988, CN.7/590(1988) at Para 3.51 at 65.

[195]Article 3(b)(i) of the Vienna Convention.

[196]Article 7 of the Vienna Convention. See also Van Jaarsveld (2011: 239), Mugarura (2012: 68) and Bell (1999: 106).

[197]Article 9 of the Vienna Convention. See also Van Jaarsveld (2011: 239).

[198]See Shams (2004: 35-37) and Gilmore (2011: 67).

[199]See Shams (2004: 35-37) and Gilmore (2011: 67).

[200]See Gilmore (2011: 67).

[201]See Shams (2004: 37).

[202]See UNCTOC, UNCAC and the EU Directives.

[203]In 2003 FATF Recommendations. EU Directives and FICA.xxxxxxxx

[204]Articles 5(3) and 7(5) of the Vienna Convention. See also Shams (2004: 37), Van Jaarsveld (2011: 240) and Gilmore (2011: 58).

It reads:

> "In order to carry out the measures referred to in this article, each Party shall empower its courts or other competent authorities to order that bank, financial or commercial records be made available or be seized. A Party shall not decline to act under the provisions of this paragraph on the ground of bank secrecy." [205]

Each state party or relevant authority is authorised to order a bank to make available financial or commercial records of customers for examination before a local judge.[206]

2.2.2 UN Convention against Transnational Organised Crime

In 2000, the United Nations adopted the Convention against Transnational Organised Crime (UNCTOC or the Palermo Convention)[207] to address the global escalation of money laundering. It is regarded as a vital initiative against organised crime following the 1988 Vienna Convention[208] and is supplemented by three Protocols.[209] The main purpose of this Convention is to promote co-operation to prevent and combat transnational organised crime.[210] It created four additional specific crimes: participation in organised crime groups,[211] money laundering,[212] corruption[213] and obstruction of justice.[214] It deals with the prevention and prosecution of various offences,

---

[205] Articles 5(3) and 7(5) of the Vienna Convention. See also Shams (2004: 37) and Van Jaarsveld (2011: 240).

[206] See Mugarura (2012: 67) and Gilmore (2011: 58-60).

[207] UNCTOC was signed on 15 November 2000. See also Mugarura (2012: 36), Gilmore (2011: 68), Ryder (2012: 26) and Leslie (2014: 9).

[208] 1988 Vienna Convention. See also Van Jaarsveld (2011: 243), Mugarura (2012: 36) and Gilmore (2011: 68).

[209] The Protocol to Prevent, Suppress and Punish Trafficking in Persons, Especially Women and Children; The Protocol against the Smuggling of Migrants by Land, Sea and Air; and the Protocol against the Illicit Manufacturing of and Trafficking in Firearms, their Parts and Components and Ammunition. See also Mugarura (2012: 70 & 103) and Gilmore (2011: 68).

[210] Article 1 of UNCTOC. See also Mugarura (2012: 103).

[211] Article 5 of UNCTOC. See also Skinnider (2006: 6).

[212] Article 6 of UNCTOC. See also Gilmore (2011: 70) and Skinnider (2006: 7).

[213] Article 8 of UNCTOC. See also Skinnider (2006: 8).

[214] Article 23 of UNCTOC. See also Mugarura (2012: 103) and Skinnider (2006: 8).

including money laundering.[215] The increase in organised criminal activity, which became an issue of international concern, was one of the main reasons for the adoption of UNCTOC. The international response to organised crime started with an action plan drafted in 1994 by the World Ministerial Conference on Organised Crime, which emphasised the need for knowledge about organised crime and for assistance to countries in drafting legislation for improved international collaboration.[216] UNCTOC promotes international co-operation in an attempt to prevent and combat international organised crime.[217] One of its main aims is to deal with the availability of the benefits of crime more effectively by concentrating on the prevention, investigation and prosecution of transnational offences by organised crime groups.[218] Unlike the Vienna Convention, the offence of money laundering is expressly included in this Convention.[219] Article 6 is phrased similarly to Article 3 of the Vienna Convention, and it also refers to the conversion or the transfer of property, with the knowledge that such property is the proceeds of crime, in order to hide its criminal origins.[220] The Vienna Convention explicitly refers to the offence of drug trafficking,[221] but Article 6 of UNCTOC has a wider application in that it deals with the proceeds of crime generally. Article 6 reads:

> "1. Each state party shall adopt, in accordance with fundamental principles of its domestic law, such legislative and other measures as may be necessary to establish as criminal offences, when committed intentionally:
>
> (a)(i) The conversion or transfer of property, knowing that such property is the proceeds of crime, for the purpose of concealing or disguising the illicit origin of the property or of helping any person who is involved in the commission of the predicate offence to evade the legal consequence of his or her action;
>
> (a)(ii) The concealment or disguise of the true nature,

215See Van Jaarsveld (2011: 243).

216See Van Jaarsveld (2011: 243) and Gilmore (2011: 67).

217See Mugarura (2012: 103).

218See Mugarura (2012: 70).

219Article 6 of UNCTOC Criminalisation of the proceeds of crime and Article 7 of UNCTOC Measures to combat money Laundering.

220Article 6 (a)(i), (a)(ii) and 6 (b)(i) and (i) of UNCTOC.

221Article 3(1)(a)(i-v) of the Vienna Convention.

source, location, disposition, movement or ownership of or rights with respect to property, knowing that such property is the proceeds of crime;

(b) Subject to the basic concepts of its legal system:

(i) The acquisition, possession or use of property, knowing at the time of receipt, that such property is the proceeds of crime;

(ii) Participation in, association with or conspiracy to commit, attempts to commit and aiding, abetting, facilitating and counselling the commission of any of the offences established in accordance with this article."[222]

Parties to this Convention are compelled to co-operate in certain instances. They are required to co-operate in the tracking of suspects who are involved in money laundering and in the tracing of the benefits of crime.[223] The Convention obligates parties to establish legislative measures to give effect to their conventional obligations.[224] Important for the legal profession are the money laundering control measures contained in Article 7 of the Convention.[225] In particular, Article 7(1)(a) provides that each State Party:

> "Shall institute a comprehensive domestic regulatory and supervisory regime for banks and non-bank financial institutions and, where appropriate, other bodies particularly susceptible to money-laundering, within its competence, in order to deter and detect all forms of money-laundering, which regime shall emphasise requirements for customer identification, record-keeping and the reporting of suspicious transactions."

Article 7 emphasises the importance of the know-your-customer standard as a tool to fight money laundering more efficiently. This Convention requires parties to institute comprehensive domestic regulatory and supervisory

[222] Article 6(a)(i), (a)(ii) and 6(b)(i) and (i) of UNCTOC.

[223] Articles 16 and 18 of UNCTOC, which deal with extradition and mutual assistance respectively.

[224] Article 7(2) of UNCTOC.

[225] Article 7(1)(a) of UNCTOC. See also Gilmore (2011: 69).

regimes. It further emphasises what is required to deter and detect all forms of money laundering, and highlights the requirements for customer identification and record-keeping. Importantly, it creates an obligation to report suspicious transactions. What is more, parties are required to establish financial intelligence units (FIUs) to collect, analyse and disseminate information on potential money laundering schemes.[226]

By ratifying UNCTOC, South Africa committed itself to taking measures against transnational organised crime. It undertook to create certain domestic criminal offences,[227] and to adopt new and sweeping legal frameworks for extradition, mutual legal assistance, and co-operation with law enforcement authorities in other countries. It is required also to promote training and building capacity within its law enforcement agencies.[228] All administrative, regulatory, law enforcement and other authorities dedicated to the combating of money laundering must have the ability to co-operate and exchange information at the national and international levels if this is permitted by national law. [229]

UNCTOC is the convention which initiates the legal profession's involvement in combating money laundering. Lawyers are referred to by implication in Article 7, which imposes a duty on non-financial institutions to report suspicious transactions.[230] However, it is Article 31 which refers particularly to the role of lawyers and notaries in combating money laundering. Paragraph 2 provides that:

> "States Parties shall endeavour, in accordance with fundamental principles of their domestic law, to reduce existing or future opportunities for organised criminal groups to participate in lawful markets with proceeds of crime, through appropriate legislative, administrative or other measures. These measures should focus on:
>
> (a) The strengthening of co-operation between law enforcement agencies or prosecutors and relevant private entities, including industry;

---

[226]Article 7 of UNCTOC.

[227]Participation in an organized criminal group, money laundering, corruption and obstruction of justice.

[228]South Africa enacted POCA, FICA and POCDATARA.

[229]Article 7(2) of UNCTOC.

[230]Article 7(2) of UNCTOC.

(b) The promotion of the development of standards and procedures designed to safeguard the integrity of public and relevant private entities, as well as codes of conduct for relevant professions, in particular **lawyers, notaries public**, tax consultants and accountants."[231]

In terms of UNCTOC, lawyers should be utilised as part of the armoury to combat money laundering. This idea is included in the KYC requirement, the STRs and explicitly in Article 31(2)(b). Lawyers are to assist in the reduction of existing or future opportunities for criminals to launder the proceeds of crime.

2.2.3 United Nations Convention against Corruption

UNCAC, adopted in 2003, is the first global instrument that addresses the issue of corruption nationally and internationally.[232] It covers five main areas: prevention, criminalisation, international co-operation, asset recovery,[233] and technical assistance.[234] The Convention requires states parties to implement corruption prevention and criminalisation measures in both the public and private sector.[235] In addition to creating a number of corruption crimes,[236] UNCAC criminalises the laundering of the proceeds of these crimes.[237]

Although UNCAC does not deal expressly with the obligation of lawyers to combat money laundering, some of its provisions are relevant to the legal profession. For example, Article 23(1)(a)(i) is in essence the same as Article 3(b)(i) of the Vienna Convention. It deals with the transformation or the transfer of the property or proceeds of corruption crimes. It includes also a knowledge requirement, which implies that a person, whilst transforming the

[231]Article 31(2)(b) of UNCTOC. Emphasis added.

[232]UNCAC signed on 14 December 2005. See also Babu (2006: 8), Schultz (2007; 3), Carr & Goldby (2011: 5), Mugarura (2012: 31) and Ryder (2012: 27).

[233]Articles 43, 51 & 57 of UNCAC. See also Schultz (2007: 2) and Mugarura (2012: 30).

[234]See Babu (2006: 8), Carr & Goldby (2011: 5) and Schultz (2007: 2).

[235]See Schultz (2007: 3) and Gilmore (2011: 73).

[236]They include active and passive corruption; corruption by foreign public officials; the embezzlement; misappropriation or diversion of property; trading in influence; and abuse of functions.

[237]Article 23 & Article 24 of UNCAC. See also Babu (2006: 13), Carr & Goldby (2011: 6) and Mugarura (2012: 31).

assets, must have known that the property derives from a crime. The person would be liable for altering the property to hide or camouflage its illegal source. A lawyer who is aware of the illicit origin of his client's income will fall in this category. Article 23(1)(a)(i) also includes conduct by a person who assists the perpetrator of the predicate offence.[238] Article 23(1)(a)(ii) refers to situations in which a person camouflages the essential characteristics of property while knowing that such property is derived from crime. The knowledge requirement in Article 23(1)(b)(i) refers to situations where assets are acquired or used by a person who knows that the property has a criminal genesis. A lawyer who has knowledge of the illegal provenance of the money with which he is paid his fee could be implicated in this manner.[239] Article 23(1)(b)(ii) covers even situations where an attempt is made to commit an offence, as well as situations where the mere association with people who commit certain offences could be punishable. It also encompasses all kinds of participation in the commission of money laundering offences including association with and conspiracy to commit such offences, as well as aiding, abetting, facilitating and counselling their commission. [240] Article 23 therefore would make it theoretically possible, with proper evidence having been adduced, to prosecute and convict lawyers who advise criminals on how to launder the proceeds of their crimes.[241]

Other UNCAC articles also refer to duties of lawyers by implication. Article 14 makes reference to customer and beneficial ownership, record-keeping, monitoring of cash movements and the reporting of suspicious activities, all of which apply to lawyers.[242] Article 14(1)(a) refers to STRs and Article 52 mentions the transfer of the proceeds of crime by financial institutions, requiring that each State Party put measures in place for financial institutions to verify the identity of customers and to determine the identity of beneficial owners of funds.[243] In order to prevent and detect the transfers of proceeds of offences, each State Party is required to implement measures to prevent banks that have no physical presence and that are not affiliated with a regulated financial group from being established in their regions.[244] Article 52(5) regulates the establishment of effective financial disclosure systems and the

[238]See Carr & Goldby (2011: 8).

[239]See Carr & Goldby (2011: 8).

[240]See Carr & Goldby (2011: 8).

[241]See Carr & Goldby (2011: 9).

[242]See Carr & Goldby (2011: 16).

[243]Article 52(1) of UNCAC.

[244]Article 52(4) of UNCAC.

creation of appropriate sanctions for non-compliance.[245] Article 58 states that FIUs must be established to receive STRs. It is thus clear that UNCAC also places certain duties on the legal profession to be vigilant against corruption and money laundering.

2.3 Regional Instruments

The European community and its member states played a pivotal role in developing both regional and international AML measures.[246] The EU always has supported international money laundering countermeasures and has requested its citizens, businesses, and institutions to help to combat money laundering.[247]

The European community participated in the drafting of a number of conventions such as the 1988 Vienna Convention, the 1990 Council of Europe Convention on Laundering, Search, Seizure, and Confiscation of the Proceeds of crime[248] and the 2005 Council of Europe Convention on Laundering, Search, Seizure and Confiscation of the Proceeds from Crime and on the Financing of Terrorism Convention against Money Laundering.[249] Member states have participated also in the deliberations of the FATF, including the conceptualisation and development of the Recommendations.[250] The EU has issued several directives against money laundering and terrorist financing.[251] The directives initially imposed stringent identification and reporting duties on all financial institutions and entities only.[252] The Council of Europe money

[245]Article 52(5) of UNCAC. See also Babu (2006: 23).

[246]See Gilmore (2011: 222), Mitsilegas & Gilmore (2007: 119), Mugarura (2012: 71) and Kirby (2008: 268).

[247]See Kirby (2008: 268), Shaughnessy (2002: 2) and Mitsilegas & Gilmore (2007: 119).

[248]Convention on Laundering, Search, Seizure, and Confiscation of the Proceeds from Crime (1990). See also Gilmore (2011: 222); Mitsilegas & Gilmore (2007: 119), Mugarura (2012:71), Kirby (2008: 268) and Shaughnessy (2002:26).

[249]Council of Europe Convention on Laundering, Search, Seizure and Confiscation of the Proceeds from Crime and on the Financing of Terrorism (2005). See also Ryder (2012: 28 –29) and Leslie (2014: 13).

[250]See Gilmore (2011: 222), Mitsilegas & Gilmore (2007: 119), Kirby (2008: 268) and Shaughnessy (2002: 26).

[251]See Gilmore (2011: 222), Mugarura (2012: 71), Mitsilegas & Gilmore (2007: 119) and Shaughnessy (2002: 25).

[252]See Gilmore (2011: 222).

laundering conventions deal with lawyers and their roles in money laundering schemes in a limited manner. The different EU directives, however, deal with the latter more comprehensively, hence the need now to focus on their content.

2.3.1 Council of Europe Money Laundering Conventions

The Council of Europe[253] was the first organisation to focus on money laundering and in 1980 it adopted a recommendation entitled Measures against the Transfer and Safekeeping of Funds of Criminal Origin.[254] This recommendation initiated the know-your-customer (KYC) rule in Europe, which presently is a pillar of the international AML regime.[255] It was incorporated in 1990 into the Convention on Laundering, Search, Seizure and Confiscation of the Proceeds from Crime.[256] This Convention brought a shift from a preventive approach to one that allowed for the implementation of criminal sanctions.[257] The main purpose of the Convention is to facilitate international co-operation as regards investigative assistance, search, seizure and confiscation of the proceeds of all types of crime, especially serious crimes, and in particular drug offences, arms dealing, terrorist offences, trafficking in children and young women, and other offences that generate large profits.[258] It broadened the scope of the 1988 Vienna Convention, which concentrated on the laundering of proceeds derived from drug offences.[259]

Interesting for the legal profession is the concern that was expressed by the drafters of the 1990 CoE Convention regarding the protection of innocent third parties.[260] This Convention includes a detailed and broad range of discretionary grounds which could be used for the refusal of requests for international co-

[253]The Strasbourg-based Council of Europe is not an EU institution and is not the same as the Council of the EU (also known as the EU Council). The Council of Europe was established in 1949. See Kirby (2009: 269) and Van Jaarsveld (2011: 259).

[254]Recommendation No.R 80(10) was adopted by the Committee of Ministers on 27 June 1980 See also Gilmore (2011: 174), Kirby (2009: 270) and Ryder (2012: 12).

[255]Recommendation (ai). See also Kirby (2008: 270).

[256]The Council in the Convention on Laundering, Search, Seizure and Confiscation of the Proceeds from Crime (1990). See also Gilmore (2011: 11, 175-184), Van Jaarsveld (2011:257) and Ryder (2012: 13).

[257]See Kirby (2008: 270).

[258]See Kirby (2009: 270).

[259]See Kirby (2009: 270).

[260]Explanatory report on the Convention on Laundering, Search, Seizure and Confiscation of the Proceeds from Crime Para 33. See also Gilmore (2011: 197).

operation.[261] One example is where the co-operation sought would be contrary to the fundamental principles of the legal system of the requested party.[262] The CoE Convention refers to proceedings on which a request is based failing to meet basic procedural requirements for the protection of human rights as contained in Articles 5 and 6 of the Convention for the Protection of Human Rights and Fundamental Freedoms.[263] The Explanatory Report to the CoE Convention confirms that certain interpretations which might raise human rights and civil liberties concerns were invalid. It expressly refers to the debate at that juncture in the United States relating to the payment of legal fees by money launderers.

> "The question has been raised, in relation to the United Nations convention, whether it would be illegal for a lawyer's fees to be paid out of funds related to a laundering offence. Some lawyers have even suggested that the United Nations convention would, by its working, make it criminal to hire a lawyer or accept a fee. In the view of the experts, the wording of the present convention cannot be misinterpreted to that effect."[264]

Evidently, as far back as 1990, it was envisaged that lawyers would be exempted from prosecution for receiving tainted fees and would be allowed to represent launderers without being subject to prosecution for doing so. In 2005, the Council of Europe adopted the Convention on Laundering, Search, Seizure and Confiscation of Proceeds from Crime and on the Financing of Terrorism (Warsaw Convention).[265] This Convention was intended to provide for the monitoring of the effectiveness of the AML regime and the measures aimed at countering the financing of terrorism. The Warsaw Convention does not mention the obligation of lawyers in the fight against money laundering,

---

261 Article 18 of the Coe Convention. See also Gilmore (2011: 197).

262 See Gilmore (2011: 197).

263 See also Gilmore (2011: 197).

264 See Paragraph 33 of Explanatory Report on the Convention on Laundering, Search, Seizure and Confiscation of the proceeds of crime. See also Gilmore (2011: 197). This matter gave rise to a huge debate in the US and resulted in various court challenges, which will be discussed in detail later.

265 See Gilmore (2011: 11 & 184).

but introduced the KYC rule[266] and the FIU requirement,[267] which were later extended to the legal profession.

2.3.2 The EU Money Laundering Directives

The EU has issued three money laundering Directives, one each in 1991, 2001 and 2005. [268] A fourth directive has been adopted by the European Council and should be ratified by the European Parliament later this year.[269] The treaty on European Union (Maastricht treaty) resulted in the creation of the basic three-pillar structure known today as the EU.[270] The treaty provides that the European Council, the European Parliament (acting jointly with the Council), and the European Commission may issue regulations, directives, decisions, recommendations, or opinions in accordance with its provisions.[271] Directives and regulations so issued constitute legislative acts of the European Union.[272]

A regulation becomes immediately and simultaneously enforceable as law in all member states.[273] It has general application and is binding in its entirety and directly applicable in all EU member states. Directives, such as the money laundering ones, must be incorporated first into national law by individual states[274] and are binding upon each member state only in regard to the result to be achieved. However, the directives leave it to the national authorities to choose the form and the method of incorporation. The EU AML directives have developed parallel to the FATF's initiatives.[275] The First Directive was adopted in 1991 and its content was influenced heavily by the measures

[266]2005 CoE Convention.

[267]Articles 12 & 46 of the 2005 Council of Europe Convention.

[268]See Mugarura (2012: 71), Gilmore (2011: 221) and Kirby (2008: 275).

[269]Cooley http://www.lexology.com.

[270]The First Pillar is also referred to as the European Communities which include the European Coal and Steel Community (ECSC) 1952, the European Atomic Energy Community (Euratom), 1958 and the European Economic Community (EEC) established under the Treaty of Rome.1957. The Second Pillar of EU law created a common foreign and security policy (CFS). The Third Pillar mandates the cooperation in justice and home affairs. See also Kirby (2007: 275).

[271]See Kirby (2008: 276).

[272]See Van der Molen www.moneytrail.eu. See also Kirby (2008:276) and Mugarura (2012:226).

[273]See Van der Molen www.moneytrail.eu. See also Kirby (2008: 276).

[274]See Van der Molen www.moneytrail.eu. See also Kirby (2008: 276) and Mugarura (2012: 226).

[275]See Gilmore (2011: 222), Mitsilegas & Gilmore (2007: 120), Kirby (2008: 268) and Levi and Reuter (2006: 307).

included in the 1990 FATF Recommendations.[276] The 1991 Directive was amended in 2001 by the Second Directive, and was replaced in 2005 by the Third Directive.[277] This study now turns to the analysis of the impact of the directives on lawyers.

2.3.2.1 The 1991 EU Money Laundering Directive

Council Directive 91/308/EEC was the first AML directive adopted by the European Commission.[278] It was a directive on the prevention of the use of the financial system for the purpose of money laundering.[279] It represented a combination of the approaches of the UN, the Council of Europe and the FATF.[280] A twofold approach followed: on the one hand, money laundering was criminalised and, on the other hand, preventive measures were put in place.[281] This Directive is regarded as the first major regional instrument to adopt a comprehensive AML framework. [282] It contains a definition of money laundering which was derived from the 1988 Vienna Convention[283] and which compelled EU member states to prohibit money laundering.[284]

Although the definition of money laundering is derived from the 1988 Vienna Convention, unlike that convention, it refers to "criminal activity" in general and is not limited to drug trafficking offences.[285] A criminal activity is defined as:

> "A crime specified in Article 3(1)(a) of the Vienna Convention (1988 UN Convention) and any other criminal activity designated as such for purposes of this directive by each member state."[286]

---

276 Recital of the 1991 EU ML Directive. See also Gilmore (2011: 223), Van Jaarsveld (2011: 270) and Ryder (2012: 13).

277 See Mitsilegas & Gilmore (2007: 120), Kirby (2008: 282) and Levi & Reuter (2006: 307)).

278 See Gilmore (2011: 222) and Van Jaarsveld (2011: 269).

279 See Kirby (2008: 276).

280 See Mitsilegas & Gilmore (2007: 119), Gilmore (2011: 222) and Kirby (2008: 278).

281 See Mitsilegas & Gilmore (2007: 119), Gilmore (2011: 222) and Kirby (2008: 278).

282 See Mitsilegas & Gilmore (2007: 120).

283 Article 3 of the Vienna Convention. See also Gilmore (2011: 223).

284 Article 1 of the 1991 EU ML Directive

285 Article 1 of the 1991 EU ML Directive. See also Gilmore (2011: 223) and Van Jaarsveld (2011: 271).

286 Article 1(e) of the 1991 EU ML Directive. See also Gilmore (2011: 223) and Kirby (2008: 278).

Member states thus are required to criminalise money laundering as so defined, especially when it comes to dealing with the proceeds of drug trafficking.[287] It was also regarded as an offence where the laundering which generated the proceeds took place in the region of another member state or in another country.[288]

All EU member states were required to ensure that laundering as defined in the 1991 Directive is prohibited and a number of preventive measures based on the 1990 FATF Recommendations were incorporated. These include obligations of credit and financial institutions to identify their customers;[289] situations where clients are offered safe custody services;[290] the collation of identification documents, evidence and existing records collected as part of the due diligence checks;[291] and the obligation not to carry out suspicious transactions.[292] The view was that the most effective means to combat money laundering was through a system of mandatory reporting of suspicious transactions and this duty was imposed on credit and financial institutions.[293] These institutions are prohibited from disclosing to customers that a report has been made and that an investigation is underway, the so-called NTO rule.[294]

Non-compliance with these obligations by credit and financial institutions would result in sanctions, the nature of which was left to the member states.[295] The 1991 Directive was to apply to the whole of the financial system,[296] as partial coverage could have resulted in launderers shifting their illicit proceeds from one kind of financial institution to another.[297] The reason for the focus on credit and financial institutions was the concern that they could be used

---

[287]Articles 1 and 2 of the 1991 EU ML Directive. See also Van Jaarsveld (2011: 272).

[288]Article 1 of the 1991 EU ML Directive.

[289]Article 3(1)-(8) of the 1991 EU ML Directive. FATF (1990) Recommendation 12.

[290]Article 3(1) of the 1991 EU ML Directive, FATF (1990) Recommendation 12. See also Gilmore (2011: 226).

[291]Article 4 of the 1991 EU ML Directive. FATF (1990) Recommendation 14. Such records must be kept for a period of at least five years. See also Gilmore (2011: 227).

[292]Article 7 of the 1991 EU ML Directive. See also FATF (1990) Recommendation 15.

[293]Article 6 of the 1991 EU ML Directive. FATF (1990) Recommendation 16. See also Gilmore (2011: 227) and Van Jaarsveld (2011: 271).

[294]Article 8 of the 1991 EU ML Directive. See Recital page 2 of the 1991 EU ML Directive. FATF (1990) Recommendation 17. See also Van Jaarsveld (2011: 272).

[295]Article 14 of the 1991 EU ML Directive.

[296]See Gilmore (2011: 225).

[297]See Gilmore (2011: 225).

to launder the proceeds of criminal activities and potentially could jeopardise the global financial system.[298] The definition of credit and financial institutions attempts to cover the entire financial system of the European Community and its provisions are not applicable only to banks, but to all types of credit and financial institutions that are or could be used by money launderers.[299]

Credit and financial institutions were required to conduct due diligence checks before they entered into any business relationship or before they perform transactions involving amounts of €15 000 or above.[300] This could include a once-off transaction in the amount of €15 000 or a series of transactions amounting to €15 000. This was obviously an attempt to discourage smurfing or structuring transactions.[301] Credit and financial institutions were required to identify clients whenever there was a suspicion of money laundering, even for transactions below €15 000.[302] A mandatory central system of reporting had to be established.[303] The confidentiality rules pertaining to the keeping of customer information had to be relaxed to allow the reporting of suspected money laundering offences.[304] Credit and financial institutions were afforded special protection in the event that they breached confidentiality rules. This protection was not limited to credit and financial institutions themselves, but was extended to employees and directors of the institutions as well.[305]

Given the fact that banks, as well as credit and other financial institutions, were subjected to AML measures, it was inevitable that launderers would seek the assistance of non-financial businesses and professions to avoid detection.[306] This brought into the frame lawyers, accountants, financial advisors, notaries and other professionals who could act as conduits for money laundering. These professional groups then were targeted by launderers to assist them in the process of disposing of their criminal profits.[307] The drafters of the 1991 Directive were well aware of this situation; hence Article 12 of the 1991 Directive obligated member states to extend its provisions, in whole or in part,

---

[298]See Gilmore (2011: 225).

[299]Article 1 of the 1991 EU ML Directive. See definition of credit and financial institutions.

[300]Articles 1 and 2 of the 1991 EU ML Directive.

[301]Article 3(2) of the 1991 EU ML Directive.

[302]Article 6 of the 1991 EU ML Directive.

[303]Article 13 of the 1991 EU ML Directive.

[304]Article 9 of the 1991 EU ML Directive.

[305]Article 9 of the 1991 EU ML Directive. FATF 1990 Recommendation 16.

[306]See Gilmore (2011: 225).

[307]See Gilmore (2011: 225).

to include the above-listed professions and to include those activities likely to be used for money laundering purposes.[308] As a consequence of the nature of the obligation in Article 12, the 1991 Directive established a contact committee whose duty it was to create a mechanism through which an element of co-ordination and harmonisation of policy could be achieved in this area.[309] In terms of Article 13 (d) one of the functions of the committee was:

> "to examine whether a profession or category or undertaking should be included in the scope of Article 12, when it has been established that such profession or category of undertaking has been used in a Member State for money laundering".[310]

The 1991 Directive, together with the 1990 FATF Recommendations, initiated the STR[311] and the NTO rules.[312] Although the need to combat the use of lawyers in money laundering schemes is not referred to explicitly in the 1991 Directive, it was realised that subsequent directives should apply to lawyers.[313]

2.3.2.2 The 2001 EU Money Laundering Directive

The adoption of the 2001 EU Directive was preceded by a major debate on whether it should be extended to other professions and non-financial businesses. The FATF revised its recommendations in 1996 with the aim of expanding the list of predicate offences for money laundering and of widening the preventive regime beyond the financial sector.[314] The customer identification system had to be updated, taking into account the challenges

[308]Article 12 of the 1991 EU ML Directive. This followed on Recommendation 9 of the 1990 FATF Reccommendations which stated that Recommendations 12-29 should not apply only to banks, but also to non-financial institutions.

[309]See Gilmore (2011: 225).

[310]Article 13(d) of the 1991 EU ML Directive.

[311]Article 6 of the 1991 EU ML Directive. FATF (1990) Recommendation 16. See also Gilmore (2011: 227) and Van Jaarsveld (2011: 271).

[312]Article 8 of the 1991 EU ML Directive. FATF (1990) Recommendation 17. See also Van Jaarsveld (2011: 272).

[313]Article 12 and 13(d) of the 1991 EU ML Directive. See also Gilmore (2011: 225).

[314]FATF (1996) Recommendation 8. See also Mitsilegas & Gilmore (2007: 123).

created by developing technologies.[315] It was realised that the existing global AML framework was not keeping pace with the changes in money laundering operations.[316] Therefore, it was proposed that the obligations previously imposed only on institutions within the financial sector be extended to other vulnerable institutions and individuals, including lawyers.[317]

Some activities of lawyers were regarded as being particularly susceptible to exploitation by money launderers, given that lawyers have the ability to incorporate legal entities, establish trusts, and provide financial advice in complex transactions.[318] Money launderers could use the client accounts of lawyers to layer and conceal dirty money which could then be hidden behind the veil of secrecy offered by legal professional privilege. These developments were monitored by the European Commission as a member of the FATF. In 1999 a proposal was tabled to implement a second AML directive that would update the first one, by incorporating the 1996 FATF revised recommendations.[319] The explanatory memorandum has this to say about the relationship with the FATF:

> "Just as the 1991 directive moved ahead of the original FATF 40 recommendations in requiring obligatory suspicious transaction reporting, the European Union should continue to impose a high standard on its member states, giving effect to or even going beyond the 1996 update of the FATF 40 recommendations. In particular the EU can show the way in seeking to involve certain professions more actively in the fight against money laundering alongside the financial sector."[320]

Before the 2001 Directive was adopted a major debate took place about the manner in which it would be extended to other professions and non-financial businesses. This is evident in Recital 13 of the 2001 Directive which states as follows:

[315]See Mitsilegas & Gilmore (2007: 123) and Gilmore (2007: 100-102).

[316]FATF (1996) Recommendation 13. See also Kirby (2008: 281).

[317]See Kirby (2008: 281), Mitsilegas & Gilmore (2007: 123) and Gilmore (2011: 230).

[318]See Kirby (2008: 281) and Shaughnessy (2002: 30).

[319]See Mitsilegas & Gilmore (2007: 123), Kirby (2008: 282) and Shaughnessy (2002: 28).

[320]See Kirby (2008: 282), Mitsilegas & Gilmore (2007: 123) and Shaughnessy (2002: 28).

> "There is evidence that the tightening of controls in the financial sector has prompted money launderers to seek alternative methods for concealing the origins of the proceeds of crime."[321]

The inclusion of the legal profession was particularly controversial.[322] The disagreement on the issue of lawyers was so vehement that it threatened to derail the proposal altogether, with the European Parliament advocating a broader exemption of the legal profession that could be accepted initially by the Council and the Commission.[323]

The negotiations on this issue lasted two years due to the concern expressed by the European Parliament regarding the impact on the legal profession.[324] It was feared that the reporting obligations would have a negative effect on the principle of attorney-client confidentiality and the right to a fair trial.[325] In November 2001, the Council of Ministers and the European Parliament reached a compromise and Directive 2001/97/EC, amending the first Directive, was adopted.[326] The 11 September 2001 attacks in the US also provided some impetus to finalise matters.[327]

The 2001 Directive amended, updated and refined the provisions contained in the 1991 Directive on the prevention of the use of the financial system for the purpose of money laundering. The scope of the latter was expanded to include various other professionals such as lawyers and independent legal professionals.[328] The amendments accorded with the revised 1996 FATF Recommendations and a broader definition of money laundering was adopted.[329] The 2001 AML Directive expanded the list of predicate offences by including serious crimes such as serious fraud, corruption, and any "offence which may generate substantial proceeds and which is punishable by a severe sentence of imprisonment in accordance with the penal law of the Member State".[330]

---

321 Recital 13 of the 2001 EU ML Directive. See also Gilmore (2011: 230).

322 See Gilmore (2011: 230).

323 See Gilmore (2011: 231).

324 See Mitsilegas & Gilmore (2007: 123) and Kirby (2008: 282).

325 See Mitsilegas & Gilmore (2007: 123) and Kirby (2008: 282).

326 2001 EU ML Directive. See also Shaughnessy (2002: 31), Mitsilegas & Gilmore (2007: 123), Kirby (2008: 282) and Ryder (2012: 14).

327 2001 EU ML Directive. See also Shaughnessy (2002: 30), Mitsilegas & Gilmore (2007: 123) and Kirby (2008: 282).

328 See Gilmore (2011: 230) and Van Jaarsveld (2011: 272).

329 Article 1(e) of the 2001 EU ML Directive. See also Kirby (2008: 283).

330 Article 3(1) of the 2001 EU ML Directive. See also Kirby (2008: 283).

The 2001 Directive imposed a more stringent application of the identification requirements underlying the KYC principle on individuals and entities subject to it.[331] Due diligence investigations are required to be performed upon all clients and the identity of clients must be established by requesting supporting evidence.[332] These due diligence investigations have to be undertaken:

> "(1) when entering into a business relationship with a new client;
> (2) when opening a client account;
> (3) when offering safe custody facilities; or
> (4) when any transaction involves €15,000 or more".[333]

However, when the entity has reason to suspect that the client is involved in money laundering, the client identification requirements must be carried out regardless of whether they have been triggered by any of the aforementioned circumstances.[334] The risks of money laundering in non-face-to-face transactions were addressed also.[335] Entities were required to take specific and adequate measures by asking for additional documentary evidence to ensure the identity of non-face-to-face clients.[336] The reporting requirement, which amounts to the filing of STRs, made it clear that the appropriate authorities must be informed of any fact which might indicate the presence of money laundering.[337] The language of the 2001 Directive has a wider implication than the 1996 FATF Recommendations regarding STRs.[338] The latter provide for an objective standard and a subjective standard that could be applied when determining the filing of a STR. The terminology used by the FATF is "suspect or have reasonable grounds to suspect".[339] The 2001 Directive requires disclosure "of any fact which might be an indication of money laundering".[340]

---

[331]See Kirby (2008: 283).

[332]See Kirby (2008: 283).

[333]Article 3(1) of the 2001 EU ML Directive. See also Kirby (2008: 283).

[334]Article 3(8) of the 2001 EU ML Directive. See also Kirby (2008: 283) and Shaughnessy (2002: 32).

[335]See Kirby (2008: 283) and Shaughnessy (2002: 32).

[336]Article 3(11) of the 2001 EU ML Directive. See also Kirby (2008: 284) and Shaughnessy (2002: 32).

[337]See Shaughnessy (2002: 33).

[338]See Shaughnessy (2002: 32) and Kirby (2008: 284).

[339]FATF (1996) Recommendation 15.FATF (2001) Special Recommendation (IV). See also Kirby (2008: 284) and Shaughnessy (2002: 33).

[340]Article 6(1)(a) of the 2001 EU ML Directive. This disclosure requirement establishes an even

Notably, the provisions of the 2001 Directive are applicable to lawyers when they engage in activities which are especially vulnerable to money laundering. These include participation in financial or corporate transactions, involving the provision of tax advice.[341] The relevant provision is Article 2a(5), which reads as follows:

> "Member States shall ensure that the obligations laid down in this Directive are imposed on the following institutions:
> 5. notaries and other independent legal professionals, when they participate, whether:
> (a) by assisting in the planning or execution of transactions for their client concerning the
> (i) buying and selling of real property or business entities;
> (ii) managing of client money, securities or other assets;
> (iii) opening or management of bank, savings or securities accounts;
> (iv) organisation of contributions necessary for the creation, operation or management of companies;
> (v) creation, operation or management of trusts, companies or similar structures;
> (b) or by acting on behalf of and for their client in any financial or real estate transaction."[342]

It was never the intention that there be blanket coverage of all the activities conducted by members of the legal profession.[343] It is only when lawyers perform the activities catalogued in Article 2a(5) that they are subject to customer identification,[344] record keeping,[345] and internal control obligations.[346] Lawyers receive special treatment in this Directive. Importantly, lawyers are

---

broader objective standard than those in the 1996 FATF Recommendations and the 2001 FATF Special Recommendations. See also Shaughnessy (2002: 34) and Kirby (2008: 284).

[341] See Gilmore (2011: 231).

[342] Article 2a(5) of the 2001 EU ML Directive. See also Shaughnessy (2002: 37) and Gilmore (2011: 230).

[343] Recital 16 of the 2001 EU ML Directive. See also Gilmore (2011: 231).

[344] Article 3 of the 2001 EU ML Directive. See also Gilmore (2011: 231).

[345] Article 4 of the 2001 EU ML Directive. See also Gilmore (2011: 231).

[346] Article 11 of the 2001 EU ML Directive. See also Gilmore (2011: 231).

exempted from obligations in respect of STRs and the NTO rule.[347] However, these exemptions are not obligatory, and the 2001 Directive gives member states a discretion in the implementation of the obligations regarding notaries and other independent legal professionals.[348]

In terms of Recital 17 of the 2001 Directive, lawyers should not be obliged to submit reports regarding their suspicions of money laundering when they ascertain the legal position of a client or when they represent clients in legal proceedings.[349] This is a very important exemption granted to lawyers in that information which is obtained before, during or after judicial proceedings, or in the course of ascertaining the legal position for a client, is regarded as privileged. The only exception, when this type of information may be divulged, is where the legal advice has the effect that the lawyer takes part in money laundering activities; where the legal advice is provided for money laundering purposes; or when the lawyer knows that the client is seeking legal advice for money laundering purposes.[350]

Recital 20 provides allows member states to take into account the professional duty of discretion that is owed to their clients by lawyers.[351] Lawyers are allowed to nominate the bar association or other self-regulatory bodies as the body to which reports on possible money laundering cases may be addressed. In terms of this recital, member states should determine the specific rules on how to deal with such reports as well as the procedure for regulating the forwarding of the reports to the appropriate bodies, and the forms of co-operation between lawyers' organisations and authorities.

In terms of the 2001 Directive, member states may designate an appropriate self-regulating body of the profession as the authority to be informed of the facts referred to in Paragraph 1a of Article 6 when situations covered in Article 2a(5) apply.[352] This confirms the position taken in Recital 20. Member states are not be obliged to apply the STR obligations laid down in Paragraph 1a of Article 6 to lawyers when they determine the legal position of a client or when

---

[347] See Kirby (2008: 286).

[348] The exemption of lawyers is regulated in Recital 17, Recital 20, Article 2a and Article 6(3) of the 2001 EU ML Directive. See also Shaughnessy (2002: 38).

[349] Recital 17 of the 2001 EU ML Directive. See also Shaughnessy (2002: 38-39), Kirby (2008: 286) and Gilmore (2011: 231).

[350] Recital 17 of the 2001 EU ML Directive. See also Shaughnessy (2002: 39) and Kirby (2008: 286).

[351] Recital 20 of the 2001 EU ML Directive.

[352] Article 6(3) of the 2001 EU ML Directive.

they are in the process of defending a client in legal proceedings. Article 6(3) thus contains two primary safeguards for the legal profession: in the event of a report being required to be made, such report must be submitted to the relevant society and not to an independent body; and if a lawyer is defending a client, no report is required.[353]

The concessions to lawyers in this Directive go even further. In terms of Article 8(2), member states have an option of excluding the legal profession from the scope of the obligation not to disclose to the client concerned, or to other parties, that information has been transmitted to the authorities or that a money laundering investigation is being carried out.[354] Gilmore states that the implication of Article 8(2) for member states who take this option is quite significant. It would allow lawyers to tip off their clients and it could be argued that such action will undermine the integrity of the investigation and subvert the purpose of the reporting obligation.[355] This exemption was omitted from the 2005 Directive.

Although the legal profession received special treatment and certain concessions, the issues regarding lawyers were not laid to rest. In terms of Article 2 of the 2001 Directive, the Commission is required to carry out an examination, within three years, of aspects relating to the implementation of the provisions regarding the treatment of lawyers and the independent legal profession.[356]

In 2004, the European Commission drafted a proposal for a third Directive, mainly to bring EC law up to date with the new FATF Recommendations following the September 2001 attacks in the US.[357] The proposal was a response to the FATF extending its provisions to combat terrorist financing and the adoption of the eight Special Recommendations in 2001 and in 2003 and the addition of the ninth Special Recommendation in October 2004.[358] Unlike the 2001 Directive, it did not take long for the Council and the European Parliament to reach agreement about the third Directive.[359]

[353]Article 6(3) of the 2001 EU ML Directive. See also Gilmore 2011: 231).

[354]Article 8(2) of the 2001 EU ML Directive.

[355]See Gilmore (2011: 234).

[356]Article 2 of the 2001 EU ML Directive.

[357]Recital 5 of the 2005 EU ML Directive. See also Kirby (2008: 288); Gilmore (2011: 236); Mitsilegas & Gilmore (2007: 125).

[358]See Kirby (2008: 288) and Gilmore (2011: 236).

[359]See Kirby (2008: 288).

2.3.2.3 The 2005 EU Money Laundering Directive

The 2005 EU ML Directive followed the FATF's revised AML and CFT standards of 2003.[360] Council Directive 2005/60/EC on the prevention of the use of the financial system for the purpose of money laundering and terrorist financing was published in November 2005, thereby repealing the earlier Directives of 1991 and 2001.[361] The 2005 Directive introduced the Financial Intelligence Units (FIUs).[362] The functions and powers of these FIUs are described in various articles of the Directive.[363] The Commission's proposal of June 2004 made it clear that the approach to the professions contained in the 2001 Directive should not be questioned, unless there was a special need to do so.[364]

Recital 19 states that:

> "Directive 91/308/EEC brought notaries and other independent legal professionals within the scope of the Community anti-money laundering regime; this coverage should be maintained unchanged in this Directive; these legal professionals, as defined by the Member States, are subject to the provisions of this Directive when participating in financial or corporate transactions, including providing tax advice, where there is the greatest risk of the services of those legal professionals being misused for the purpose of laundering the proceeds of criminal activity or for the purpose of terrorist financing."

The activities of lawyers are dealt with in Article 2(1)(3)(b) of the 2005 Directive. It is based on Article 2a(5) of the 2001 Directive, with minor amendments.[365] The 2005 Directive has tightened the European Union's AML regime and the scope of the Directive includes not only professionals such as lawyers, but also accountants, real estate agents, casinos, and trust

---

[360] Commission Directive 2006/70/EC of 1 August 2006. See also Mugarura (2012: 73), Gilmore (2011: 239), Mitsilegas & Gilmore (2007: 125) and Ryder (2012: 14).

[361] See Kirby (2008: 288).

[362] Article 21(1) of the 2005 EU ML Directive. See also Gilmore (2011: 237), Van Jaarsveld (2011: 263) and Mitsilegas & Gilmore (2007: 125).

[363] Articles 21(2), 37 & 38 of the 2005 EU ML Directive. See also Gilmore (2011: 237).

[364] See Gilmore (2011: 239).

[365] See Gilmore (2011: 239).

and company services. Further it requires enhanced customer due diligence measures for politically exposed persons and their immediate families or close associates.[366] Article 2(1)(3)(b) provides as follows:

> "This Directive shall apply to ...
> (b) notaries and other independent legal professionals, when they participate, whether by acting on behalf of and for their client in any financial or real estate transaction, or by assisting in the planning or execution of transactions for their client concerning the:
> (i) buying and selling of real property or business entities;
> (ii) managing of client money, securities or other assets;
> (iii) opening or management of bank, savings or securities accounts;
> (iv) organisation of contributions necessary for the creation, operation or management of companies;
> (v) creation, operation or management of trusts, companies or similar structures."

This article is applicable to lawyers when they participate in financial business or transactions on behalf of companies, including their giving advice on tax matters. The 2005 EU Directive makes provision for performing due diligence on the identity of clients.[367] There must be verification regarding beneficial ownership and information must be obtained about the purpose and intended nature of the business relationship. Member states should encourage professionals who are unable to comply with their obligations not to establish any business relationship or terminate the business relationship[368] with a suspected client and thereafter send a statement to the FIU.[369] Member states must require that, where the institution or person concerned is unable to comply with due diligence obligations,[370] such institution or person may not carry out a transaction through a bank account, establish a business relationship or carry out the transaction, or must terminate the business

[366] See Van Jaarsveld (2011: 275)

[367] Article 8(a) of the 2005 EU ML Directive.

[368] Article 9(1)(5) of the 2005 EU ML Directive.

[369] Article 22 of the 2005 EU ML Directive.

[370] See Article 8(1)(a)-(c) of the 2005 EU ML Directive.

relationship, and must consider making a report in relation to the customer to the FIU.[371] This requirement does not apply to lawyers in situations where they are in the course of ascertaining the legal position for their client or performing their task of defending or representing the client in, or concerning judicial proceedings, including advice on instituting or avoiding proceedings.[372]

The 2005 Directive proposes a simplified customer due diligence procedure for low-risk transactions involving public authorities or public bodies, if their identity and activities are publicly available. It further proposes on-going monitoring of such transactions.[373] In terms of the Directive, independent legal professionals have the duty to inform the FIU promptly if they "know, suspect or have reasonable grounds to suspect" that an act of money laundering or an act of terrorist financing is being or has been committed or attempted.[374]

The exemption in the 2001 Directive regarding the defence of clients is repeated in the 2005 Directive.[375] The reporting obligation is not applicable to lawyers if they obtain information whilst determining the legal position of a client, or if they are defending a client. This includes advice on instituting or avoiding proceedings, and the information could have been received or obtained before, during or after such legal proceedings. The same exemption is referred to in Recital 20. However, in the event of lawyers taking part in money laundering or terrorist financing, or the legal advice is provided for money laundering or terrorist financing purposes, or the lawyer knows that the client is seeking legal advice for money laundering or terrorist financing purposes or the exemption will not be applicable.[376] But in all other circumstances it would not be appropriate to put the legal profession under obligation to report suspicious transactions. The 2001 Directive also allows member states to designate a self-regulating body as an authority to receive the information in place of the FIU.[377] There is a difference in the treatment of lawyers in the 2005 Directive and the 2001 Directive. Article 11(2)(b) of the 2005 Directive provides that member states may allow lawyers not to apply customer due diligence in respect of:

---

[371]See Article 22 of the 2005 EU ML Directive.

[372]Article 9(5) of the 2005 EU ML Directive.

[373]See Van Jaarsveld (2011: 275).

[374]Article 22(1)(a) of the 2005 EU ML Directve.

[375]Article 23(2) of the 2005 EU ML Directive.

[376]Recital 20 of the 2005 EU ML Directive.

[377]Article 23(1) of the 2005 EU ML Directive.

> "beneficial owners of pooled accounts held by notaries and other independent legal professionals from the Member States, or from third countries provided that they are subject to requirements to combat money laundering or terrorist financing consistent with international standards and are supervised for compliance with those requirements and provided that the information on the identity of the beneficial owner is available, on request, to the institutions that act as depository institutions for the pooled accounts".

The 2005 Directive brought a number of changes in respect of the legal profession.[378] The first change deals with the controversial NTO clause in the 2001 Directive. Article 8(2) of the 2001 Directive exempts the legal profession in respect of the NTO rule.[379] It allows lawyers to inform their clients that a report was made, thus tipping them off. There is no such clause in the 2005 Directive. It was not part of the FATF 2003 Recommendations. The exemption of lawyers from reporting duties remains, but the tipping off provision has been amended. This was done because there was the possibility of member states exempting lawyers from this obligation. Such possibility was not considered to be in line with the revised FATF Recommendations and consequently was omitted from this Directive.

The second substantial change in the 2005 Directive is contained Article 28(6), which states that attempts by lawyers to dissuade clients from engaging in illegal activity will not amount to tipping off. Article 28(6) also includes a provision that prohibits the disclosure to the client or third party that an investigation may be carried out. This provision has sealed off a potential loophole, since the NTO rule previously was limited to situations where investigations were underway. In terms of the 2005 Directive, the lawyer may not disclose to the client that an STR has been filed. In the 2001 Directive, Article 6(3) allowed lawyers to make a report to an appropriate self-regulating body, rather than to the normal national competent authority.[380] Article 23(1) of the 2005 Directive limits the role of such self-regulating body in particular where the legal profession is concerned. Member states may designate an appropriate self-regulatory body of the profession to be informed rather than a FIU, but

[378] See Gilmore (2011: 240).

[379] Article 8(2) of the 2001 EU ML Directive.

[380] Article 6(3) of the 2001 EU ML Directive.

the self-regulating body is required to forward the unfiltered information to the FIU. This was not mandated by the applicable FATF Recommendation, which merely requires that countries using this indirect reporting method put in place "appropriate ... co-operation between these organs".[381] Although the 2005 Directive did make some changes pertaining to lawyers it did not result in radical shifts in the overall position of the legal profession.

2.3.3 Report from the Commission to the European Parliament and the Council

This Report was produced in response to Article 42 of the 2005 Directive. It was completed in 2012.[382] In Article 42, the Commission was requested to present a report to the European Parliament and the Council, which report had to include a specific examination of the treatment of lawyers and other independent legal professionals.[383] The Report had to cover the following: the Article 23(2) exemption for notaries and other legal professional in respect of the obligation to report suspicious transactions; the appointment of appropriate self-regulating bodies of the profession, and the receipt by such bodies of STRs which they then submit to the FIU.[384] It confirmed the procedure stipulated in the 2005 Directive that entities are obliged to inform the FIU promptly if there are reasonable grounds to suspect money laundering or terrorist financing.[385] Lawyers, as non-financial professionals, are allowed to report via a self-regulating body, which must deliver the report promptly and unfiltered to the FIU.[386] The Report also confirms that Article 37(5) of the 2005 Directive allows self-regulating bodies in sectors such as the legal profession to monitor and ensure compliance with AML requirements. Article 23 allows the designated self-regulating body to channel STRs to the FIU.[387]

---

[381]See Gilmore (2011: 240).

[382]Report from the Commission to the European Parliament and the Council [2012 Commission Report] dated 11 April 2012. This report was in response to Article 42 of the 2005 EU ML Directive referred to above.

[383]2012 Commission Report (Para 2).

[384]Article 23(1) of the 2005 EU ML Directive.

[385]Article 22(1) of the 2005 EU ML Directive. 2012 Commission Report (Para 2.7) 10.

[386]Article 22(1) of the 2005 EU ML Directive. 2012 Commission Report (Para 2.7) 10.

[387]2012 Commission Report (Paras 2 & 3). The report confirmed that a self-regulating body has the responsibility to forward the information to the FIU "promptly and unfiltered".

The Report noted that all member states have included the Article 23(2) exemption for lawyers in their national legislation and that the profession is anxious that the STR obligation imposed by the 2001 and 2005 Directives allegedly violates the lawyer's right to professional secrecy or confidentiality and the fundamental right to a fair trial and a fair defence.[388] The Report referred with approval to the decision of the European Court of Justice, which has ruled on this issue.[389] Although this judgment concerned the 1991 EU ML Directive, the main findings remain valid for the 2005 Directive.[390] The Court found that the obligations imposed on legal practitioners do not infringe the right to a fair trial as guaranteed in Article 6 of the ECHR and Article 47 of EU Charter of Fundamental Rights.[391] The Report confirmed that the STR obligations in the 2005 Directive apply only to lawyers when they are advising clients in preparation or execution of certain transactions, referred to in Article 2(1)(3)(b) when they act on behalf of or for clients in financial and real estate transactions.[392] The nature of these proceedings is such that they take place with no link to judicial proceedings and therefore fall outside the scope of the right to a fair trial.[393]

Importantly, the Report confirms the safeguard of the right to a fair trial in the following instances. In the event of a legal professional acting in connection with a real estate transaction or a financial transaction, and he is called upon to assist the client by defending or representing the client before court, or is asked for advice as to the manner of instituting proceedings or how to avoid judicial proceedings, the exemption applies.[394] The Report further refers to a study conducted by Deloitte which found that DNFBPs such as lawyers do not file many STRs and that there should be consideration given to ways of improving such reporting.[395] The Report found that it would appear to be unnecessary to revise the treatment of lawyers fundamentally in a new

[388]2012 Commission Report (Para 3) 15.

[389]ECJ C305/05 *Ordre des barreaux francophones et germanophone et al V Conseil des Ministries*, Judgment 26 June 2007.The court held that there was no infringement of the right to a fair trial as guaranteed by Article 6 of the ECHR.

[390]See Gilmore (2011: 233).

[391]2012 Commission Report (Para 3.1) 16. Article 47 of the 2005 EU ML Directive.

[392]2012 Commission Report Para (3.1) 16.

[393]2012 Commission Report Para (3.1) 16.

[394]2012 Commission Report Para (3.1) 16. Exemption in Articles 9(5), 23(1), 23(2) of the 2005 EU ML Directive.

[395]2012 Commission Report Para (3.2) 16.

Directive. The only matter that requires further consideration is how deal with the under-reporting of STRs.[396]

2.3.4 Proposed Fourth EU Money Laundering Directive

On 5 February 2013 a proposal was released for a fourth EU ML Directive.[397] This arose as a result of the FATF's update of its Recommendations in 2012. The Directive was approved by the European Council on 20 April 2015 and it is expected to be adopted by the European Parliament without any amendments.[398] Due to the extensive coverage of lawyers in the 2001 Directive, the 2005 Directive, the response of the Commission to Parliament, and decisions of various European Courts,[399] the position of lawyers regarding money laundering is not amended substantially. The Directive confirms its application to lawyers when they are involved in assisting clients in real estate and financial matters.[400] STRs can be submitted to self-regulatory bodies instead of a FIU and it is confirmed that member states should take into account professional secrecy, confidentiality and privacy when dealing with the reporting obligation of lawyers.[401] The exemption for lawyers not to report STRs if information is obtained from clients where there is a link to litigation once again is allowed.[402]

2.3.5 African Union Convention on Preventing and Combating Corruption

The AU Convention on Preventing and Combating Corruption (AU Convention) contains a number of provisions that deal with preventing and combating money laundering. Article 6 is titled Laundering of the Proceeds of Corruption and in essence is identical to Article 3 of the Vienna Convention. It confirms that states parties are to adopt legislative and other measures to create certain criminal offences. The conversion, transfer or disposal

[396]2012 Commission Report Para (3.4).17.

[397]Van der Molen www.moneytrail.eu.

[398]Cooley http://www.lexology.com.

[399]ECJ C305/05 *Ordre des barreaux francophones et germanophone et al V Conseil des Ministries,* Judgment 26 June 2007.

[400]Article 2(1)(3)(b)(i-v) of the proposed Fourth EU AML Directive.

[401]Recital 27 of the proposed Fourth EU AML Directive.

[402]Article 34(2) of the proposed Fourth EU AML Directive.

of property, known to be the proceeds of corruption or related offences, is a crime. Furthermore, conversion or transfer which is done to conceal or disguise the illicit origin of the property or to assist someone else involved in the commission of the offence to evade the law is criminalised also.[403]

The provisions of Article 7 confirm the principle contained in the Vienna Convention regarding the invoking of bank secrecy.[404] This Convention, however, is silent on suspicious transacting reports, customer due diligence, tipping off and the legal profession's obligation to combat money laundering. The only matter related to the legal profession is the stipulation in Article 14 that any person alleged to have committed corruption is entitled to a fair trial. The Convention does not confront the problem of the use of lawyers as conduits in money laundering schemes.

2.4 The Financial Action Task Force

The Paris-based FATF was established in 1989 as the flagship body to combat money laundering.[405] Its coming into being coincided with the commemoration of the 200th anniversary of the French Revolution in July 1989.[406] The FATF has formulated a set of guidelines, now known as the FATF Recommendations, to give structure and direction to the international AML crusade. [407] The primary purpose of the FATF is to co-ordinate efforts to prevent money laundering at both the international and domestic level.[408] The original FATF Recommendations were drafted in 1990 and were revised in 1996, 2003 and 2012.[409] In June 2013, the FATF published a typology report

---

403 Article 6(a) of the AU Convention.

404 Article 17(2) and 17 (3) of the AU Convention.

405 Established in 1989 by the Organisation for Economic Development and Cooperation at the G7 Economic Summit in Paris. See also Richards (1999: 226), Mugarura (2012: 80), Hamman & Koen (2012: 69), Terry (2010: 6), Paton (2010: 169), Cummings & Stephnowsky (2011: 10), Gilmore (2011:91) and Christensen (2006: 302).

406 See Shepherd (2009: 609) and Gilmore (2011: 91).

407 FATF International Standards on Combating Money Laundering and Financing of Terrorism & Proliferation.(2012). See also Terry (2010: 3), Mugarura (2012: 79), Richards (1999: 226), Paton (2010: 166), Van Jaarsveld (2011: 19), Shepherd (2012: 34), Healy *et al* (2009: 798) and Gregory (2003: 31).

408 FATF "About us" http://www.FATF-gafi.org/pages/aboutus. See also Shepherd (2009: 609), Paton (2010: 169) and Ryder (2012:14).

409 See Paton (2010: 169).

in which it described the extent to which the legal profession is vulnerable to money laundering and terrorist financing.[410]

The FATF Recommendations subject the legal profession to a range of obligations with respect to AML and CFT.[411] Lawyers, whom the FATF classifies amongst the DNFBPs,[412] are regarded as "gatekeepers" who can facilitate or prevent money laundering and terrorist financing.[413]

This section focuses on the FATF Recommendations pertaining to what lawyers should do to combat money laundering. It also considers whether the Recommendations succeed in striking a balance between the traditional values that undergird the practice of law, on the one hand, and the obligations placed upon them in the fight against money laundering, on the other hand. This section also evaluates the FATF's 2008 document titled RBA *Guidance for Legal Professionals.*[414]

2.4.1 What is the FATF?

The FATF is an intergovernmental policy-making body whose aim is to develop and promote national and international policies to combat money laundering and terrorist financing.[415] It attempts to convince and encourage politicians to bring about legislative and regulatory reforms in these areas. It has no independent ability to enact laws, but it relies on its political power to accomplish reforms in money laundering and terrorist financing.[416] The FATF can expel members that do not comply with its policies and recommendations.[417] It concentrates its efforts on the following matters: setting standards; ensuring effective compliance with those standards; and identifying money laundering and terrorist financing threats.[418] The United States of America, the United Kingdom, France, Italy and Germany are charter

---

410FATF Report (2013|).

411See Shepherd ((2009: 611), Terry (2010: 9) and Paton (2010: 166).

4122008 FATF *Lawyer Guidance* Para 8 at 5. See also Hill (2010: 154).

413See Terry (2010: 9) and Paton (2010: 166).

414See Terry (2010: 13) and Paton (2010: 166).

415FATF "About us" http://www.FATF-gafi.org/pages/aboutus/whoweare. See also Shepherd (2009: 614), Terry (2010: 5), Shepherd 2012: 34) and Paton (2010: 166).

416See Shepherd (2009: 614).

417Its edicts and recommendations are "soft law," rather than "hard law. See also Terry (2010: 6).

418FATF "About us" http://www.FATF-gafi.org/pages/aboutus/whoweare. See also Shepherd (2009: 614).

members of the FATF, which at present consists of 36 members, amongst which are 34 countries and territories and two regional organisations.[419] FATF members are required to declare in writing that they endorse and support its recommendations and policies at the political level, and they agree to undergo periodic mutual evaluations and rating.[420]

The FATF, whose Secretariat is based at the Organisation for Economic Co-operation and Development (OECD) headquarters in Paris,[421] has a president with a one-year term of office. For the fiscal year 2014, the FATF's annual budget exceeded €3.5 million. The FATF originally was supposed to operate until December 2012, but the member states have extended its existence to 2020.[422] The FATF conducts mutual evaluations of its members on a regular basis to assess their compliance with its Recommendations.[423] The evaluation reports are publicly available on the FATF webpage.[424]

2.4.2 The FATF Recommendations for Lawyers

In April 1990 the FATF issued a wide ranging action plan known as the Forty Recommendations[425] to combat money laundering. These Recommendations form the basic framework for AML efforts and are applicable universally. They consist of four major parts, namely: the role of national legal systems in controlling money laundering; the role of financial systems in controlling money laundering; the measures necessary to combat money laundering and terrorist financing; and international co-operation.[426] The Recommendations have been amended several times.[427]

---

[419]FATF "About us" http://www.FATF-gafi.org/pages/aboutus/membersandobservers. During 1991 and 1992, the FATF expanded its membership from the original 16 to 28 members. In 2000 the FATF expanded to 31 members, and has since expanded to its current 36 members. See also Terry (2010: 8), Shepherd (2009: 614) and Paton (2010: 169).

[420]See Shepherd (2009: 615), Terry (2010: 7) and Healy *et al* (2009: 799).

[421]FATF "About us "http://www.FATF-gafi.org/pages/aboutus/FATFpresidency/. Gilmore (2011: 94).

[422]FATF "2020 Mandate "http://www.FATF-gafi.org/media.

[423]FATF "Mutual Evaluations" http://www.FATF-gafi.org/topics/mutualevaluations/. See also Paton (2010: 170), Healy et al (2009: 799) and Gregory (2003: 32).

[424]FATF "Mutual Evaluations" http://www.FATF-gafi.org/topics/mutualevaluations/.

[425]See Richards (1999: 226), Terry (2010: 9), Gilmore (2011: 96) and Paton (2010: 169).

[426]The Forty Recommendations were adopted in 1990, revised in 1996, in 2003 and again in 2012. See also Paton (2010: 169).

[427]See Shepherd (2012: 34) and Paton (2010: 169).

In October 2001, a month after the 11 September 2001 terrorist attacks in the United States, the FATF expanded its mandate to address terrorist financing and issued *Special Recommendations on Terrorist Financing.*[428] They originally comprised eight recommendations, but one was added late, which made them the 40 + 9 Recommendations, presently referred to as the FATF AML/CFT Recommendations or Standards. They have been accepted by more than 180 jurisdictions, as well as the World Bank and the International Monetary Fund.

The most important 2012 Recommendations applicable to lawyers are criminalising of money laundering,[429] measures to prevent money laundering and terrorist financing,[430] the reporting of suspicious transactions[431] and the NTO rule.[432] The STR requirement and the NTO rule are two FATF Recommendations that have elicited strong criticism from lawyers and lawyers' associations.[433]

The FATF Recommendations made no mention of lawyers initially. The situation started to change when the G7 finance ministers, in their report to the heads of state and government meeting in Okinawa, Japan, in July 2002, called upon the FATF to revise its Recommendations.[434] In particular, their report suggested that the FATF should examine the position of "gatekeepers" to the financial system, namely, professionals such as lawyers and accountants.[435] Fortunately, at that stage 15 of its member states were also members of the EU, which already had begun, in its 2001 EU ML Directive, to address the need for the legal profession to combat money laundering.[436] The 15 countries had published a Consultation Paper in May 2002 which identified a number of areas in which the AML framework could be amended.[437] The Consultation

---

[428]See Shepherd (2012: 34), Paton (2010: 169) and Ryder (2012: 16).

[429]FATF (2012) Recommendation 3 was FATF (2003) Recommendation 1.

[430]Recommendation 22-28 legal practitioners are regarded as Designated Non Financial Business Professionals (DNFBP's). See also Shepherd (2012: 34).

[431]FATF (2012) Recommendation 20. See also Shepherd (2012: 34).

[432]FATF (2012) Recommendation 21 was FATF (2003) Recommendation 14. See also Shepherd (2012: 34).

[433]See Shepherd (2012: 34) and Paton (2010: 170).

[434]See Gilmore (2011: 106).

[435]The FATF (2001-2) Report par 32. See also Gilmore (2011: 106) and Christensen (2006: 31).

[436]See Gilmore (2001: 112) and Kirby (2008: 268).

[437]FATF 40 Recommendations. See also Christensen (2006: 31), Kirby (2008: 272) and Shaughnessy (2002: 27).

Paper brought the legal profession into the vanguard of the fight against money laundering. Comments were requested from non-FATF members as well as from the private sector on the review process.[438] The FATF then used the provisions in the 2001 EU Directive to assist it in the drafting of the 2003 Recommendations. It issued a revised set of the 40 Recommendations in June 2003. The revised Recommendations, complemented by its interpretive notes, brought lawyers into the AML system explicitly for the first time.[439]

Matters such as customer due diligence, STRs and increasing vigilance, beneficial ownership and control of corporate vehicles, and the application of AML obligations to DNFBPs were included in the Recommendations.[440] One of the main reasons for including DNFBPs, such as legal professionals, was the FATF's recognition of the strategic role that they could play in keeping an eye on money launderers. The FATF Consultation Paper made this point in the following words:

> "Professionals such as lawyers, accountants, and financial advisors are believed to be in a unique position to observe transactions and identify potential suspicious activities that may indicate money laundering, terrorist financing, or even unlawful conduct. These gatekeeper professionals, however, are subject to confidentiality commitments, professional secrecy, or legal privileges that underlie the very professional relationship that allow them to perform these necessary gatekeeper roles."[441]

The concern was that criminals could make use of "gatekeeper professionals" such as lawyers to help them launder their ill-gotten gains by acting as intermediaries or by giving the criminals expert legal advice.[442]

The objective of the record-keeping requirements is to make it easier for government officials to probe and prosecute violations. FATF Recommendation 22(d) of 2012, which is quite similar to the articles in the EU Directives, states explicitly that lawyers, notaries, and other independent

---

[438]See Christensen (2006: 31).

[439]FATF (2003) Recommendation 12 and 16. See also Gilmore (2011: 112), Christensen (2006: 305) and Kirby (2008: 273).

[440]FATF (2002) Consultation PaperPara 5 at 3. See Shepherd (2009: 620).

[441]FATF (2002) Consultation Paper Para 5 at 3. See Shepherd (2009: 620).

[442]FATF (2001), FATF (2006), FATF (2007) FATF (2013). See also Shepherd (2009: 620).

legal professionals, as DNFBPs, are subject to customer due diligence and record-keeping requirements when they prepare or execute transactions for a client with respect to the following activities:

> "1. buying and selling of real estate;
> 2. managing of client money, securities or other assets;
> 3. management of bank, savings or securities accounts;
> 4. organisation of contributions for the creation, operation or management of companies;
> 5. creation, operation or management of legal persons or arrangements, and buying and selling of business entities."[443]

The implications of Recommendation 22 are that lawyers are not only under an obligation to file STRs when representing clients in respect of the matters listed above, but also not to divulge the making of the STRs to their clients.[444] These two requirements have affected the legal profession[445] and its capacity and willingness to represent a certain group of clients. However, the provisions are applicable only to lawyers in private practice, which means that they exclude in-house counsel. The recommendations refer to "legal privilege" but it is not stipulated clearly when and how legal privilege applies during suspicious transaction reporting.[446] Lawyers are not required to file STRs in matters covered by professional secrecy or legal professional privilege.[447]

2.4.3 The Risk-Based Approach to Customer Due Diligence

The development of the risk-based approach (RBA) for the legal profession was initiated at a meeting of the FATF held in November 2006.[448] The theory behind the RBA is that there must be a concerted effort by lawyers to ensure that limited resources are made available to combat money laundering and

---

[443]FATF (2012) Recommendation 22(d). Same as in the 2001 and 2005 EU ML Directives. See also Hill (2010: 155), Kirby (2008: 273) and Christensen (2006: 308).

[444]FATF (2003) Recommendation 14. See also Shepherd (2009: 617).

[445]Regarded as controversial by Shepherd (2009: 618).

[446]See Terry (2010: 10).

[447]FATF (2003) Recommendation 16.

[448]See discussion by Shepherd, who was one of the negotiators of the ABA for a detailed account of the various meetings which resulted in the drafting of the risk-based approach of lawyers. See Shepherd (2009: 625), Shepherd (2012: 35), Healy *et al* (2009: 799) and Ryder (2012: 23).

terrorist financing.[449] The greatest possible risks must receive the highest attention.[450]

By contrast, a rules-based approach requires lawyers to comply with particular laws, rules, or regulations, irrespective of the underlying degree of risk.[451] The legal profession's representatives argued against being subjected to the RBA when conducting client due diligence, maintaining that the legal profession is fundamentally different from the traditional financial institutions and many of the risk factors for financial institutions as contained in the *Financial Institution Guidance* do not apply to it.[452] The most important concern was that guidance for the legal profession would need to be subject to attorney-client privilege, attorney-client confidentiality and legal professional privilege. Representatives argued that guidance for the legal profession in applying the RBA had to take into account that sole practitioners and medium-sized firms have limited resources.[453] They emphasised that such practitioners lack the expertise and resources to adopt and implement an effective RBA.[454] Lawyers and the FATF also engaged in discussions regarding the STR requirement and the NTO rule.[455] United States lawyers were opposed fiercely to any form of guidance that would impose the STR obligation or NTO rule on the legal profession.[456] Lawyers were adamant that such imposition would infringe the attorney-client privilege and the principles of client confidentiality and legal professional privilege.[457]

The FATF's attitude was that its Recommendations mandated the imposition of the STR obligation on lawyers and that there could not be a guidance that ignored such Recommendations.[458] The FATF reiterated that the guidance for the other DNFBP sectors would include an STR obligation and was against excluding it from a lawyer guidance.[459] The matter was resolved finally when the FATF and the lawyers acknowledged that STRs are not part of a risk-

---

[449]See Shepherd (2009: 625), Shepherd (2012: 35) and Healy *et al* (2009: 799).

[450]See Shepherd (2009: 625), Shepherd (2012: 35) and Healy *et al* (2009: 799).

[451]See Shepherd (2009: 625), Shepherd (2012: 35) and Healy *et al* (2009: 799).

[452]See Shepherd (2009: 629).

[453]See Shepherd (2009: 633).

[454]See Shepherd (2009: 633).

[455]See Shepherd (2009: 633).

[456]See Shepherd (2009: 633.

[457]See Shepherd (2009: 635) and Healy *et al* (2009: 795).

[458]FATF (2003) Recommendations 16 and 13. See also Shepherd (2009: 635).

[459]See Shepherd (2009: 636).

based assessment.[460] They agreed that STRs represent a response mechanism once a suspicion of money laundering has been formed.[461] An important development was the agreement by the FATF that a mandatory STR obligation would not be imposed on the legal profession.[462] The FATF agreed to this only because the lawyer guidance took a risk-based approach as opposed to a rules-based approach.[463] But this agreement was subject to a provision that in those jurisdictions in which a law or regulation mandates the filing of an STR, the RBA is not applicable and the legal profession must comply with the demands of the rules-based approach. Individual countries were left to decide whether to adopt either a risk-based or rules-based approach on STRs for lawyers. The *Lawyer Guidance* provides as follows:

> "This Guidance does not address FATF Recommendations relating to suspicious transaction reporting (STR) and the proscription against "tipping off" those who are the subject of such reports. Different countries have undertaken different approaches to these Recommendations of the FATF. Where a legal or regulatory requirement mandates the reporting of suspicious activity once a suspicion has been formed, a report must be made and, therefore, a risk-based approach for the reporting of the suspicious activity under these circumstances is not applicable. STRs are not part of risk assessment, but rather reflect a response mechanism—typically to an SRO or government enforcement authority—once a suspicion of money laundering has been identified. For those reasons, this Guidance does not address those elements of the FATF Recommendations."[464]

Lawyers thus were exempted to some extent from STRs and the NTO rule.[465] The STR requirement, however, applies without exception to the other DNFBP sectors, but the formulation differs from sector to sector.[466]

---

[460]See Shepherd (2009: 636).
[461]See Shepherd (2009: 636).
[462]See Shepherd (2009: 636).
[463]See Shepherd (2009: 636).
[464]FATF (2008) *Lawyer Guidance* (Para 120).
[465]See Healy *et al* (2009: 799).
[466]See Shepherd (2009: 637).

2.4.4 The FATF Risk-Based *Lawyer Guidance*

The *Lawyer Guidance* was eventually approved at the October 2008 plenary meeting of the FATF in Rio de Janeiro.[467] It contains 125 paragraphs which outline the various risk factors that lawyers are required to take into account when developing a risk-based system.[468] This *Lawyer Guidance* does not apply to every form of legal representation or legal advice.[469] It applies only when lawyers perform transactions on behalf of their clients in one or more of the five categories of activities listed above in §2.4.2.

It is, however not clear what lawyers should do when they receive extra instructions in addition to those listed in §2.4.2. For example, a client's initial instructions could be a request to be represented in court, but that same client could instruct the lawyer later to attend to the transfer of property or draft a will or any other type of contract. Furthermore, neither the FATF Recommendations nor the Guidance for lawyers addresses the issues pertaining to the financing of such transactions or assisting of a client with the drafting of lease agreements.[470] It is thus clear that lawyers who perform transactions concerning the buying and selling of property will have to perform the CDD and record keeping requirements on their clients, regardless of the type of financing obtained for the properties.[471]

2.4.5 Country, Client and Service Risk

The *Lawyer Guidance* identifies the three most commonly used CDD risk criteria associated with the services that lawyers offer. The risks relate to the country or geographical area, the kind of service offered, and the client.[472]

Country risk refers to whether a particular country or a certain geographical area represents higher risks than others.[473] Although there is no evidence that

[467]FATF (2008) *Lawyer Guidance* (Para 5) 4. This guidance has been described as complex by various authors. See also Shepherd (2009: 647), Hill (2010: 152), Shepherd (2012: 35), Terry (2010: 16) and Healy *et al* (2009: 799).

[468]See Shepherd (2009: 648), Shepherd (2012: 35), Terry (2010: 16) and Hill (2010: 152).

[469]See Shepherd (2009: 648), Terry (2010: 16) and Hill (2010: 152).

[470]See Shepherd (2009: 648) and Shepherd (2012: 36).

[471]See Shepherd (2009: 648) and Shepherd (2012: 36).

[472]FATF (2008) *Lawyer Guidance* (Para 108) 26. See also Shepherd (2009: 651) and Healy *et al* (2009: 800).

[473]FATF (2008) *Lawyer Guidance* (Para 108) 26. See also Terry (2010: 17), Shepherd (2009: 651),

one country is riskier than another, there are certain high risk indicators. In terms of *Lawyer Guidance,* there is no agreement amongst designated competent authorities, self-regulatory organisations (SROs) and legal professionals as to whether a transaction which emanated from a particular country or a certain geographical area represents a higher risk.[474] Factors that could influence the risk of money laundering are a client's residence or domicile, or the location where the transaction is concluded, or the country from which the funding or the finances for the agreement emanates.[475] It is thus important for lawyers to ascertain these factors to determine the risk attaching to the transaction.[476]

The *Lawyer Guidance* mentions the countries which pose a higher risk of money laundering than others.[477] Countries with high risks could be those subject to UN sanctions, embargoes or similar measures, and those that are known for their high incidence of corruption or crime, or for their financial support of terrorist organisations.[478] Lawyers are required to be particularly vigilant when, for example, they represent clients who acquire businesses or properties in a country such as Zimbabwe,[479] which is regarded as a high-risk country because it is subject to UN sanctions.[480]

Client risk refers to the risk that is associated with certain categories of clients and the risk they pose as potential money launderers or as funders of terrorist activities.[481] The *Lawyer Guidance* lists several situations which may indicate whether a client's activities represent a high risk or not.[482] The categories include politically exposed persons in certain situations;[483] cash intensive businesses;[484] clients requesting services to be rendered in unconventional

---

Shepherd (2012: 36) and Healy *et al* (2009: 800).

474FATF (2008) *Lawyer Guidance* (Para 108) 26. See also Shepherd (2009: 651), Shepherd (2012: 36) and Healy *et al* (2009: 800).

475FATF (2008) *Lawyer Guidance* (Para 108) 6. See also Shepherd (2009: 651) and Shepherd (2010: 120).

476See Terry (2010: 17), Shepherd (2012: 35) and Healy *et al* (2009: 800).

477FATF (2008) *Lawyer Guidance* (Para 108) 26. See also Shepherd (2009: 651).

478See Shepherd (2009: 651) and Shepherd (2012: 35).

479See Shepherd (2009: 651).

480See Shepherd (2009: 651).

481See Shepherd (2012: 36) and Healy *et al* (2009: 800).

482See Terry (2010: 17), Shepherd (2012: 36) and Healy *et al* (2009: 800).

483FATF (2008) *Lawyer Guidance*. See also Terry (2010: 18), Shepherd (2012: 36)and Healy *et al* (2009: 800).

484This will include money services businesses and casinos. See Healy *et al* (2009: 800).

ways;[485] clients dealing with structures whose beneficial owner's identity is difficult to establish; charities and non-profit organisations; clients who are not subject to monitoring or supervision by competent authorities;[486] clients who change their settlement instructions without any appropriate explanation; clients with no address or who have multiple addresses without legitimate reasons and clients who make use of financial institutions, financial intermediaries or legal professionals not subject to adequate AML/CFT laws.[487]

Service risk refers to the potentially high risks that are dependent on the service rendered by lawyers who receive funds.[488] The *Lawyer Guidance* states that there are 18 factors that lawyers need to consider when providing legal services and dealing with cash. [489]

Thus, for example, lawyers should be sceptical when a transaction, such as the transfer of a commercial property, takes place in an unusually short time compared to similar transactions. [490] Conveyancers should be extra careful where the beneficial owner of the property is concealed from the authorities.[491] A situation where an existing client suddenly prefers to be anonymous should be regarded as being abnormal. The lawyer should then inquire into the rationale for this.[492] The source of funds for transactions and the client's source of wealth are also factors that should be scrutinised by lawyers.[493] The type of transaction where it is apparent that inadequate consideration is paid or where the client does not identify legitimate reasons for the amount of the consideration should be regarded as irregular.[494]

However, sole practitioners are not expected to devote an equivalent amount of resources as do large law firms to create, implement and manage a reasonable RBA[495] But all lawyers are required to consider whether the client and the proposed work would be unusual, risky or suspicious.[496] This factor must be

---

[485]See Terry (2010: 17), Shepherd (2012: 36) and Healy *et al* (2009: 800).

[486]See Terry (2010: 17), Shepherd (2012: 36) and Healy *et al* (2009: 800).

[487]See Terry (2010: 18), Shepherd (2012: 36) and Healy et al (2009: 800).

[488]FATF (2008) *Lawyer Guidance* (Para 110) 28. See also Shepherd (2012: 36).

[489]FATF (2008) *Lawyer Guidance* (Para 110) 28. See also Shepherd (2012: 37).

[490]FATF (2008) *Lawyer Guidance* (Para 110) 28. See also Shepherd (2012: 37).

[491]FATF (2008) *Lawyer Guidance* (Para 110) 28. See also Shepherd (2012: 36).

[492]FATF (2008) *Lawyer Guidance* (Para 110) 28.

[493]FATF (2008) *Lawyer Guidance* (Para 110) 28.

[494]FATF (2008) *Lawyer Guidance* (Para 110) 28.

[495]FATF (2008) *Lawyer Guidance* (Para 111) 29.

[496]FATF (2008) *Lawyer Guidance* (Para 112) 29.

evaluated in the context of the lawyer's specific practice.[497] There are a number of risk variables that may affect the risk determination and there are 13 factors that have been identified that may influence the risk assessment.[498] The presence of one or more of the variables may require the lawyer to perform enhanced due diligence and monitoring or, conversely, reduce, modify, or simplify it.[499] Legal persons that are well known and have operated for a number of years without being convicted of money laundering may pose a lower risk.[500]

The regularity or duration of an attorney-client relationship can be an indication of a possible risk. [501] A long-standing relationship which involves frequent client contact poses less risk; by contrast, client relationships of a temporary or short duration may suggest more risk.[502] A dramatic change in the legal services being sought by a client may increase the risk of representing the client, unless the client gives a satisfactory explanation for the sudden deviation in instructions.

As already noted, the 2008 *Lawyer Guidance* does not address the suspicious transaction requirement.[503] Because the STR is not regarded as being part of the risk assessment process, the FATF and lawyers' representatives have agreed to discuss the STR requirement at a later date and accordingly have omitted STR requirements from the 2008 *Lawyer Guidance.*[504]

2.5 Other Bodies

2.5.1 The Basel Principles

The Basel Committee on banking regulations and supervisory practices operates under the auspices of the Bank for International Settlements in Basel, Switzerland.[505] In 1988, after recognising that banks are being exploited

[497]FATF (2008) *Lawyer Guidance* (Para 112) 29.

[498]FATF (2008) *Lawyer Guidance* (Para 112) 29. See also Shepherd (2012: 37).

[499]FATF (2008) *Lawyer Guidance* (Para 112) 30.

[500]FATF (2008) *Lawyer Guidance* (Para 112) 30. See also Shepherd (2012: 37).

[501]FATF (2008) A *Lawyer Guidance* (Para 112) 30. See also Shepherd (2012: 37).

[502]FATF (2008) RBA *Lawyer Guidance* (Para 112) 30.

[503]FATF (2008) RBA *Lawyer Guidance* (Para 120) 33.

[504]Healy *et al* (2009: 799 & 801).

[505]Basel Committee on Banking supervision_See also Van Jaarsveld (2011: 213), Richards (1999: 241) and Shams (2004: 38).

as money laundering vehicles, the Basel Committee issued a statement of principles that encourages banks to put measures in place to thwart money laundering.[506] This was followed by the issuing of other important documents pertaining to the KYC standard and CDD.[507] Although the Basel Principles concern primarily the banking industry, they paved the way for roping in the legal profession to perform a gate-keeping function too. The relevant documents do not refer to lawyers explicitly, but they address issues such as CDD and STRs, which are relevant also to the legal profession.

2.5.1.1 Statement of Principles

The 1988 Statement of Principles issued by the Basel Committee called for the prevention of the criminal use of the banking system for the purpose of money laundering.[508] The Committee concentrated on the preventive aspect of AML law,[509] and proposed that banks prohibit unidentified accounts, and implement procedures to protect the financial system against money laundering. [510] The principles emphasise the integrity of bank managers, who are required to watch that banks do not become associated with criminals or be used as conduits for money laundering.[511] Proper client identification

[506]The Basel Committee on Banking Supervision sat at the same time as the Vienna Convention. This legal development took place in Basel Switzerland. Its main aim was to regulate the prevention of criminal use of banking systems for the purpose of money laundering. In the preamble of the principles one can notice that there is an assumption that banks are being used for money laundering purposes. See also Van Jaarsveld (2011: 213), Shams (2004: 37-38), Bell (1999: 108), Hinterseer (1997: 162) and Ryder (2012: 18).

[507]These are: the Basel Core Principles for Effective Banking Supervision (1997); the Basel Core Methodology for Effective Banking Supervision (1999), Client Due Diligence for Banks (2001); and a General Guide to Account Opening and Client Identification (2003). See also Van Jaarsveld (2011: 213), Shams (2004: 38) and Leslie (2014: 162).

[508]Statement of Principles (1988). See also Van Jaarsveld (2011: 214).

[509]The Vienna Convention 1988 was more focused on money laundering control whilst the Basel principles attempted to develop consensus on laws to prevent money laundering. The four principles concern the Purpose of the statement, customer identification, compliance with laws, cooperation with law enforcement authorities and adherence to the statement. See also Shams (2004: 37).

[510]Statement of Principles (1988). See also Van Jaarsveld (2011: 214).

[511]Statement of Principles (1988). Preamble S 6. See also Van Jaarsveld. (2011: 214).

procedures are proposed, and banks are advised to avoid transactions which they believe are pipelines for money laundering.[512]

2.5.1.2 Basel Core Principles

The Basel Core Principles for Effective Banking Supervision were drafted in 1997, in collaboration with banking supervisors from different countries.[513] They are intended mainly to reinforce accurate banking supervision and to support countries in assessing the quality of their respective supervisory and regulatory systems.[514] The Core Principles consist of 25 supervisory criteria and are supplemented by the Basel Core Methodology of 1999.[515] The Basel Committee further undertook to monitor the implementation of the Core Principles in conjunction with, among others, the IMF and the World Bank.[516] Supervisors are urged to comply with the FATF Recommendations regarding adequate customer identification, record-keeping and the reporting of suspicious transactions.[517]

2.5.1.3 Basel Core Methodology

The Core Methodology was drafted in 1999 and reaffirmed the goals of the Core Principles which directed when bank assessments should be performed.[518] The Core Principles require banks to have internal policies[519] that provide for the following: a customer acceptance policy; customer identification and due diligence programmes;[520] processes to monitor suspicious transactions; referrals to senior management of decisions to contract with high-risk customers; and unambiguous rules concerning the keeping of customer

---

[512]Statement of Principles (1988). Preamble S 6 Basel Principle II. See also Van Jaarsveld. (2011: 214).

[513]Basel Core Principles for Effective Banking Supervision (1997). See also Van Jaarsveld (2011: 216).

[514]For a complete list of countries see Basel Core Principles for Effective Banking Supervision (1997 1-3.

[515]The Core Principles consist of 25 supervisory criteria.

[516]Basel Core Principles for Effective Banking Supervision (1997).See also Van Jaarsveld (2011: 216).

[517]Basel Core Principles for Effective Banking Supervision (1997). See also Van Jaarsveld (2011: 217).

[518]Basel Core Methodology for Effective Banking Supervision (1999).

[519]Basel Core Methodology for Effective Banking Supervision (1999.

[520]Basel Core Methodology for Effective Banking Supervision (1999). See also Van Jaarsveld (2011: 218).

records. [521] The Core Methodology is one of the first documents in which the Basel Committee advises banks to file STRs to local FIUs for the purposes of money laundering control.[522]

The Basel Committee did not take into account the bank confidentiality controversy and failed to advise banks on the issue.[523] The Core Methodology did not resolve the tension between bank confidentiality rules and the duty of banks to file STRs. A situation that remains unresolved concerns the legal profession and client confidentiality.

2.5.1.4 Client Due Diligence

In 2001, the Basel Committee issued two further documents that relate exclusively to customer identification.[524] The Client Due Diligence for Banks and the General Guide to Account Opening contain the standards and guidelines which banks must comply with when conducting business with both existing and new customers.[525] The two documents refer to customer acceptance policies,[526] customer identification[527] and risk management in general.[528] They recommend that banks insist that customers identify themselves with valid documents, that accounts should be closed if the customer's identity cannot be verified, and that banks should note whether persons who refer other customers to them are "fit and proper" persons themselves.[529]

2.5.1.5 The General Guide to Account Opening

The General Guide to Account Opening of 2003 was issued to assist banks to identify customers accurately. The information contained in the Guide is similar to the contents of documents published by the FATF.[530] It states that

[521]Basel Core Methodology for Effective Banking Supervision (1999). See also Van Jaarsveld (2011: 218).

[522]Basel Core Methodology for Effective Banking Supervision (1999). Van Jaarsveld (2011: 219).

[523]Basel Core Methodology for Effective Banking Supervision (1999). Van Jaarsveld (2011: 219).

[524]Client Due Diligence for Banks (2001). Van Jaarsveld (2011: 219).

[525]Client Due Diligence for Banks (2001). Para 2-30. Van Jaarsveld (2011: 219).

[526]Client Due Diligence for Banks (2001). Para 20.

[527]Client Due Diligence for Banks (2001). Paras 21-51.

[528]Client Due Diligence for Banks (2001). Paras 19.23,25,28,32-33,38 and 45.

[529]Client Due Diligence for Banks (2001). Para 36.

[530]General Guide to Account Opening and Client Identification (2003).

transactions and customers must be scrutinised carefully to determine the extent of detail verification that is required. Banks that fail to enforce KYC standards may suffer legal consequences.[531]

2.5.2 The Egmont Group of Financial Intelligence Units

The Egmont Group was formed when a collection of FIUs organised themselves to deal with information about STRs and money laundering.[532] The Group derives its name from the Egmont-Arenberg palace in Belgium where it held its first meeting in June 1995. These FIUs meet regularly to find ways to co-operate, especially in the areas of information exchange, training and the sharing of expertise. They receive, analyse and disseminate information regarding the proceeds of money laundering.[533] The Egmont Group issued a statement of purpose in June 1997, including a number of guidelines that were revised in June 2001.[534]

The Egmont Group fills a vacuum which existed in both the 1991 EU ML Directive and the 1996 FATF Recommendations.[535] Both these documents called for mandatory suspicious transaction reporting to the relevant national authorities, without specifying what form such national authorities should take.[536] Although countries had FIUs, they differed in model.[537] There is the police model in the United Kingdom, where STRs are made to the police;[538] the judicial model in Portugal, where disclosures are addressed to the office of the public prosecutor;[539] and a mixed model, where reports are made to the police and the judiciary jointly.[540] Then there is the intermediary/ administrative model, for example, the USA's Financial Crimes Enforcement

---

[531]General Guide to Account Opening and Client Identification (2003).

[532]See Richards (1999: 239,240), Mugarura (2012: 93), Gilmore (2011: 81), Madinger (2012: 72), Van Jaarsveld (2011: 250), Ryder (2012: 20) and Leslie (2014: 163).

[533]Egmont Group Statement of Purpose (2001) Preamble Paras 1–4. See also Mugarura (2012: 93), Madinger (2012: 72) and Van Jaarsveld (2011: 250).

[534]Egmont Group Statement of Purpose (2001) Para 2. See also Van Jaarsveld (2011: 250).

[535]Article 58 of UNCAC also requires that FIU's must be established to receive STR's. Articles 3(6) and 6 of the 1991 EU ML Directive. 1996 FATF Recommendation 16. See also Mitsilegas & Gilmore (2007: 122) and Gilmore (2011: 82).

[536]See Gilmore (2011: 82) and Van Jaarsveld (2011: 250).

[537]See Gilmore (2011: 82) and Ryder (2012: 21).

[538]See Gilmore (2011: 82) and Mitsilegas & Gilmore (2007: 122).

[539]See Gilmore (2011: 82) and Mitsilegas & Gilmore (2007: 122).

[540]See Gilmore (2011: 83) and Mitsilegas & Gilmore (2007: 122).

Network (FinCEN)[541] and the Australian Transaction Reports and Analysis Centre (Austrac).[542] In South Africa it is the Financial Intelligence Centre (FIC)[543] which is an intermediary model.

FIUs act as a buffer between the private sector and the law enforcement authorities.[544] However, the different models created difficulties in achieving international co-operation in the fight against money laundering.[545] There is a request from the FATF that its members improve international information exchange relating to STRs.[546]

At its November 1996 meeting, the Egmont Group defined an FIU as:

> "a central, national agency responsible for receiving (and as permitted requesting), analysing and disseminating to the competent authority disclosure of financial information concerning suspicious proceeds of crime, or required by national legislation or regulation in order to counter money laundering".[547]

The Egmont Group established a permanent secretariat in 2008 in Toronto, Canada, and in 2014 the Group issued its 2014-2017 strategic plan, which sets out how it will be tackling its responsibilities and objectives over the stated period.[548] It has strong ties with the FATF[549] and was granted observer status at the FATF in February 2002.[550] The Egmont Group has made it possible that the potential for enhanced international co-operation through national FIUs becomes a reality.[551] Its role is recognised universally now.[552] The UN and the IMF/World Bank encourage international co-operation among FIUs.[553] The

---

[541]See Richards (1999: 240), Madinger (2012: 72), Levi & Reuter (2006: 340) and Kirby (2008: 304).

[542]See Richards (1999: 240) and Madinger (2012: 72).

[543]See Madinger (2012: 72).

[544]See Gilmore (2011: 82).

[545]See Mitsilegas & Gilmore (2007: 122).

[546]1996 FATF Recommendation 32. See also Gilmore (2011: 83).

[547]The Egmont Group of Financial Intelligence Units. www.egmontgroup.org. See also Mitsilegas & Gilmore (2007: 122).

[548]The Egmont Group www.egmontgroup.org.

[549]See Gilmore (2011: 83).

[550]See Gilmore (2011: 83).

[551]See Gilmore (2011: 83).

[552]The Egmont Group of Financial Intelligence Units. www.egmontgroup.org. See also Levi & Reuter (2006: 320), Gilmore (2011: 84), Mugarura (2012: 93) and Madinger 2012: 72).

[553]See Gilmore (2011: 84).

vacuum which existed in both the 1991 EU ML Directive and the 1996 FATF Recommendations[554] regarding the form of FIUs has been filled in that the Egmont Group prescribes the nature of FIUs.

2.5.3 The Wolfsberg Principles

The Wolfsberg Principles were published in 2000 and were revised in 2002 and again in 2012. Their name stems from the Wolfsberg Group, which consists of 11 international banks that met at the Château Wolfsberg in Switzerland in 2000 to develop standards in the financial services sector regarding KYC and AML and CFT policies.[555] The FATF has a close relationship with the Wolfsberg Group.[556] The Group publishes papers on the financing of terrorism and AML principles.[557] It also issues guidelines on AML with the aim of providing guidance in the areas of banking activity where the need exists. [558] In 2007, the Group issued a Guidance on Corruption, together with Transparency International and the Basel Institute of Governance.

Although the Basel Principles, the Egmont Group and the Wolfsberg Principles do not refer expressly to legal practitioners, they contain lessons and invaluable experiences that can be utilised by the profession. These bodies had to grapple with CDD and the filing of STRs, as well as FIUs. They also had to cope with the impact of hard law and soft law on the erosion of client confidentiality and the disclosure of confidential information to third parties. The legal profession, which works very closely with banks and financial institutions, is indirectly affected by the challenges that these bodies face, and is also bound to file reports to FIUs.

---

[554]Article 58 of UNCAC also requires that FIU's must be established to receive STR's. Articles 3(6) and 6 of the 1991 EU ML Directive. 1996 FATF Recommendation 16. See also Mitsilegas & Gilmore (2007: 122) and Gilmore (2011: 82).

[555]See www.wolfberg-principles.com. See also Mugarura (2012: 91), Van Jaarsveld (2011: 248), Ryder (2012: 19) and Leslie (2014: 162).

[556]See Mugarura (2012: 91).

[557]See Mugarura (2012: 91).

[558]See Mugarura (2012: 92).

2.6. Conclusion

There is no gainsaying the fact that lawyers are utilised to perform gatekeeper roles. However, the application of all the international instruments unambiguously excludes conduct which will affect an accused person's right to a fair trial. This means that although lawyers are essential for combating money laundering, there are strong indicators that the right to a fair trial of an accused should not be infringed and that whenever a client seeks advice that may lead to litigation, lawyers are under no obligation to submit STRs and CTRs to the appropriate authorities. There is no justification also to prosecute lawyers for being paid a tainted fee. The next chapter discusses the vulnerability of South African lawyers to money laundering.

3

THE SOUTH AFRICAN ANTI-MONEY LAUNDERING FRAMEWORK

3.1 Introduction

This chapter analyses the South African legal framework pertaining to money laundering and its impact on the legal profession. There are certain encumbrances placed on lawyers by AML legislation which infringe not only on the right to the free exercise of law as a profession, but also on the constitutional and statutory right to legal representation. This chapter points out the consequences and contradictions of requiring lawyers to act against the ethos of their profession. Attorneys have to comply with a number of important AML statutory measures in addition to the traditional obligations imposed on them by the Attorneys Act 53 of 1979 and the rules of their respective law societies.[559]

South Africa has developed a comprehensive legal structure to combat money laundering.[560] The principal AML statutes are the Prevention of Organised Crime Act (POCA),[561] the Financial Intelligence Centre Act (FICA),[562] and the Protection of Constitutional Democracy against Terrorism and Related Activities Act (POCDATARA).[563] FICA creates a range of AML

[559]See Dendy (2006: 33).

[560]See De Koker(2003: 83), Van Jaarsveld (2011: 461),Burdette (2010: 1), Van der Westhuizen (2011: 25) and Van Wyk (2001: 419).

[561]Act 121 of 1998.

[562]Act 38 of 2001.

[563]Act 33 of 2004.

obligations, including customer identification, record keeping requirements, and suspicious transaction reporting for financial institutions and DNFBPs such as lawyers and accountants. The main objective of FICA is to identify the proceeds of unlawful activities and to combat money laundering schemes. The overall purpose of POCA is to regulate racketeering and to outlaw the criminal activities of gangs. It also criminalises money laundering and contains a reporting obligation for businesses coming into possession of suspicious property. POCDATARA prohibits the facilitating and financing of terrorism and criminalises terrorist financing. It makes terrorist financing a predicate offence for money laundering.[564] A financial intelligence centre (FIC) was established explicitly to implement the AML mechanisms set out in both FICA and POCA.[565] Collectively, POCA and FICA form the backbone of the South African AML regime. POCA sets out substantive AML provisions, whilst FICA provides the administrative arrangements, deemed necessary to curb money laundering.

In this chapter the main issues regarding lawyers and money laundering, such as CDD, STRs and record keeping, and the payment of fees with tainted money, are covered. Although South Africa has implemented a comprehensive AML framework, the position of legal practitioners is not defined clearly. South African courts have not had the opportunity yet to consider challenges to money laundering legislation to the extent that their American and Canadian counterparts have.[566] This chapter thus gives special attention to the right to legal representation in relation to lawyers' right to practise their profession and the problem of tainted fees. The chapter also considers the impact of STRs on legal professional privilege and the effect on the independence of the legal profession of the expectation that lawyers collect evidence which could be used against their clients.

The chapter takes a close look at the impact that POCA and FICA have on the legal profession in South Africa. The fact of the matter is that it is possible for lawyers to be prosecuted for receiving and accepting dirty money as payment for fees. The question is whether this threat of being prosecuted has an impact on the right to legal representation and the right of lawyers

---

[564] FATF Mutual Evaluation Report 7. In the context of money laundering, a predicate offence is a crime (such as theft, fraud, robbery) which produces the proceeds to be laundered and which found the charge of money laundering. See further Article 2(h) of UNCAC.

[565] In the long title of FICA, the stated aim is: "To establish a Financial Intelligence Centre".

[566] See *Estate Agency Affairs Board v Auction Alliance* 2014 (4) BCLR 373 (CC) para 73 where Section 45B of FICA was declared unconstitutional.

to exercise their profession. Lawyers are required to file STRs against their clients. Failure to file such an STR renders the lawyer liable to prosecution. The question to answer here is what impact such reporting has on the confidential relationship that underpins interaction between lawyers and their clients. In addition, the law places an obligation on lawyers to ensure that their clients are identifiable. Clients' identities must be verified and stored, making it possible for the state to gain access to the information collected and stored by lawyers. Such information could be used against a client in subsequent criminal proceedings. All these matters are dealt with in this chapter. The discussion starts with the lawyer's receipt of fees paid with money deriving from a crime. Such a fee is referred to as a tainted fee.

3.2 Tainted Fees

3.2.1 Prevention of Organised Crime Act 121 of 1998

POCA came into operation on 21 January 1999 and includes AML measures that make it possible for lawyers to be prosecuted for accepting tainted fees.[567] It criminalises racketeering and money laundering and imposes an obligation on businesses to report certain information and provide for the recovery of the proceeds of unlawful activities.[568] The money laundering offence is committed when certain acts are performed in respect of "unlawful activities".[569] Provision is made also for the attachment and forfeiture of the instrumentalities of an offence.[570]

"Unlawful activity" includes:

> "any conduct which constitutes a crime or which contravenes any law whether such conduct occurred before or after the commencement of this act and whether such conduct occurred in the Republic or elsewhere".[571]

[567]Act 121 of 1998. See also Burdette (2010: 11), Van Jaarsveld (2011: 466), Ndzengu & Von Bonde (2013: 309) and De Koker (2003: 83).

[568]See long title POCA. See also Burdette (2010: 11), Van Jaarsveld (2011: 466), De Koker (2003: 83) and Van Wyk (2001: 420).

[569]See De Koker (2003: 84), Van Wyk (2001: 420) and Van Jaarsveld (2011: 467).

[570]*NDPP v Geyser* 2008 ZASZC and *NDPP v Vermaak* 2008 1 SACR 157 SCA. See also De Koker (2003: 83) and Van Wyk (2001: 420).

[571]Section 1 of POCA.

The "proceeds of unlawful activity" is defined as:

> "any property or any service, advantage, benefit or reward which was derived, received or retained, directly or indirectly in the Republic or elsewhere, at any time before or after the commencement of this act, in connection with or as result of any unlawful activity carried on by any persons, and includes any property representing property so derived". [572]

The definition of property in the Act is wide and illustrates that it is not only money that can be laundered.[573] The definition of property encompasses:

> "money or any other movable, immovable, corporeal or incorporeal thing, any rights, privileges claims and securities and any interest therein and all proceeds thereof".[574]

It is obvious that should a client pay his lawyer with money that constitutes the proceeds of an unlawful activity, such payment will fit within the ambit of the definition. A number of provisions in POCA could apply to lawyers representing criminal clients. Section 2 deals with racketeering,[575] Section 4 addresses the offence of money laundering,[576] Section 5 deals with persons who assist another to benefit from the proceeds of unlawful activity,[577] and Section 6 covers the acquisition, possession or use of the proceeds of unlawful activities.[578] POCA also includes penalties for convictions in terms of certain sections.[579] The applicability of these various provisions to money deposited into an attorney's trust account, or handed to an attorney for such deposit,

[572]Section 1 of POCA. See also Burdette (2010: 12) and Van Jaarsveld (2011: 467).

[573]See Sections 1, 4-6 of POCA. See also Burdette (2010: 12), Van Jaarsveld (2011: 467), De Koker (2003: 84) and Van Wyk (2001: 420).

[574]Section 1 of POCA.

[575]See Dendy (2006: 33), Burdette (2010: 13), Van Jaarsveld (2011: 470) and Van Wyk (2001: 420).

[576]See Burdette (2010: 13), Van Jaarsveld (2011: 470) and Van Wyk (2001: 420).

[577]Section 5(a) and 5(b) of POCA. See also Dendy (2006: 33), Burdette (2010: 13), Van Jaarsveld (2011: 470) and Van Wyk (2001: 420).

[578]Section 6 of POCA substituted by Section 8 of Act No. 24 of 1999. See also Dendy (2006: 33), Burdette (2010: 13), Van Jaarsveld (2011: 470) and Van Wyk (2001: 420).

[579]Section 3. & Section 8 of POCA. See also Dendy (2006: 33), Burdette (2010: 13), Van Jaarsveld (2011: 470) and Henning & Ebersohn (2001: 120).

is obvious.[580] It must be noted, however, that where a person is charged with any of the offences set out in Sections 2, 4, 5 and 6 of POCA, that person may raise as a defence the fact that he reported knowledge or suspicion in terms of Section 29 of FICA.[581]

In Section 4 of POCA, money laundering is described and criminalised in the following terms:

> "Any person who knows or ought reasonably to have known that property is or forms part of the proceeds of unlawful activities and-
>
> (a) enters into any agreement or engages in any arrangement or transaction with anyone in connection with that property, whether such agreement, arrangement or transaction is legally enforceable or not; or
> (b) performs any other act in connection with such property, whether it is performed independently or in concert with any person, which has or is likely to have the effect-
> (i) of concealing or disguising the nature, source, location, disposition or movement of the said property or the ownership thereof or any interest which anyone may have in respect thereof; or
> ii) of enabling or assisting any person who has committed or commits an offence, whether in the Republic or elsewhere
> (aa) to avoid prosecution
> (bb) to remove or diminish any property acquired directly, or indirectly, as a result of the commission of an offence shall be guilty of an offence."[582]

There is a knowledge requirement in this section as well as in the definition of money laundering in FICA. POCA deals firstly with a person who knows or ought to have known that the property at issue is part of the proceeds of unlawful activities.[583] It covers both intention and negligence as a requirement for guilt. It is not only actual knowledge that is defined, but also wilful

---

[580] See Dendy (2006: 33) and Itsikowitz (2006: 86).

[581] See Dendy (2006: 33).

[582] See also Burdette (2010: 14), Henning & Ebersohn (2001: 120) and De Koker (2003: 84).

[583] See De Koker (2003: 84) and Van Jaarsveld (2011: 470).

blindness and negligence regarding general knowledge, skill, training and experience that a person in that position reasonably may be expected to have. This knowledge is coupled with the general knowledge, skill, training and experience he in fact has. A lawyer who suspects that a monetary transaction may include the benefits of crime and proceeds with the transaction therefore could be in trouble. If he did not take reasonable steps to obtain further information, he will be deemed to have known that the money was acquired by illegal means.[584] The definition of knowledge in POCA[585] can mean that if the lawyer proceeds with the action, despite the property being tainted, the court may find that he acted with criminal knowledge.[586] Lawyers thus are vulnerable to possible prosecution if they acted with such knowledge.[587] This means that lawyers can be prosecuted simply for the fact that their fees were paid with dirty money.

Section 5 and Section 6 are applicable also to lawyers, since they embrace the conduct of their clients and hence, by necessary implication, the conduct of the lawyer himself.[588] They subsume the attorney-client relationship if the lawyer knows or ought to have known that his client has obtained the proceeds of unlawful activities. Section 5 reads:

> "Any person who knows or ought reasonably to have known that another person has obtained the proceeds of unlawful activities, and who enters into any agreement with anyone or engage in any arrangement or transaction whereby-
>
> a) the retention or the control by or on behalf of the said person of the proceeds of unlawful activities is to facilitate; or
> b) the said proceeds of unlawful activities are used to make funds available to the said other person or to acquire property on his or her behalf or to benefit him or her in any way, shall be guilty of an offence."[589]

[584]See Van Jaarsveld (2011: 471).
[585]Section 1(2) of POCA.
[586]See De Koker (2003: 85).
[587]See *Roestof v Cliffe Dekker Hofmeyr Inc* ZAGPPHC 219 (2012) and *S v Wei & Others*, pending case before the Western Cape High Court.
[588]See Burdette (2010: 13).
[589]Section 5 of POCA. See also Van Wyk (2001: 420), Van Jaarsveld (2011: 471) and De Koker (2003: 85).

A scenario like this played out in the case of *Roestof v Cliffe Dekker* where a lawyer was instructed by a client to claim money that was purported to be a debt.[590] An amount of R350 000 was fraudulently transferred out of the plaintiff's personal account, and R200 000 thereof was cleaned via the trust account of the defendant law firm. One of the directors of the firm was led to believe that the firm was receiving payment of a debt due to one of its clients. It was the client who used the law firm's trust account as a conduit to decontaminate the criminal proceeds of a phishing scam and caused the onward transmission of the money to another party. In this case, the law firm, in fact, assisted the client to benefit from his unlawful activities. Fortunately for the particular lawyer in question, the court found that there was no negligence on his part when he authorised that the amount be transferred to the launderer. [591]

In *S v Rossouw,* an attorney was charged with money laundering for allegedly assisting his client with unlawful activities.[592] The charge related to Rossouw's alleged participation in the financial schemes of the client.[593] It was alleged that Rossouw acceded to his client's request to have investors deposit their investments into his trust account. The money laundering charge against Rossouw was formulated in terms of Section 5 of POCA in that it was alleged that Rossouw assisted another person, his client, to retain or enjoy the proceeds of his client's unlawful activities. [594]

Section 6 of POCA similarly could implicate lawyers who receive the proceeds of unlawful activities. It reads:

> "Any person who
> (*a*) acquires;
> (*b*) uses; or
> (*c*) has possession of,
> property and who knows or ought reasonably to have known that it is or forms part of the proceeds of unlawful activities of another person, shall be guilty of an offence."[595]

[590]*Roestof v Cliffe Dekker Hofmeyr Inc* ZAGPPHC 219 (2012).

[591]*Roestof v Cliffe Dekker Hofmeyr Inc* ZAGPPHC 219 (2012). See also Hamman (2013: 43)

[592]*S v Rossouw*, unreported, case number: B1679/09, SHD163/09, Wynberg Regional Court.

[593]Greyling negotiated a plea bargain independently of Rossouw and accepted a sentence of eight years' imprisonment, three of which were suspended for five years. He also agreed to testify against Rossouw.

[594]See detailed discussion of *S v Rossouw* later in this chapter at Para 3.8.

[595]Section 6 of POCA.

The payment of legal fees could have the effect that when a lawyer acquires, uses or possesses money with a criminal origin, he commits a crime. If it is proved that the lawyer had knowledge of the origin of the tainted money, it could be argued that he acquired the proceeds of crime and could be guilty of contravening Section 6 of POCA.

The punishment for a conviction of one of the money laundering offences under Section 2, 4, 5 or 6 of POCA is a maximum fine of R100 million or imprisonment for a period not exceeding 30 years.[596] Thus, if a client pays his lawyer with tainted money and the paying of the fee is regarded as a transaction or an agreement, it could be argued that the proceeds of crime were used by the criminal to pay his lawyer.[597] Similarly, if it is proved that the lawyer knowingly acquired the proceeds of the unlawful activities as a fee, he can be prosecuted for accepting such a fee.

3.2.2 Financial Intelligence Centre Act 38 of 2001

The possibility of prosecution for accepting tainted fees is covered in Section 1(1) of FICA, where money laundering is defined as "an activity which has or is likely to have the effect of concealing or disguising the nature, source, location, disposition or movement of the proceeds of unlawful activities or any interest which anyone has in such proceeds".[598] The receipt or payment of legal fees can be regarded as an activity that has the effect of concealing or disguising the nature and source of unlawful activities.[599] Nowhere in the Act is there any indication that a lawyer will not be prosecuted for being paid with dirty money. In terms of Section 28 of FICA, an attorney is required to submit to the Financial Intelligence Centre a CTR in respect of all cash transactions constituting payments to and receipts from a client or his agent in excess of the prescribed threshold of R24 999-99.[600] The receipt of this amount in cash could well be the proceeds of an illegal activity. In such a case, the attorney, in

[596]Sections 3 & 8 of POCA. See also Henning & Ebersohn (2001: 120).

[597]Section 1 of FICA defines a "transaction". See also De Koker (2003: 88), Itsikowitz (2006: 78-79), Van Jaarsveld (2011: 489) and Hamman & Koen (2012: 73).

[598]See also Itsikowitz (2006: 78).

[599]See *S v Rossouw* , unreported, case number: B1679/09, SHD163/09, Wynberg Regional Court and *S v Wei & Others*, pending case before the Western Cape High Court.

[600]Regulation 22B of the regulations to FICA. See also Hamman & Koen (2012: 73), Henning & Ebersohn (2001: 124) and Millard & Vergano (2013: 399).

addition to being required to submit a CTR, will have been paid a tainted fee if the money was derived from unlawful activities.

Criminals always will look for means to facilitate the cleaning of their money, including enlisting the skills and resources of legal professionals.[601] Such skills and resources could be abused by launderers appointing counsel with the aim of cleaning money by paying huge fees.[602] It is thus quite possible that legal fees can be paid from the proceeds of crime and that legal practitioners can become involved in the money laundering process by accepting dirty money as fees. It is in the nature of a legal practitioner's work that large amounts of money are handled on a daily basis. Although some clients will pay their fees by cheque or by electronic remittances, amongst a certain category of clientele cash remains the most popular method of payment. Thus, for example, both the attorney who acts for a drug dealer in a criminal matter and the attorney who attends to a contractual or commercial matter for a drug dealer face the prospect of being offered tainted money in settlement of their fee accounts.

Tainted fees invariably place the lawyer in an invidious position, both ethically and legally. The problem is exacerbated in respect of criminal lawyers. Defence practitioners routinely deal with clients who are shady and suspect, and who may deposit the "proceeds of unlawful activities" into the practitioner's trust account to be defrayed later in respect of legal advice and representation provided by the practitioner. Indeed, the criminal lawyer is much more likely to be paid with dirty money than practitioners in other professions. He likely knows or suspects that many of his clients are villains whose funds are obtained nefariously. Such a conclusion is inevitable, more or less, when the client or his agent hands over to the lawyer large sums of cash in the caricatured suitcase, as a fee retainer or as bail money. However, it well may be reached also in those situations where a felonious client uses an electronic method of transferring tainted funds into his lawyer's trust account.[603] So it is quite evident that in terms of both POCA and FICA, attorneys face the possibility of prosecution because of being paid with dirty money. There is the real possibility that an attorney can be prosecuted for facilitating the cleaning of the money in terms of Sections 4, 5 and 6 of POCA and Sections 1 and 28 of FICA. This has repercussions for lawyers themselves as well as their clients.

---

[601]FATF Report (2013). See also Burdette (2010: 36).

[602]In *S v Wei & Others* it is alleged that the poaching syndicate paid the attorney exorbitant fees for legal representation.

[603]*Roestof v Cliffe Dekker Hofmeyr Inc* ZAGPPHC 219 (2012).

The criminalisation of accepting tainted legal fees has significant implications for the right to legal representation. This issue is discussed below.

3.2.3 The Effect on the Right to Legal Representation

Whereas all accused persons have a constitutional right to paid legal representation,[604] South African law does not protect attorneys who are paid with tainted funds and attorneys thus are vulnerable to prosecution as money launderers in respect of such funds. What is more, the legislature amended FICA in 2008 with the insertion of Section 43A which empowers the Financial Intelligence Centre (FIC) or a supervisory body such as a Law Society to issue Directives to attorneys to provide information, reports or statistical returns as requested and to surrender any document as required. Section 43A has been described as a crackdown on dirty money,[605] and well may be enlisted as a mechanism to police the acceptance of tainted fees in the legal profession. The receipt of tainted fees is not limited to attorneys who specialise in criminal work and can include civil lawyers who assist clients who have connections with organised crime. It is highly likely that a practitioner at some stage in his career will be confronted with this possibility.

This possibility of the receipt of tainted fees puts a lawyer in an unenviable position. He must decide whether to accept money which is tainted by criminality or whether he should represent a client whom he either knows or suspects will pay his fees with such money. It has been regarded by some writers as unethical for a lawyer to take dirty money as fees.[606] The practitioner is faced with the following legal conundrum: is the acceptance of such fees equivalent to money laundering, and does he, by accepting tainted money as fees, become complicit in a money laundering scheme. These ethical and legal questions ultimately affect an accused's constitutional right to legal representation. Every person has a right to legal representation and it is crucial for lawyers to provide such representation. To prevent lawyers from accepting tainted fee payments could violate a person's constitutional right to legal representation.[607] In the United States a huge debate took place regarding

---

[604]Section 35(3)(f) of the Constitution of 1996.

[605]See Mabanga & Pile www. *secure.financialmail.co.za*.

[606]See Orentlicher (1999: 1339-1376).

[607]See Bussenius (2004: 30).

the prosecution of lawyers for accepting dirty money as a fee payment.[608] This question has not been raised in South Africa yet, although there presently is a case before the Western Cape High Court, *S v Wei & Others*,[609] in which a lawyer who represents an abalone poaching syndicate, has been charged, along with members of the syndicate, with money laundering for allegedly being paid with tainted fees:

> "Bellville attorney Anthony Broadway, who allegedly helped Barends with his financial affairs, and who represented several syndicate members since 2001, was also a defendant in the restraint proceedings. His assets, listed on an annexure to the order, include properties in Kenridge and Bellville, a Mercedes-Benz, a Hyundai i20, a trailer, two motorcycles and the contents of nine bank accounts in his name. His wife, Helena, who lives in Kent in the UK, has been cited as a respondent, as was close corporation Royal Albatross Investments, in which Barends and two of his co-accused hold members' interests."[610]

The accused have been charged with several contraventions of the Marine Living Resources Act,[611] POCA and FICA, including money laundering and racketeering. His charges include the receiving or retention of property whilst he knew that such property was derived from a pattern of racketeering activity[612] and with contravening Sections 4, 5, and 6 of POCA[613] and the provisions of FICA.[614]

The fact is that an accused is entitled to legal representation under the Constitution.[615] Supposing the defence attorney suspects that the fee that he is paid stems from a crime, he has the following dilemma: must he decline the brief? If he does, and if other attorneys, too, decline the brief on the same basis,

---

[608]*United States v Monsanto* 491 US 600 (1989), *Caplin & Drysdale, Chartered, Petitioner v United States* 491 US 617 (1989) and *USA v Velez, Kuehne and Ochoa* US District Court, Southern District of Florida, Miami Division, Case No. 05-2-770-CR-COOKE.

[609]*S v Wei & Others*, pending case, Western Cape High Court.

[610]Schroeder F http://www.iol.co.za.

[611]Marine Living Resources Act 18 of 1998.

[612]Section 2(1)(b) of POCA.

[613]The charges relate to money laundering and offences relating to the proceeds of unlawful activities.

[614]*S v Wei*; Summary of facts Para F7.

[615]Section 35(2) & 35(3) of the Constitution of 1996.

what avenue is open to the accused? His right to legal representation of his choice would have been nullified. Can the accused then apply for legal aid on the basis that no one wants to defend him and that he is entitled to legal aid, not because he lacks the means, but purely on the ground that a substantial injustice could result otherwise?[616] There is case law to support the view that Legal Aid South Africa, the national body that administers legal aid, has no authority to decline an application for legal aid purely on the ground that the application does not satisfy the means test.[617] The Constitutional Court has held that a substantial injustice overrides the means test. It has identified a number of factors to be considered in deciding whether a substantial injustice would occur where the accused is not represented legally. These include the complexity or simplicity of the case, the ability of the accused to defend himself and the gravity of the possible consequences of being found guilty.[618] In practice, the courts generally have construed the phrase "substantial injustice" to include instances where "direct imprisonment is the likely punishment to be imposed".[619] In the event that the Legal Aid Board, decides not to assist a poor person, the court may overrule this decision if, in its view, the provision of a defence lawyer is essential to a fair trial.[620] A court may order the appointment of a defence lawyer at state expense irrespective of the view taken by the Legal Aid Board, "for the right to legal aid at state expense is most certainly one of the notions of a fair trial".[621]

Does this mean that an accused, despite having money to pay for a lawyer of his choice, must accept a legal aid lawyer who is allocated to him, who earns substantially less than a privately-appointed lawyer and who might not be experienced in handling money laundering cases?[622] Does this not undermine his constitutional right to legal representation, which has been interpreted by the courts to mean competent legal representation? Why must an accused who can afford a lawyer of choice be put in the same position as someone

---

[616]This means that a term of imprisonment of more than three months could be imposed if he is found guilty. See also (Meadows (1995: 454).

[617]Meadows (1995: 468).

[618]*S v Vermaas, S v Du Plessis* 1995 (2) SACR 125 (CC) Para 15.

[619]*S v Cornelius and Another* 2008 (1) SACR 96 (C) at Paras 102, 103a. See also *S v Moos* 1998 SACR 372 (C) and *Legal Aid Board v Msila and Others* 1997 (2) BCLR 229 (E). See also Legal Aid South Africa, Legal Aid Guide 2012 Para 4.4.2 at 47.

[620]See Eilman (2004: 319) and Cole (2011: 108).

[621]*S v Du Toit and Others* 2005(2) SACR 411 at 425.

[622]See remarks of Jaftha J in *National Director of Public Prosecutions v Elran* 2013 (4) BCLR 379 (CC): Money laundering legislation is complex even for judges.

who cannot afford such a lawyer? Conversely, why must the South African taxpayer fund, by way of legal aid, the criminal defence of someone accused of defrauding the economy of revenue? This person has money and if he is granted legal aid, it would mean that he is entitled to legal representation at state expense – without his having to pay a cent.

Another question is whether a lawyer must enquire from the accused where the money comes from which is used to pay his fee? Does this not immediately undermine the client's confidence in the lawyer? Will it not, as was pointed out in chapter one, make the client hesitant to disclose all the facts, thereby weakening the lawyer's ability to conduct an effective defence? If a lawyer declines a brief in the belief that his fee will be paid from dirty funds, he remains under obligation to report to the FIU as there is a reporting obligation under FICA even where the transactions did not take place between the lawyer's office and the client.[623] A further contentious issue is the fact that it is permissible, at least in some cases, for a lawyer who is representing someone who is contesting a preservation order, to be paid his legal fees out of the frozen illegal assets, whereas the lawyer who is defending someone charged with money laundering may not be paid out of dirty funds.[624]

3.2.4 The Effect on a Lawyer's Right to Exercise his Profession

As mentioned earlier, criminal defence lawyers, by definition, must enter into transactions with accused persons, many of whom have engaged in money-generating criminal enterprises. If the state is allowed to prosecute lawyers who represent criminals on the strength of POCA and FICA, it could spell the end of the criminal defence bar. Young lawyers could be discouraged from wanting to do criminal work. If it means the end of the criminal defence bar, what about the right of its members to earn a living and to exercise their profession? In terms of Section 22 of the Constitution, everyone is entitled to earn a living from his profession. It reads as follows:

> "Every citizen has the right to choose their trade, occupation or profession freely. The practice of a trade occupation or profession may be regulated by law."[625]

---

[623]Section 29(2) of FICA.

[624]See discussion of Sections 26(6) and 44(4) of POCA in § 3.4 below.

[625]Section 22 of the Constitution of 1996.

Law graduates have a right to choose the sphere of legal practice in which to specialise. It often happens in practice that new graduates enter the profession by becoming state prosecutors in the Department of Justice. This is the route to attain valuable criminal court and litigation experience. Some of them, after working a few years for the state, decide to join either the attorneys' or the advocates' profession. They, in all probability because of their experience gained, then will specialise in criminal law in defence of clients. There are also a number of Justice Centres in South Africa that offer articles of clerkship to candidate attorneys.[626] If there is a reluctance or hesitation on the part of these newly qualified lawyers, once their period of clerkship is finalised, to become criminal lawyers, they will be lost to the criminal defence bar. It will affect those who want to specialise in criminal law and it could lead to a situation that an accused person is unable to secure competent representation. The practitioner's right to choose to become a criminal defence lawyer is at risk here. It is submitted that such a restriction on the freedom to choose and practice criminal law as a profession will not pass constitutional muster. It is difficult to comprehend that the restriction on the freedom of choice of profession will be justifiable in terms of Section 36 of the Constitution, which deals with the limitation of rights.[627]

3.3 Reporting Suspicious Transactions

FICA establishes two types of reporting obligations: an obligation on all businesses to report suspicious transactions;[628] and additional reporting obligations for accountable institutions and reporting institutions.[629] The risks of attorneys' practices falling prey to the plotting of money launderers are addressed predominantly in Sections 28 and 29 of FICA, which provide for mandatory cash threshold reporting (CTR)[630] and mandatory suspicious

---

[626]See Meadows (1995: 456)

[627]This Section states that rights may be limited only in terms of a general law provided "the limitation is reasonable and justifiable in an open an democratic society based on human dignity, equality and freedom".

[628]Section 29 of FICA. See also Van Jaarsveld (2011: 489).

[629]Section 1 of FICA. See also De Koker (2003: 88), Itsikowitz (2006: 78-79), Van Jaarsveld (2011: 489) and Hamman & Koen (2012: 73).

[630]Section 28(a)-(b) of FICA. See also Millard & Vergano (2013: 399), Van Jaarsveld (2011: 490), Hamman & Koen (2012: 73) and Henning & Ebersohn (2001: 125).

transaction reporting (STR) respectively.[631] Sections 28 and 29 have implications for lawyers in that there is the possibility of criminal prosecution for a failure to report suspicious and unusual transactions to the FIC. Section 28 deals with transactions for which a cash threshold of R24 999-99 is prescribed.[632] An attorney is required to submit to the Financial Intelligence Centre a CTR in respect of all cash transactions constituting payments to and receipts from a client or his agent in excess of the prescribed threshold of R24 999-99.[633] Interestingly, the CTR obligation relates to both single transactions and to a series of transactions, each of which is below the threshold but which, if aggregated, constitute a fraction of a composite transaction which amounts to R25 000-00 or more.[634] The CTR must be filed within two working days of the attorney or a member of his practice becoming aware that a cash transaction exceeding the threshold has been concluded.[635] It would seem that Section 28 operates upon the principle that cash transactions in excess of the prescribed threshold are suspicious *ipso facto* and must be brought to the attention of the FIC.[636] The CTR may be understood as an effort to deploy a quantitative dictate in order to impede opportunities for money laundering.

Section 29 of FICA places an obligation on any "person who carries on a business, who manages a business or is in charge of a business or who is employed by a business" to submit an STR to the FIC.[637] Thus, in terms of Section 29(1), legal practitioners, as DNFBPs, have a reporting obligation in that, in addition to identifying and verifying each customer, they must keep updated client profiles and records and must report all suspicious transaction to the FIC.[638] Section 29(1)(a) places an obligation on any such legal practitioner to file an STR pertaining to his knowledge or suspicion of the receipt or imminent receipt by the business of the proceeds of unlawful activities; Section 29(1)(b) creates identical STR obligations in respect of those

---

[631] Section 29 of FICA. See also Van Jaarsveld (2011: 490), Hamman & Koen (2012: 73). Henning & Ebersohn (2001: 126) and Millard & Vergano (2013: 400).

[632] See Hamman & Koen (2012: 73) and Millard & Vergano (2013: 399).

[633] Regulation 22B of the regulations to FICA. See also Hamman & Koen (2012: 73), Henning & Ebersohn (2001: 124) and Millard & Vergano (2013: 399).

[634] This amounts to an attempt to prevent smurfing or structuring. See also Hamman & Koen (2012: 73).

[635] See Hamman & Koen (2012: 73).

[636] See Hamman & Koen (2012: 74) and Kilbourn (2008: 18.3).

[637] See De Koker (2003: 103) and Itsikowitz (2006: 78).

[638] See Van der Westhuizen (2003: 3) and De Koker (2003: 103).

business transactions which facilitate or are likely to facilitate the transfer of the proceeds of unlawful activities, or which are not manifestly lawful, or which are aimed at evading any FICA reporting duty, or which may pertain to tax evasion;[639] and Section 29(1)(c) replicates the STR duty in relation to the use or imminent use of the business for money laundering purposes.[640] As already intimated Section 29(1) creates a reporting onus in respect of suspicious and unusual transactions. The compass of its onus is wider than that of Section 28 in that it applies to any person who runs, manages or works for DNFBPs. All the personnel constituting an attorney's practice would fall within this compass, and thereby incur a legal obligation in respect of STRs.[641]

Lawyers are required to file the STR within 15 working days of having become aware of the transaction in question,[642] and the report must contain the particulars prescribed by Regulation 23 of the regulations to FICA.[643] Section 29(2) prescribes a similar STR duty in respect of dodgy transactions which, if concluded, may have caused the business to be used, *inter alia*, for money laundering purposes.[644] Section 29 makes the reporting to the FIC of unlawful or suspicious transactions, as well as money laundering transactions, mandatory for all members of a business, including a legal practice.[645] In the case where a practitioner or his firm receives dirty money it will indicate that he or the firm is party to a transaction or a series of transactions involving ill-gotten gains. This is viewed as facilitating the transfer of the proceeds of unlawful activities. It will have the effect that the business has been used, or is about to be used, for money laundering purposes, which is prohibited strictly by FICA.

Knowledge and suspicion are the effective stimuli for Section 29 and thus necessitate some consideration. The knowledge criterion is bivariate: it is "real" or "constructive" according to whether the person who is required to file the STR knew of or reasonably ought to have known of the money laundering character of the transaction in question.[646] Section 1(2) delineates

---

[639]See Van der Westhuizen (2008: 18).

[640]See Hamman & Koen (2012: 74) and Van der Westhuizen (2008: 18).

[641]*S v Mushimba* 1977 (2) SA 829 (A).

[642]FIC 2001 www.fic.gov.za. Regulation 24 of the regulations to FICA.

[643]See Hamman & Koen (2012: 74).

[644]See Van Jaarsveld (2011: 492), Burdette (2010: 18), Hamman & Koen (2012: 74) and Itsikowitz (2006: 80).

[645]See Hamman & Koen (2012: 74) and Itsikowitz (2006: 77).

[646]See Hamman & Koen (2012: 75).

real knowledge to include both positive or actual knowledge and negative knowledge constituted by wilful ignorance,[647] that is, a conscious choice to turn a blind eye to a contaminated transaction in order to fabricate an absence of knowledge. Section 1(3) is concerned with constructive knowledge and approaches it in terms of the standard of the reasonable person. It provides, essentially, that a person reasonably ought to have known that a business transaction was tainted if the conclusions he ought to have drawn would have been the conclusions of a reasonably diligent and vigilant person with his attributes and in his position. In other words, a person is deemed to have constructive knowledge of a money laundering transaction if a reasonable person in his shoes would have adjudged the transaction to be tarnished.[648] The fact is that a lawyer, armed with knowledge, whether real or constructive, of a money laundering transaction in his place of business has a legal obligation to file an STR with the FIC.[649]

As alluded to above, the Section 29 reporting obligations arise also if a person who runs, manages or works for a business reasonably ought to have suspected that a given transaction was contaminated by the malodour of money laundering.[650] The criteria contained in Section 1(3) apply also to the determination of whether or not a person reasonably ought to have had the suspicion which entrains a reporting obligation.[651] The legal consensus seems to be that the suspicion in question should be an objectively reasonable one, that is, a suspicion which a reasonable person in the same position would have formed and entertained.[652] Putting it differently, a person who runs, manages or works for a business is burdened with a legal obligation to file an STR in respect of any transaction which a reasonable person in his position would have considered suspicious and unusual.[653]

The AML reporting regime of FICA revolves not only around Section 29, but also Section 28.[654] An attorney must be aware of and comply with the requirements of both sections in order to avoid being prosecuted as a money launderer. Needless to say, there will be some overlap in practice, sometimes

---

[647]See Van der Westhuizen (2004(1): 37) and Hamman & Koen (2012: 75).

[648]See Hamman & Koen (2012: 75).

[649]See Hamman & Koen (2012: 75).

[650]See Hamman & Koen (2012: 75).

[651]See Hamman & Koen (2012: 75).

[652]See Itsikowitz (2006: 78-79), Van der Westhuizen (2004b): 37) and Hamman & Koen (2012: 75).

[653]See Hamman & Koen (2012: 75).

[654]See Hamman & Koen (2012: 76).

considerable, between his obligations under the two sections, in the sense that a transaction which exceeds the threshold of R24 999-99 prescribed in Section 28 well may qualify as a suspicious and unusual transaction under Section 29.[655] In such a case, the attorney would have to submit a CTR as an accountable institution as well as an STR as a person running or managing or employed by a business. Be that as it may, Sections 28 and 29 constitute a tandem effort to produce an AML climate and to enlist the support of attorneys in doing so. What is more, it is an endeavour which has a strong comminative dimension.[656] Thus, failure by an attorney to file a CTR in terms of Section 28 and an STR in terms of Section 29 is criminalised by Section 51 and Section 52 respectively, and Section 68 prescribes maximum penalties for such non-reporting, namely, 15 years' imprisonment or a fine of R10 million.[657] As intimated above, there is the real possibility that, in addition to being prosecuted for facilitating the cleaning of the money, as tainted fees, in terms of POCA and FICA, an attorney can face a charge of failing to report a suspicious transaction if he should have known thereof in terms of Sections 28 and 29.

Section 29 contains an additional sting in the tail for attorneys. Section 29(3) prohibits a person who has filed or must file an STR from revealing this fact or anything about the contents of said STR to anybody, including the person who is the subject of the STR. This is the NTO clause.[658] The prohibition is given prominence in Section 29(4), which forbids a person from disclosing any knowledge or suspicion that an STR has been or must be submitted, or from disclosing anything about the contents of the said STR. Again, the prohibition is all-embracing and includes disclosure to the person who is the subject of the STR in question. Together, Sections 29(3) and 29(4) constitute a comprehensive injunction against tipping off. Both subsections make provision for four identical exceptions, when disclosure of the STR or its contents may be permissible.[659]

However, these exceptions are limited and do not detract significantly from the NTO principle embedded in Section 29. This principle means that once an

[655]See Hamman & Koen (2012: 76).

[656]See Hamman & Koen (2012: 76).

[657]See Hamman & Koen (2012: 76), Burdette (2010: 21) and Millard & Vergano (2013: 402).

[658]See Itsikowitz (2006: 81).

[659]Section 29(3) and 29(4) of FICA prohibits tipping off, unless it is allowed: in terms of legislation, to carry out FICA's provision, for legal proceedings or in terms of a court order.

attorney has reported or is about to report a client in terms of Section 29, he may not inform the client that he has made or is about to make the STR, nor may he give the client any information about the contents of the STR.[660] The same would apply to any other member of the attorney's practice who knows or suspects that an STR has been or must be filed in relation to a specific client. The prohibition against tipping off makes eminent sense within the AML purpose of FICA. Warnings by attorneys or their staff to dodgy clients of STRs and their contents undermine this purpose directly by giving such clients the opportunity to take evasive action in relation to possible investigations by the FIC. Consequently, tipping off in contravention of Sections 29(3) and 29(4) is criminalised by Sections 53(1) and 53(2) respectively.[661] A person convicted of tipping off may be punished with imprisonment not exceeding 15 years or a fine not exceeding R10 million.[662] It is quite evident that the legislature regards tipping off a dodgy client to be as serious an offence as not filing an STR on such a client. A further reporting obligation is contained in Section 31 of FICA, which creates a reporting duty in respect of electronic funds transfers in excess of a prescribed threshold into and out of the country.[663] It applies to attorneys as accountable institutions. The provision obviously is a response to the internationalisation and ever-increasing digitalisation of money laundering referred to earlier and to the concomitant magnification of the vulnerabilities of accountable institutions.

Regardless of the route by which the monies find their way into his trust or business account, the attorney is obliged to report such suspicious transactions to the FIC or face the prospect of prosecution as a money launderer. There, is however, no indication as yet that South Africa is considering amending the STR requirement for lawyers, despite the worldwide debate in the FATF and the development of the RBA, which does not include compulsory STRs for lawyers.

3.3.1 Client Confidentiality and Legal Professional Privilege

FICA's reporting regime calls for attorneys to provide the FIC with information about their clients. This information may have been obtained

[660] See Hawkey (2011: 9). Similar provisions as in FATF Standards and the EU ML Directives.

[661] Section 53(1) and 53(2) of FICA.

[662] Section 68 of FICA. See also Hamman & Koen (2012: 77).

[663] Section 31 of FICA. See also Hamman & Koen (2012: 77) and Van der Westhuizen (2011: 36).

from or supplied in the course of the conduct of the attorney-client relationship. FICA seeks to allay the fears of attorneys to a certain extent by expressly protecting the legal professional privilege.[664] Section 37(2) states that the FICA reporting requirements trump whatever secrecy and confidentiality obligations an attorney may owe his client.[665] Fortunately, the legal professional privilege between attorney and client has survived. However, this protection afforded to the legal professional privilege is not a blanket one, but limited to confidential attorney-client communications made in respect of legal advice or litigation in progress, pending or proposed; and to confidential attorney-third party communications made in respect of litigation in progress, pending or proposed.[666] The latter protection would include, for example, confidential communications between an attorney and an advocate and an attorney and witnesses. Confidential attorney-client communications which do not resort under Section 37(2) are not privileged and thus not protected.[667]

Theoretically, FICA's reporting obligations do not contravene the well-established common law right to legal professional privilege. In fact, Section 37(2) confirms the common law in this regard. In practice, however, there is every likelihood that an attorney's complying with his duty to render a CTR or STR will violate the trust relationship with his client. Whereas the legal professional privilege may be crucial, the attorney-client relationship transcends it, comprehending also such decisive ethical matters as trust, confidence, security and reliability. In the run-of-the-mill world of legal practice, the distinction between legal professional privilege and attorney-client confidentiality is a purely formal one.[668] The theoretical distinction between privileged and unprivileged confidences is a practical restraint upon the requirement of an unencumbered attorney-client relationship as a vital element of the fair trial right to legal representation. Certainly, clients are inclined to expect that all communications with attorneys will be confidential and therefore privileged; they conflate confidentiality and privilege.[669] The fact is that the reporting requirements of FICA present the attorney with a most unpleasant choice: betray your client's confidence or betray your legal

[664]Section 37(2) of FICA.

[665]See De Koker (2003: 107), Itsikowitz (2006: 80) and Millard & Vergano (2013: 404).

[666]Section 37(2)(a) of FICA. See also Millard & Vergano (2013: 405).

[667]See Itsikowitz (2006: 81).

[668]See Itsikowitz (2006: 73-75) and Burdette (2010: 38).

[669]See Millard & Vergano (2013: 391).

obligations to report. FICA makes no attempt to regulate or resolve this issue. The attorney is left to his own devices. If he fails to comply with his reporting duties he runs the risk of being prosecuted as a launderer for his omission. If he does comply, he almost certainly will undermine the principle of attorney-client confidentiality.[670] That is a most unenviable ethical burden with which to saddle an attorney.

Nonetheless, there is no negating the fact that confidential attorney-client communications are not protected by the legal professional privilege if they do not relate to legal advice or litigation. The attorney features as a gatekeeper in international AML discourse and strategy. The reporting obligations of FICA require attorneys to take seriously their gatekeeper designation. All in all, these requirements give effect to the FATF recommendation that DNFBPs be drafted as troopers in the AML crusade.

As noted, although FICA overrides most of the secrecy and confidentiality obligations in South African law, the legal professional privilege between attorney and client has been protected explicitly in FICA.[671] In the case of *A Company and Two Others v The Commissioner for the South African Revenue Services*, it was held that the record of accounts can be protected by legal professional privilege if it contains legal advice.[672] The privileged information in respect of the seeking advice or of the giving of the advice was contained in a fee note and it was held that those parts where the fee note refers to the legal advice given would receive protection under legal professional privilege.

3.3.2 Customer Identification Obligation

The object of FICA was to complement POCA by introducing mechanisms and measures aimed at preventing and combating money laundering activities.[673] A key AML strategy in this connection is the KYC system. To this end, FICA creates a range of AML obligations, including customer identification, record-keeping requirements, and internal controls for banks, securities and investment firms, insurance companies, *bureaux de change*, money remitters, casinos, dealers in travellers' cheques and money orders, as

---

[670]See Van der Westhuizen (2008:18).

[671]Section 37 of FICA. See also Hamman & Koen (2012: 77) and Itsikowitz (2006: 84).

[672]*A Company and Two Others v The Commissioner for the South African Revenue Services* 2014 (4) SA 549 (WCC).

[673]Preamble to Act 38 of 2001.

well as for lawyers and accountants.[674] It imposes obligations on accountable institutions, *inter alia*, to establish and verify the identity of their clients;[675] retain these records for at least 5 years;[676] report suspicious and unusual transactions;[677] implement internal rules; appoint a compliance officer;[678] and train employees with regard to their money laundering control obligations.[679] This KYC system copies international AML measures.

The obligation to establish and verify the identity of clients and retain records is, however, somewhat abated by the exemptions provided for attorneys in respect of certain transactions.[680] Attorneys are exempted from this in respect of all business relationships and transactions with clients other than those listed in the regulations.[681] The obligations do apply in respect of clients, *inter alia*, who instruct an attorney in respect of transactions related to property, commercial, investment, trust and litigation work in respect of which the client deposits in excess of R100 000 for attorneys' fees over a 12-month period.[682] It is questionable whether practitioners are even aware of this requirement and, if they are, it would be interesting to find out whether they are complying with this obligation. The obligations do not apply in respect of parties who are not clients of the attorney.

These obligations are applicable then mostly to conveyancing attorneys and attorneys specialising in finance and real estate matters.[683] This is because money launderers tend to launder the dirty money through financial institutions or by buying and selling real estate. There is the obligation to establish and verify the identity of customers.[684] There is also the prohibition

---

[674]See Van der Westhuizen (2003: 33) and Millard & Vergano (2013: 396).

[675]Section 21 of FICA. See also Millard & Vergano (2013: 396) and Van der Westhuizen (2011: 35).

[676]Section 23 and 24 of FICA. See also Millard & Vergano (2013: 396).

[677]Section 29 of FICA. See also Millard & Vergano (2013: 396).

[678]Section 43 of FICA. See also Millard & Vergano (2013: 397).

679Section 42 of FICA. See also Millard & Vergano (2013: 397).

[680]Regulation 10 of Part 4 of Schedule to Regulations of FICA.

[681]Regulation 10 of Part 4 of the Schedule to the Regulations to FICA. The items listed in Regulation 10 of Part 4 of the FICA Regulations essentially reproduce those identified in the FATF Recommendations, and the 2001 EU ML 2001 Directive and the 2005 EU ML Directive.

[682]Regulation 10 of Part 4 of the Schedule to the Regulations to FICA.

[683]Regulation 10 of Part 4 of the Schedule to the Regulations to FICA is the same as the 2012 FATF Recommendation 22(d), Article 2(a)(5) of the 2001 EU ML Directive and Article 23(b) of the 2005 EU ML Directive.

[684]Section 21(1)(a) of FICA. see also Millard & Vergano (2013: 396), Henning & Ebersohn (2001: 124), De Koker (2003: 101) and Van der Westhuizen (2011: 35).

on an attorney entering into a business relationship with a client unless he knows the identity of the client and has verified the client's identity.[685]

The Regulations to FICA include the manner in which identification and verification of various categories of customers should be conducted.[686] In essence, FICA's identification obligation comprises two parts. The Regulations set out the information to be obtained about South African citizens and people resident in South Africa.[687] The Regulations also stipulate how the information must be verified.[688] It is submitted that lawyers, for their own good, must obtain these details from clients. They are required in terms of the rules of the various law societies and also for their protection, should they be sued for negligence where they fail to act on behalf of a specific client or if a client was defrauded.[689]

3.3.3 Record-Keeping Obligation

Lawyers, as accountable institutions, are required by FICA to keep detailed records of their clients and the transactions entered into by their clients.[690] This duty commences when a lawyer establishes a business relationship or enters into a transaction with a client. FICA also requires that lawyers keep records of the identity of a client and the manner in which the identity of the client was established. Details such as the nature of the business relationship or the transaction, the amount involved and parties to the transaction must be kept also. A further requirement is that any document or copy thereof used to verify a person's identity must be retained by a lawyer.[691] The obtained records must be kept for at least five years after a transaction has been concluded[692] and for a minimum of five years after the date on which a business relationship was terminated.[693] Records may be kept in electronic format.[694] The records

[685]See Van der Westhuizen (2003: 33), Millard & Vergano (2013: 398), De Koker (2004: 715) and Van der Westhuizen (2011: 37).

[686]Section 77(1)(b) of FICA.

[687]Regulation 3(1) of FICA.

688Regulation 44(1) of FICA. See also Van der Westhuizen (2003: 3).

[689]See Millard & Vergano (2013: 398).

[690]Section 22 of FICA.

[691]Section 21(1) and 21(2) of FICA.

[692]Section 22 of FICA.

[693]Section 23 of FICA.

[694]Section 22(2)) of FICA.

may be kept by third parties as long as the accountable institution has free and easy access to them,[695] and it is an offence to destroy or tamper with such records.[696]

3.3.4 Third Party Access to Client Records

In terms of Section 26 of FICA, an authorised representative of the FIC has access, during ordinary working hours, to any records kept by or on behalf of an accountable institution.[697] The FIC may examine, make extracts from or make copies of any such records.[698] The representative of the FIC, except in the case of records to which the public is entitled, may have access to the records only by virtue of a warrant issued by a magistrate or regional magistrate or judge within the jurisdiction where the records are kept, or within the jurisdiction where the accountable institution conducts business.[699]

A warrant may be issued by a presiding officer only if it appears to him, from information obtained under oath or affirmation, that there are reasonable grounds to believe that the records may assist the FIC to identify the proceeds of unlawful activities or to combat money laundering activities.[700] The warrant may contain such conditions regarding access to the relevant records as the magistrate, regional magistrate or judge may deem appropriate.[701] In fact, accountable institutions may allow representatives of the FIC to access any records only if such representatives are in possession of a warrant issued by a judge.[702]

Sections 45A and 45B, provide for both administrative and criminal sanctions for non-compliance with AML obligations.[703] Section 45B(7) allows for warrantless searches of the offices of accountable institutions. There is thus an anomaly between Section 26 and Section 45B of FICA. The new Sections 45A and 45B provide for the appointment of inspectors[704] and give

[695]Section 24 of FICA.

[696]Section 48(d) of FICA. See also Henning & Ebersohn (2001: 125).

[697]See Van der Westhuizen (2011: 38) and Burdette (2010: 22).

[698]Section 26(1) of FICA. See also Van der Westhuizen (2011: 38) and Burdette (2010: 22).

[699]Section 26(2) of FICA. See also Burdette (2010: 22).

[700]Section 26(3) of FICA. See also Van der Westhuizen (2011: 39).

[701]Section 26(4) of FICA.

[702]Section 27(1) & (2) of FICA. See also Henning & Ebersohn (2001: 125) and Van der Westhuizen (2011: 38).

[703]Section 45A and 45B of FICA Inserted by Financial Intelligence Centre Amendment Act 11 of 2008 (FICAA) and came into force 1 December 2010. See also Millard & Vergano (2013: 394).

[704]Section 45A(1) of FICA.

them onerous powers to ensure compliance with FICA. Some of the powers allow that inspectors, at any reasonable time and on reasonable notice, may enter and inspect any premises at which the FIC or, the supervisory body,[705] "reasonably believes that the business of an accountable institution, reporting institution or other person to whom the provisions of this Act apply, is conducted".[706] An inspector has the authority to direct that a person appear for questioning before him at a time and place determined by him.[707] He can order any person to produce a document relating to the affairs of the business[708] and to furnish him with information in respect of that document.[709] He may open or order someone to open any strong room, safe or other container in which he suspects any document relevant to the inspection is kept.[710] Furthermore, he may use any computer system or equipment to access any data contained therein and reproduce any document from that data;[711] he may examine or make extracts from or copy any document[712] and seize any document which he regards as evidence of non-compliance with a provision of FICA or any order, determination or directive in terms of FICA.[713]

An accountable institution must provide reasonable assistance to an inspector acting in terms of Section 45B(2).[714] The one advantage for lawyers is that the inspector, in respect of any accountable institution regulated or supervised by a supervisory body such as the LSSA, may conduct an inspection only if the supervisory body failed to do so despite a recommendation of the FIC made in terms of Section 44(B) or failed to conduct an inspection within the period recommended by the FIC.[715] Section 45B(6)(b) allows that "an inspector of a supervisory body may conduct an inspection, other than a routine inspection in terms of this section, only after consultation with FIC on that inspection".[716]

---

[705]In the case of lawyers the Law Societies of South Africa (LSSA).

[706]Section 45B(1) of FICA. See critique hereof in Van der Westhuizen (2008: 18).

[707]Section 45B(2)(a) of FICA.

[708]Section 45B(2)(b)(i) of FICA.

[709]Section 45B(2)(b)(ii) of FICA.

[710]Section 45B(2)(c) of FICA.

[711]Section 45B(d) of FICA.

[712]Section 45B(e) of FICA.

[713]Section 45B(2)(f) of FICA.

[714]Section 45B(3) of FICA.

[715]Section 45B(6)(a) of FICA.

[716]Section 45B 6)(a) of FICA.

Most alarmingly, for this kind of inspection no warrant is required.[717] If Section 45B had been applicable to law offices, it would have meant that a FIC inspector or a representative of LSSA could have entered the premises of any lawyer and taken any computer document to be used as evidence against a client at a later stage. It effectively would have meant that warrantless searches of law offices were sanctioned by legislation. Fortunately, in *Estate Agency Affairs Board v Auction Alliance,* the Constitutional Court declared Section 45B of FICA to be unconstitutional.[718] Although this matter did not specifically deal with lawyers, the judgment is crucial for lawyers who do not want their offices subjected to warrantless searches. In this case, the Estate Agency Affairs Board, wanted to conduct a warrantless search of the offices of Auction Alliance, an estate agency. Auction Alliance then approached the Western Cape High Court to declare both Section 32A of the Estate Agency Affairs Act (EAAA) and Section 45B of FICA unconstitutional. In the Western High Cape Court both sections were held to be unconstitutional and the matter went the Constitutional Court for confirmation of the High Court order. The Constitutional Court confirmed the invalidity of both sections but held that invalidity was not retrospective and the order was suspended for 24 months to give the legislature a chance to rectify the situation. The current situation is that, before FICA is amended, warrantless searches are not allowed and a supervisory body as well as inspectors from the FIC must obtain a warrant before they can conduct non-routine inspections. This is in accordance with the sentiment expressed by Bester, that the mere notion of the "conscription of attorneys to spy on and report on the activities of their unsuspecting clients to a government agency and to be designated the repository of the clients rights no matter how noble the cause, is morally and ethically repugnant".[719]

3.4 The Release of Legal Expenses

The two sections in POCA which deal with the release of money for legal expenses will now be discussed.[720] Sections 26(6) and 44 deal with the

[717]Section 45B(7) of FICA.

[718]*Estate Agency Affairs Board v Auction Alliance (Pty) Ltd and Others* [2014] ZACC 3 Para 65. This case is analysed in detail in §3.6.2 below.

[719]Bester (2002: 29). See also Millard & Vergano (2013: 409), Burdette (2010: 34) and Klaff (2004: 5).

[720]Sections 26(6) and 44 of POCA.

application for the release of legal expenses from property under restraining orders. The situation seems a bit strange in that, in terms of Sections 2, 4, 5 and 6 of POCA and Section 1 of FICA, attorneys could be charged because their fees are paid with dirty money. However, if one contrasts this with the release of legal expenses under Sections 26 and 44 of POCA, payment of fees from money where there is at least a suspicion that it is tainted, is allowed. It is submitted that a lawyer at least should suspect that his money is the proceeds from unlawful activities if his client's property is either restrained or the subject of a forfeiture application. If the application is for the forfeiture of property and it is alleged that the defendant has been drug dealer or a dealer in any other prohibited substance, one can assume that the suspicion has turned into knowledge. So it seems that in certain parts of POCA and FICA it is a crime to be paid with tainted fees, whereas in two sections of POCA it is not.

There is an argument that if a person has suffered a loss through, for example, a theft, he should not pay for the thief's defence.[721] Initially, the position of the courts was that a criminal should not be permitted to spend the proceeds of crime and benefit from the proceeds of crime.[722] Thus, it was held in *DPP v Aerobe and Others* that the proceeds of crime cannot be used for the defence of an accused.[723] Likewise, in *NDPP v Macasa* it was held that a claimant has no right to dissipate assets to discharge his reasonable legal expenses.[724]

Be that as it may, Section 26 and Section 44 of POCA contain provisions regarding the payment of legal expenses out of forfeited property.[725] Section 26(1) reads as follows:

> "The National Director may by way of an *ex parte* application apply to a competent High Court for an order prohibiting any person, subject to such conditions and exceptions as may be specified in the order, from dealing in any manner with any property to which the order relates."

Section 26(6), which contains the legal expenses clause, provides:

---

[721] See Ndzengu & Von Bonde (2011: 311).

[722] See Ndzengu & Von Bonde (2011: 311).

[723] *DPP v Aerobe and Others* 2000(1) SACR 366 (N).

[724] *NDPP v Macasa* 2000 (1) SACR 287 TKH para 81. See also Ndzengu & Von Bonde (2011: 311).

[725] See Freedman (2012: 445) and Ndzengu & Von Bonde (2011: 312).

> "Without derogating from the generality of the powers conferred by subsection (1), a restraint order may make such provision as the High Court may think fit—
> (*a*) for the reasonable living expenses of a person against whom the restraint order is being made and his or her family or household; and
> (*b*) for the reasonable legal expenses of such person in connection with any proceedings instituted against him or her in terms of this Chapter or any criminal proceedings to which such proceedings may relate, if the court is satisfied that the person whose expenses must be provided for has disclosed under oath all his or her interests in property subject to a restraint order and that the person cannot meet the expenses concerned out of his or her unrestrained property".

Section 26 will regulate a situation where there is an application for a restraining order against the property.

Section 44 also contains a legal expenses clause:

> "A preservation of property order may make provision as the High Court deems fit for—
> (*a*) reasonable living expenses of a person holding an interest in property subject to a preservation of property order and his or her family or household; and
> (*b*) reasonable legal expenses of such a person in connection with any proceedings instituted against him or her in terms of this Act or any other related criminal proceedings.
> (2) A High Court shall not make provision for any expenses under subsection (1) unless it is satisfied that—
> (*a*) the person cannot meet the expenses concerned out of his or her property which is not subject to the preservation of property order; and
> (*b*) the person has disclosed under oath all his or her interests in the property and has submitted to that Court a sworn and full statement of all his or her assets and liabilities."

Unfortunately, neither Section 26 nor Section 44 refers to the issue of legal aid for which a claimant may apply.[726] It is unclear whether a person first

[726] See Ndzengu & Von Bonde (2011: 314).

should exploit the avenue of obtaining legal aid and, if unsuccessful, apply for legal expenses or *vice versa.* In terms of Section 26, a court can grant a restraining order simultaneously with the order to release legal expenses. Section 26(6) has two requirements which must be met: the inability to meet expenses out of unrestrained property and a full disclosure of interest in the restrained property.[727] Although Section 44(2) requires an applicant to furnish the court with a full list of assets and liabilities, Section 26(6) does not require such a list to be lodged.[728] In neither Section 26 nor Section 44 is there a provision that assets proved to be the proceeds of unlawful activity may not be released to cover legal expenses. Ndzengu & Von Bonde argue that this is an indication that if the legislature wanted to exclude it, it would have provided so expressly.[729]On reading both sections it can be deduced that a discretion is allowed the courts to grant an order for the release of legal fees. The word "may" in both sections is indicative thereof. This discretion has been interpreted in the recent Constitutional Court judgment of *NDPP v Elran* and it is important to examine the case to understand how the Court dealt with this matter.[730]

3.5 Additional Duties of Lawyers under FICA

There are a number of other obligations imposed on lawyers by the AML legislation which do not require an in-depth analysis, but of which lawyers should be aware. Those will be discussed briefly in this section.

3.5.1 Training Obligation

Section 43 of FICA requires that lawyers educate their employees to comply with the Act and the internal AML rules of the practice. Failure to observe FICA's training obligation is not only an offence, but also may be raised as a defence by an employee charged with money laundering.[731] An employee of a

---

[727]*National Director of Public Prosecutions v Elran* 2013 (4) BCLR 379 (CC) Para 56. See also Ndzengu & Von Bonde (2011: 313).

[728]Section 44(2) of POCA.

[729]See Ndzengu & Von Bonde (2011: 313) and Freedman (2012: 445).

[730]*National Director of Public Prosecutions v Elran* 2013 (4) BCLR 379 (CC). This case is analysed in §3.6.1 below.

[731]Section 43(a) read with Section 62 of FICA. See also Dendy (2006: 33) and Van Jaarsveld (2011: 500).

law firm, when charged with a reporting offence, may as a defence argue that the firm failed adequately to train him to comply with the provisions of FICA or the firm's internal AML rules.[732] It is therefore in the best interests of lawyers to ensure that their employees are trained properly, as required by FICA. FICA also requires the appointment of a person whose main responsibility is to ensure compliance with AML measures by both fellow employees and his employer.[733] This person is responsible for evaluating, preparing and, where good cause exists, reporting suspicious transactions to the FIC.[734]

3.5.2 Development of a Set of Internal Rules

Attorneys' firms, irrespective of the nature of their practice activities, must develop a set of internal rules setting out the procedures and duties as per FICA.[735] The rules must be confirmed by the management of the firm by way of a resolution. Such internal rules must be documented in a manual which must be made available to the FIC at its request. [736] An attorney, like other accountable institutions, must formulate and implement internal rules regarding the verification of the identity of persons whom the attorney is obliged to identify, the information to be kept in terms of FICA, the manner in which and place at which such records must be kept, and the steps to be taken to determine when a transaction is reportable so as to ensure compliance with the Act.[737] The internal rules must be made available to employees.[738]

3.6 Litigation against AML Legislation

Since the promulgation of POCA and FICA, litigation against the legislation has not taken place on any significant scale. There is a paucity of cases challenging the constitutional validity of certain sections of POCA and FICA. In this section, two cases relevant to this study will be discussed. The

[732]Section 43(a) of FICA. See also Van Jaarsveld (2011: 501).

[733]Section 43(b)(i) & (b)(ii) of FICA. See also Van Jaarsveld (2011: 501).

[734]See Van Jaarsveld (2011: 501).

[735]Section 42 of FICA. See also Millard & Vergano (2013: 396).

[736]Section 42(4) of FICA .see also Law Society of Free State http://www.fs-law.co.za.

[737]Section 42(1) of FICA. See also Kilbourn (2008: 18.3).

[738]Section 42(3) of FICA.

first is *NDPP v Elran*[739] relating to the release of legal expenses; and the other is *Estate Agency Affairs Board v Auction Alliance,*[740] regarding the warrantless searches of the offices of accountable institutions.

3.6.1 *NDPP v Elran*

In this case, the Constitutional Court analysed Sections 26 and 44 of POCA as to how they relate to the payment of legal fees and what preconditions, if any, have to be met before an order for the payment of fees is made.[741] In 2006, a preservation order under POCA was obtained by the National Director of Public Prosecutions (NDPP) against Elran. At that stage the NDPP had reasonable grounds to believe that the Elran's property represented the proceeds of illegal activity. In June 2009, Elran applied to the High Court for an order for the release of funds to cover his legal expenses from the property covered by the preservation order. In his founding affidavit he denied having any funds or property not subject to the preservation order. He attached his two previous affidavits from May and June 2006 and provided no further update. The NDPP opposed the application on the grounds that Elran relied only on affidavits from 2006 and failed to provide any detailed information about charity and loans that he claimed to have received since 2006. The NDPP argued that he did not fulfil the precondition in Section 44(2)(b) which required that he submit "a sworn and full statement" of all his assets".

Elran's original application to the High Court was successful and this was confirmed by the full bench of the High Court on appeal. Both courts were satisfied that Elran had met the statutory requirements, and accordingly granted payment of legal expenses. The NDPP, however, dissatisfied with the outcome, lodged an appeal to the Constitutional Court.

The majority of the Court, for which Cameron J delivered the judgment,[742] held that the outcome reached at the High Court level was incorrect and that the wording of Section 44(2) is clear about the preconditions that must be fulfilled before a court may grant living and legal expenses. It held that Section 44(2)

---

[739]*National Director of Public Prosecutions v Elran* 2013 (4) BCLR 379 (CC).

[740]*Estate Agency Affairs Board v Auction Alliance (Pty) Ltd and Others* [2014] ZACC 3.

[741]The important judgment fot purposes of this research is the minority judgment delivered by Jaftha J. Cameron J wrote the majority judgment. Zondo J delivered a separate one with which Cameron J concurred.

[742]Concurred in by Mogoeng CJ, Froneman J, Van der Westhuizen J and Zondo J.

expressly stipulates two preconditions for the exercise of the power conferred in Section 44(1). The first is need and the second is disclosure.[743] The person must aver that he cannot meet the expenses concerned out of his property and he must declare under oath his interests in the property and submit a sworn statement of all his assets and liabilities. Without these preconditions being fulfilled to the court's satisfaction, the power does not exist. The court held that the words "shall not" do not leave enough space to manoeuvre for "interpreting the provision to mean that the conditions thereafter specified are merely factors to be taken into consideration in exercising a discretion that can be exercised regardless of their existence".[744] The majority disagreed with the minority who held that the precondition in Section 44(2)(a) is met even though it accepts that Elran did not comply with Section 44(2)(b).[745]

In a separate judgment, Zondo J concurred in Cameron J's judgment and found that Section 44 does not confer a discretion on a High Court to grant or refuse living expenses. He held that if a person in Elran's position was found to have no unpreserved property from which he could meet his legal or living expenses and was also found to have disclosed his full interest in the preserved property and to have submitted a statement of his assets and liabilities as required by Section 44, there could be no basis for the Court to refuse a provision of living or legal expenses. He found that Section 44(1) confers power on the High Court, which granted the preservation order, to provide for the living and legal expenses of a person holding an interest in the preserved property.[746] However, in terms of Section 44(2), the High Court is precluded from making provision for any living or legal expenses in favour of the person contemplated in Section 44(1) unless the two two preconditions are met.[747]

Unfortunately, the majority did not canvas the issues that are relevant to this thesis. Its main focus was on the validity of the preconditions as set out in Section 44(2). The majority failed to link the release of legal fees to the right to legal representation, whereas Jaftha J, in his the minority judgment, discusses the sections in relation to the right to legal representation. Therefore Jaftha J's judgment, although the minority one, is considered in more detail than those of Cameron J and Zondo J.

---

[743] *National Director of Public Prosecutions v Elran* 2013 (4) BCLR 379 (CC) Para 80.

[744] *National Director of Public Prosecutions v Elran* 2013 (4) BCLR 379 (CC) Para 80.

[745] *National Director of Public Prosecutions v Elran* 2013 (4) BCLR 379 (CC) Para 83.

[746] *National Director of Public Prosecutions v Elran* 2013 (4) BCLR 379 (CC) Para 97.

[747] *National Director of Public Prosecutions v Elran* 2013 (4) BCLR 379 (CC) Para 97.

Jaftha J[748] concluded that he would have dismissed the appeal and held that the requirements in Section 44(2), that the accused cannot meet his living expenses and the submission of a sworn statement of all his assets and liabilities, is a minimum threshold that has to be fulfilled. He held that the requirements are not preconditions, but merely considerations to be balanced in exercising the statutory discretion. Thus, even though Elran's disclosure was incomplete, Jaftha J was of the view that this did not bar the High Court from granting him legal expenses. He held that the Constitutional Court is bound by its interpretation of Section 26(6) that the right to legal representation must be recognised.[749] Accordingly it should be followed, unless it is shown to be wrong. He held that Section 44(1) confers a similar discretion on the court,[750] to direct that funds for reasonable legal expenses be paid from the seized property.[751] The interest in the property must be disclosed by the applicant in a sworn statement setting out fully his assets and liabilities. Section 44(2) also requires proof of his inability to meet his expenses from property falling outside the preservation order. The judge was of the opinion that the stipulation in Section 44(2) that the full list of assets and liabilities must be provided operated to assist the court to determine Elran's inability to pay.[752]

As alluded to earlier, Jaftha J's judgment is the only one which expressly referred to the right to legal representation. He stated that to construe Section 44(2) in the manner that was contended for by the NDPP, and also by the majority, would undermine the very purpose of by Section 44.[753] He held that without the recognition of the right to legal representation, the relevant chapter of POCA would be unconstitutional. He referred to the *Fraser* matter in which the Constitutional Court held that:

> "Without the recognition of the right to legal representation in Section 26(6), the scheme of the restraint embodied in POCA might well have been unconstitutional."[754]

---

[748]Moseneke DCJ, Nkabinde J and Yacoob J concurred.

[749]*Fraser v Absa Bank* 2007 (3) BCLR 219 (CC) Para 68.

[750]*National Director of Public Prosecutions v Elran* 2013 (4) BCLR 379 (CC) Para 62.

[751]*National Director of Public Prosecutions v Elran* 2013 (4) BCLR 379 (CC) Para 29.

[752]*National Director of Public Prosecutions v Elran* 2013 (4) BCLR 379 (CC) Para 31.

[753]*National Director of Public Prosecutions v Elran* 2013 (4) BCLR 379 (CC) Para 35.

[754]*National Director of Public Prosecutions v Elran* 2013 (4) BCLR 379 (CC) Para 35. See also *Fraser v Absa Bank* 2007 (3) BCLR 219 (CC) Para 68.

Jaftha J further held that the interpretation advanced by the NDPP is inconsistent with the promotion of the right to legal representation and the purpose of Section 44. It would lead also to absurd results.[755] He stated that the effect on the right to legal representation of not ordering legal expenses was not canvassed by the majority. He noted also that a court would be disempowered and precluded from authorising payment of expenses if the applicant failed to submit a list of assets, even if there are no assets to list, and this would have fatal consequences to applications of this nature.[756]

Jaftha J submitted that to avoid such absurdity, an interpretation of Section 44(2) should allow a court to authorise payment of expenses if it was satisfied that the applicant could not meet his expenses from his unpreserved property and he is entitled to receive payment of expenses from the property subject to the preservation order.[757] He held further that such an interpretation is in accordance with the purpose of Section 44 and advances the right to legal representation. He again referred to *Fraser* which laid down a similar approach:

> "The circumstances of each case have to be considered in order to reach a determination which is fair and just in view of the objects and wording of POCA, together with an accused person's constitutionally protected fair trial rights, existing rules and principles of the law of insolvency and other relevant areas of law. The High Court should seek as best as possible to ensure that a defendant neither benefits unduly from the terms of a restraint order, nor is prejudiced as far as reasonable legal and/or living expenses are concerned."[758]

Jaftha J found that proceedings involving POCA are complex because the Act is complex and difficult to interpret and therefore legal representation is necessary.[759] There is no indication in the record that Elran was aware that he could ask for a rescission of the judgment. Jaftha J said even if he was so aware,

---

[755] *National Director of Public Prosecutions v Elran* 2013 (4) BCLR 379 (CC) Para 36.

[756] *National Director of Public Prosecutions v Elran* 2013 (4) BCLR 379 (CC) Para 36.

[757] *National Director of Public Prosecutions v Elran* 2013 (4) BCLR 379 (CC) Para 37.

[758] *National Director of Public Prosecutions v Elran* 2013 (4) BCLR 379 (CC) Para 37. See also *Fraser v Absa Bank* Para 72.

[759] *National Director of Public Prosecutions v Elran* 2013 (4) BCLR 379 (CC) Para 52.

in all likelihood he would have battled to understand POCA which is difficult to interpret, even for judges. He made a crucial point regarding the right to legal representation, positing that the importance of the right in complex court proceedings in South Africa cannot be overemphasised.[760] He held that the interpretation of the majority is that Section 44(2) sets preconditions for the exercise of the discretion conferred by Section 44(1).[761] If these preconditions were absent, the power to authorise payment of legal expenses was non-existent. He agreed, given that the court is concerned with the exercise of a narrow discretion, interference would be justified only if one of the recognised grounds exists. He accepted that if Section 44(2) created preconditions which must be met before a court may exercise the discretion, then the High Court ought not to have granted the order because the respondent had not submitted a list of liabilities pertaining to loans he received from friends and family for his living expenses. But he noted that the question of whether Section 44(2) lays down preconditions or jurisdictional facts lies at the heart of his disagreement with the majority.[762]

It is unfortunate that the argument regarding the right to legal representation was not highlighted more by counsel and that the court did not deliberate this issue further. The court's focus was on whether it had a discretion to grant the order and whether the preconditions for the order were met. It is submitted that the majority could have been more critical regarding the preconditions. Surely the question of whether an application for legal expenses should fail or succeed should not depend on the failure to make a full disclosure on affidavit? Should the question not be whether an accused is entitled to legal expenses and the declaration under oath of a full list of assets and liabilities only a factor in determining whether he should be awarded legal expenses? The Constitutional Court could have been more critical in its discussion of Sections 26 and 44 and could have made recommendations or read down the sections to construct an equitable dispensation for the accused.

3.6.2 *Estate Agency Affairs Board v Auction Alliance*

In this matter the Constitutional Court had to consider the constitutionality

---

[760] *National Director of Public Prosecutions v Elran* 2013 (4) BCLR 379 (CC) Para 52.

[761] *National Director of Public Prosecutions v Elran* 2013 (4) BCLR 379 (CC) Para 53.

[762] *National Director of Public Prosecutions v Elran* 2013 (4) BCLR 379 (CC) Para 54.

of Section 32A of the Estate Agency Affairs Act (EAAA)[763] and of Section 45B of FICA.[764] Both provisions conferred wide powers of search and seizure on regulatory bodies. The application in the Western Cape High Court was brought by Auction Alliance (Pty) Ltd, an estate agency, as an accountable institution under FICA.[765] In terms of both Section 32A of the EAAA and of Section 45B of FICA, the Estate Agency Affairs Board is authorised, as a supervisory body, to conduct searches of the premises of accountable institutions without first obtaining a warrant.

The facts of the case are briefly as follows: In early 2012 Rael Levitt, the founder and former chief executive of Auction Alliance, was the subject of a television exposé that, if accurate, implicated Auction Alliance in activities constituting gross and wide-ranging violations of the EAAA and FICA.[766] The producers of the television programme forwarded the information that they had gathered to the Estate Agency Affairs Board and an investigation commenced. During the period that the Board was devising a strategy with the FIC, it learned that Auction Alliance was destroying documents and information.

The Board then decided to conduct an urgent search of Auction Alliance's offices in Cape Town, Johannesburg and Durban, unannounced and warrantless. The inspectors of the Board demanded entry to the offices.[767] Auction Alliance refused their request and launched an application for both interim relief, to prevent the Board from conducting the warrantless search and seizure operation, and for final relief through its constitutional challenge to the two provisions.[768] The Board's affidavits contained details of the evidence against Levitt and Auction Alliance and the High Court found that this evidence strongly suggested that Auction Alliance, as part of its operations, had committed serious breaches of both the EAAA and of FICA.[769] Auction Alliance chose not to tender any rebuttal and instead focused on the constitutional validity of the provisions. The High Court then found that the

---

[763] Act 112 of 1976.

[764] *Auction Alliance (Pty) Ltd v Estate Agency Affairs Board and Others* [2013] ZAWCHC 105.

[765] Schedule 1 of FICA sets out the categories of persons and institutions that are "accountable institutions". Item 3 specifies estate agents as defined in FICA.

[766] "Rael Levitt steps down as CEO of Auction Alliance & Investec responds to accusations" http:// www.myproperty.co.za.

[767] *Estate Agency Affairs Board v Auction Alliance (Pty) Ltd and Others* [2014] ZACC 3 Para 8.

[768] *Estate Agency Affairs Board v Auction Alliance (Pty) Ltd and Others* [2014] ZACC 3 Para 9.

[769] *Estate Agency Affairs Board v Auction Alliance (Pty) Ltd and Others* [2014] ZACC 3 Para 11.

Board's allegations had to be accepted as true and that the litigation proceed by accepting that Auction Alliance had committed grave infringements of the laws which regulated its business.

The High Court noted that Auction Alliance did not challenge "routine" inspections of its premises. Its challenge was limited to warrantless "non-routine" (or targeted") inspections. Such inspections were based on a particular suspicion of wrongdoing and it is these that Auction Alliance opposed.[770] The High Court referred to the decision of *Magajane*,[771] where the Constitutional Court held that all statutorily authorised inspections limit the constitutional right to privacy.[772] The High Court had to consider whether the inspections were reasonable and justifiable limitations under the Constitution.[773] It concluded that those engaged in the estate-agency industry have a reduced expectation of privacy. It found further that the search which the Board tried to conduct was, as under *Magajane*,[774]a search aimed at enforcement and concluded that Section 32A of the EAAA is overbroad. This was because it authorised a warrantless search of "any place" which an inspector has reason to believe "is connected with an act performed by an estate agent".[775] The Court held that this language was so wide that it could include even the private homes of estate agents' former clients. The provision also did not include any requirement of prior notice, or any guidance about how a search should be conducted. It was overbroad also because it required an estate agent to produce "any . . . document" demanded by an inspector, without limitation as to relevance.[776] The Court held that this overreach meant that the "provision did not survive scrutiny under the 'less restrictive means' rubric of the limitations clause".[777] In terms of Section 36(1)(e) of the Constitution, rights can be limited only "in terms of law of general application to the extent that the limitation is reasonable and justifiable in an open and democratic society based on human dignity, equality and freedom, taking

[770]*Estate Agency Affairs Board v Auction Alliance (Pty) Ltd and Others* [2014] ZACC 3 Para 13.

[771]*Magajane v Chairperson, North West Gambling Board* [2006] ZACC 8.

[772]*Estate Agency Affairs Board v Auction Alliance (Pty) Ltd and Others* [2014] ZACC 3 Para 14. Section 14 of the Constitution of 1996.

[773]Section 36(1) of the Constitution of 1996.

[774]*Magajane v Chairperson, North West Gambling Board* [2006] ZACC 8 at Para 70.

[775]Section 32A(1)(a)(ii) of the EAAA.

[776]Section 32A(1)(b)(ii) of the EAAA.

[777]*Estate Agency Affairs Board v Auction Alliance (Pty) Ltd and Others* [2014] ZACC 3 Para 15. Section 36(1)(e) of the Constitution of 1996.

into account all relevant factors, including less restrictive means to achieve the purpose."[778] The court thus implied that there are less restrictive means available to achieve the purpose of the EAAA and that the prohibition is too broad and therefore unconstitutional.

There was negligible evidence that "requiring a warrant for targeted searches would hinder the Board's work".[779] Despite the fact that industry participants have a reduced expectation of privacy in non-routine warrantless searches, it could not be justified when the searches were conducted with the "intention of enforcing statutory provisions that could eventually include criminal or quasi-criminal sanctions".[780]

The High Court then dealt with the constitutionality of Section 45B of FICA, which was found also to be defective, but less so.[781] It held that corporate entities such as Auction Alliance, operating in a closely regulated industry, would have a reduced expectation of privacy.[782] FICA's provisions were found not to be overbroad, although the inspection was targeted and non-routine, aimed at criminal investigation, and possibly could result in prosecution and penal sanction.[783] The section required that the inspection, whether routine or targeted, be for the purpose of determining compliance with FICA[784] and that reasonable notice be given and that searches be conducted at reasonable times. Inspections were limited also to determinable business premises, and guidance was provided to inspectors. The documents subject to inspection were limited to those relating to the institution's affairs. Although the Court noted that an inspection may be conducted at a private home where there was a reasonable belief that a business of the kind contemplated was being conducted, and that the provisions cover a large number of industries, the Court nevertheless concluded that the purpose of FICA requires this breadth.[785]

The Court deemed the section well-tailored to the ends it sought to accomplish, but held that there were less restrictive means available to obtain the information.[786] It held that the respondents had not shown that

---

[778] Section 36(1)(e) of the Constitution of 1996.

[779] *Estate Agency Affairs Board v Auction Alliance (Pty) Ltd and Others* [2014] ZACC 3 Para 15.

[780] *Estate Agency Affairs Board v Auction Alliance (Pty) Ltd and Others* [2014] ZACC 3 Para 15.

[781] *Estate Agency Affairs Board v Auction Alliance (Pty) Ltd and Others* [2014] ZACC 3 Para 17.

[782] *Estate Agency Affairs Board v Auction Alliance (Pty) Ltd and Others* [2014] ZACC 3 Para 17.

[783] *Estate Agency Affairs Board v Auction Alliance (Pty) Ltd and Others* [2014] ZACC 3 Para 17.

[784] *Estate Agency Affairs Board v Auction Alliance (Pty) Ltd and Others* [2014] ZACC 3 Para 18.

[785] *Estate Agency Affairs Board v Auction Alliance (Pty) Ltd and Others* [2014] ZACC 3 Para 18.

[786] It failed the "less restrictive means" component of the limitations clause; Section 36 of the Constitution of 1996.

requiring a warrant for targeted non-routine inspections would defeat the purpose of inspections.[787] Section 45B of FICA, like Section 32A of the EAAA, therefore was declared to be unconstitutional.[788] However, because of the substantial public interest considerations that were at issue, the declaration of unconstitutionality was suspended for 18 months to allow the Legislature to amend Section 45B.[789]

This matter then went to the Constitutional Court to pronounce on the validity of Section 32A of the EAA and Section 45B of FICA. The Court stated that this type of matter did not require any reinvention as the same issues had been dealt with in *Gaertner*,[790] where the Court invalidated provisions of the Customs and Excise Act.[791] This Act had authorised warrantless searches of premises and allowed inspectors to demand books and documents from persons believed to have them or to have control over them. The Act also permitted the breaking open of doors, windows and walls of premises in order to search and to open any room or safe if locked and the keys were not available. The sole qualification was that the premises could be entered only "for the purposes of" the statute. Beyond this, the provisions gave officials far-reaching powers that could be exercised at any place, at any time and in relation to whomsoever. There was a requirement that a reasonable suspicion should have existed, irrespective of the type of search.[792]

The Court held that the provisions of the EAAA and FICA were less conspicuously in conflict with constitutional rights than those at issue in *Gaertner*.[793] The provisions do not authorise the destruction of property in their execution [794] and the documents that inspectors may demand were are not limited to those linked to the business of estate agency.[795] The court held that Section 45B of FICA,[796] like Section 32A of the EAAA, limits searches to

---

[787]*Estate Agency Affairs Board v Auction Alliance (Pty) Ltd and Others* [2014] ZACC 3 Para 19.

[788]*Estate Agency Affairs Board v Auction Alliance (Pty) Ltd and Others* [2014] ZACC 3 Para 19.

[789]*Estate Agency Affairs Board v Auction Alliance (Pty) Ltd and Others* [2014] ZACC 3 Para 19.

[790]*Estate Agency Affairs Board v Auction Alliance (Pty) Ltd and Others* [2014] ZACC 3 Para 33. See also *Gaertner and Others v Minister of Finance and Others* [2013] ZACC 38.

[791]Customs and Excise Act 91 of 1964.

[792]*Gaertner and Others v Minister of Finance and Others* [2013] ZACC 38 Para 66. See also *Estate Agency Affairs Board v Auction Alliance (Pty) Ltd and Others* [2014] ZACC 3 Para 33.

[793]*Estate Agency Affairs Board v Auction Alliance (Pty) Ltd and Others* [2014] ZACC 3 Para 35.

[794]*Estate Agency Affairs Board v Auction Alliance (Pty) Ltd and Others* [2014] ZACC 3 Para 35.

[795]*Estate Agency Affairs Board v Auction Alliance (Pty) Ltd and Others* [2014] ZACC 3 Para 37.

[796]FICA was enacted in 2001, and Section 45B was inserted by Section 16(b) of the Financial Intelligence Centre Amendment Act 11 of 2008.

reasonable times.[797] In addition, it requires that, where appropriate, reasonable notice of the search be given.[798] Section 45B defines the premises that may be targeted and sets out, in some detail, the powers and obligations of inspectors during inspections.[799] The Court held that although the section refers to "any premises",[800] the search may be exercised only when the FIC or a supervisory body like the Estate Agency Affairs Board,[801]reasonably believes that the business of an accountable institution is being conducted there. In addition, the provision requires that non-routine inspections by a supervisory body, like the Board, may be conducted only after consultation on that inspection with the FIC.[802]

The Constitutional Court agreed with the High Court that because of the abovementioned features and given the pressingly important objectives of FICA in combating money laundering and the financing of terrorism, Section 45B was not overbroad.[803] However, it confirmed that Section 45B failed the "less restrictive means" component of the limitations analysis contained in Section 36 of the Constitution. A warrant was necessary for non-routine inspections and while surprise was often crucial, that could be attained by allowing warrants to be issued without notice to other parties (*ex parte*) and by providing limited exceptions. The Court found nevertheless that in starting from the premise that no searches need warrants, Section 45B went too far. Without modulation, that premise was not acceptable constitutionally.[804] The Constitutional Court held that: "It follows that the High Court's conclusion that the provisions must be declared incompatible with the Constitution and therefore invalid was correct."[805]

The High Court had suspended its declaration of invalidity of Section 45B for 18 months, to give Parliament a chance to fix the provision. The

---

[797]Section 45B(1) of FICA. See also *Estate Agency Affairs Board v Auction Alliance (Pty) Ltd and Others* [2014] ZACC 3 Para 38.

[798]*Estate Agency Affairs Board v Auction Alliance (Pty) Ltd and Others* [2014] ZACC 3 Para 38.

[799]*Auction Alliance (Pty) Ltd v Estate Agency Affairs Board and Others* [2013] ZAWCHC 105 Para 50.

[800]Section 45B(1) of FICA.

[801]Section 45B(1) of FICA.

[802]Section 45B(6)(b) of FICA. *Estate Agency Affairs Board v Auction Alliance (Pty) Ltd and Others* [2014] ZACC 3 Para 38.

803*Estate Agency Affairs Board v Auction Alliance (Pty) Ltd and Others* [2014] ZACC 3 Para 39.

[804]*Estate Agency Affairs Board v Auction Alliance (Pty) Ltd and Others* [2014] ZACC 3 Para 43

[805]*Estate Agency Affairs Board v Auction Alliance (Pty) Ltd and Others* [2014] ZACC 3 Para 43.

Constitutional Court felt it advisable to grant the Legislature a 24-month period of suspension, six months more than the High Court.[806]

The following order was made by the Constitutional Court:

> "1. The declaration of constitutional invalidity of Section 32A of the EAAA, and of Section 45B of FICA, made by the Western Cape High Court, Cape Town is confirmed.
> 2. The declaration of invalidity is not retrospective and
> 3. The declaration of invalidity is suspended for 24 months to afford the Legislature an opportunity to cure the invalidity."[807]

Although this case dealt with estate agents, it is applicable to lawyers as accountable institutions under FICA, and lawyers definitely can benefit from the order of invalidity. It emphasises the need for lawyers' offices and their contents to be protected against warrantless searches by the FIC and the law societies. Lawyers deal with much more confidential information than estate agents. Their files contain intimate details of clients, giving credence to the proposition that lawyers' office should not be utilised for gathering evidence against their clients for onward transmission to the prosecution authorities.

3.7 Response by Legal Profession

Although the association of law societies has not challenged the AML legislation in court, representations were made on the Financial Intelligence Centre Amendment Act (FICAA).[808] The representations were made at the Bill stage of the amendment and Parliament was urged to respect professional legal confidentiality, the independence of the profession and the rule of law.[809]

The submissions were made to the parliamentary Portfolio Committee on Finance. The LSSA delegation was led by Marilese Van der Westhuizen, who emphasised that, although the legal profession supported the campaign against money laundering and terrorism, the Bill represented a significant

[806] *Estate Agency Affairs Board v Auction Alliance (Pty) Ltd and Others* [2014] ZACC 3 Para 60.

[807] *Estate Agency Affairs Board v Auction Alliance (Pty) Ltd and Others* [2014] ZACC 3 Para 73.

[808] Financial Intelligence Centre Amendment Act (FICAA) 11 of 2008.

[809] See Van der Westhuizen (2008: 18) and Millard & Vergano (2013: 395).

attack on basic rights.[810] Parliament was requested to take the steps necessary to recognise the independence of the legal profession and the rule of law in the Bill. It was argued that measures in the Amendment Bill, such as those regulating access to attorneys' offices, would impose unreasonably onerous and impractical obligations on attorneys, which might affect adversely and seriously attorneys' ability and their right to conduct their profession in a business-like and effective way.[811] The Bill was regarded as a threat to legal professional privilege and attorney-client confidentiality, on the one hand, and to the independence of the profession, on the other.

3.7.1 Professional Privilege and Confidentiality

Van der Westhuizen pointed out that attorneys had difficulties in distinguishing confidential information from privileged information. She stated that practical experience has taught that it is a complicated exercise to differentiate between a transaction required to be reported to the FIC in terms of Section 29 of FICA and one not to be reported.[812] The danger exists that an attorney may report a client mistakenly for fear of non-compliance, thereby depriving the client both of an existing privilege and of the opportunity to obtain advice as to the existence and breach of such privilege.[813] In addition, the LSSA's concern was heightened by the proposed amendment which would empower the FIC to make available any information obtained by it during an inspection. The LSSA warned that, if the protection afforded to information and documents covered by legal professional privilege were not extended to the sections sought to be introduced by the Bill, a constitutional challenge may ensue.[814]

3.7.2 The Rule of Law and the Independence of the Legal Profession

The LSSA maintained in its submissions that an independent legal profession which requires that attorneys are free to carry out their work

---

[810] See Van der Westhuizen 2008: 18), Millard & Vergano (2013: 395) and. LSSA submissions Para 2.

[811] See Van der Westhuizen (2008: 18) and Millard & Vergano (2013: 395).

[812] See Van der Westhuizen (2008: 18) and Millard & Vergano (2013: 396).

[813] See Van der Westhuizen (2008: 18) and Millard & Vergano (2013: 395).

[814] See Van der Westhuizen (2008: 18).

without interference or fear of reprisal is fundamental to the doctrine of the separation of powers and the rule of law and to the profession's role in the proper administration of justice.[815] Van der Westhuizen, on behalf of the LSSA, stated:

> "Lawyers have a duty, within the law, to advance the interests of their clients fearlessly and to assist the courts in upholding the law. To enable them to perform these duties it is necessary that lawyers enjoy professional independence. Challenges to such independence may arise where attorneys are not able to form independent professional organisations, are limited in the clients whom they may represent, are threatened with disciplinary action, prosecution or sanctions for undertaking their professional duties or are subjected to unreasonable interference in the way they perform their duties. Independence is not provided for the benefit or protection of the legal profession as such. Nor is it intended to shield lawyers from being held accountable in the performance of their professional duties and to the general law. Instead, its purpose is the protection of the people, affording them an independent legal profession as a fundamental principle of justice." [816]

The provisions of the Bill which threatened this independence included the powers of the FIC to issue written directives to cease or refrain from engaging in an act, omission or conduct not necessarily related to the implementation or the provisions of FICA, and the proposal that the costs incurred in complying with such directives were to be borne by the accountable institution, in this case the attorney.[817] Also, the Bill contained the provision that any directive issued by the FIC would trump an Act of Parliament, a notion that, according to the LSSA, offended the principles underlying the rule of law.[818] Apart from the submissions made to Parliament and guidance given to lawyers, no court application was initiated from the legal profession's side to declare any part of the AML legislation unconstitutional.[819]

---

[815]See Van der Westhuizen (2008: 18).

[816]See Van der Westhuizen (2008: 18).

[817]See Van der Westhuizen (2008: 18).

[818]See Van der Westhuizen (2008: 18).

[819]The LSSA makes available guidance notes and videos to attorneys.

3.8 Prosecuting Lawyers as Launderers

There are very few South African cases in which attorneys have been prosecuted for money laundering. This well may indicate that South African attorneys are honest generally and have resisted successfully the dangers and lures of becoming money launderers or becoming entangled in the designs of money launderers. Alternatively, the dearth of cases may mean that money launderers have not turned their attention to the trust accounts of South African attorneys in any significant way yet. There is also, of course, the cynic's perspective according to which South African attorneys rarely are prosecuted for money laundering, not because they are vigilant gatekeepers, but because they are adept at concealing their money laundering shenanigans from auditors and other prying eyes. Be that as it may, there are only two reported South African cases at this stage in which attorneys faced criminal charges founded upon their participation in a money laundering scheme.

In the case of *Price*,[820] the attorney was charged with fraud in connection with the theft and laundering of two cheques. Price was part of a crime syndicate that stole two cheques drawn by Mercantile Registrars Limited, one for the amount of R325 000 and the other for the amount of R1 620 000. The first stolen cheque was deposited into Price's trust account at Standard Bank. The cheque was deposited with Price's knowledge, and was cleared for payment to his account by a syndicate member who worked for Standard Bank. Another member of the syndicate intercepted and destroyed the paid cheque when it was returned to Mercantile Registrars Limited.

After the money had been paid into his trust account, Price drew a trust cheque for the amount of R323 632,[821] payable to Tjeriktik Eiendomsbeleggings Bpk. This cheque was deposited into a bank account by yet another syndicate member and the bulk of the money was withdrawn periodically.[822] Price undertook a layering exercise in respect of the money by creating a dummy file in the name of the EM Gorton Trust. He used this dummy file to document fraudulently that one of the trustees had deposited the cheque into his trust account for a property transaction, that the transaction had fallen through

[820]*S v Price and Another* 2003 (2) SACR 551 (SCA).

[821]Price held back R1 368 (R1 200 plus VAT) as a fee.

[822]By the time the scheme was exposed, all but R8 964-01 of the R323 632 had been withdrawn.

and that, at the trustee's request, he had refunded the money to Tjeriktik Eiendomsbeleggings Bpk.[823]

The second stolen cheque was not deposited into Price's trust account. Instead, it was deposited into the trust account of Stephen Martin, a tyro attorney whom Price had recruited to help wash the stolen funds. Martin was supposed to be paid R25 000 for accepting the R1 620 000 into his trust account as payment for a fake business transaction and then repaying the money (to the second appellant, a certain Labuschagne) by way of an uncrossed trust cheque when the transaction supposedly collapsed.[824] However, Martin later withdrew from the scheme and he was then instructed to issue a trust cheque in favour of Good Hope Financial Services Trust for the full amount of R1 620 000. In the meanwhile, Martin had reported the scheme to the police, and when Price and his cohorts went to collect the cheque from Martin, they were arrested.[825] Thereby, the loss of the R1 620 000 was averted. Price was charged with and convicted of two counts of fraud. He received a prison sentence of 15 years on each count (to run concurrently)[826] and was ordered to pay R326 140-10 to Standard Bank as compensation for its loss in respect of the first cheque.[827] In dismissing Price's appeal against his sentence, Farlam JA held that:

> "The crime was carefully planned. Its execution involved the co-operation of a number of accomplices. In addition, the use of an attorney's trust account for what amounts to the laundering of the proceeds of crime is an important aggravating factor. Conduct of this kind by a practising attorney is reprehensible and cannot be tolerated."[828]

The trial judge had commented similarly on Price's involvement in the criminal enterprise, and on his attempt to corrupt a junior colleague:

---

[823]Price was supposed to have been paid R100 000 for his role in the scheme, but apparently he was swindled by the syndicate and ended up only with the fee of R1 200 (plus VAT).

[824]The idea was that Labuschagne would cash the uncrossed trust cheque at a bank.

[825]*S v Price and Another* 2003 (2) SACR 551 (SCA) Para 14.

[826]These were minimum sentences prescribed by Section 51(2)(a)(i) of the Criminal Law Amendment Act 105 of 1997.

[827]The compensation order was made in terms of Section 300 of the Criminal Procedure Act 51 of 1977.

[828]*S v Price and Another* 2003 (2) SACR 551 (SCA) Para 32.

> "He was part of a syndicate. He knew exactly how the crimes were to be committed. He related to attorney Martin that a person would steal a cheque and that the cheque would then be deposited into a trust account, and further steps would be taken. On one occasion accused No 1 made his trust account available for the stolen cheque. He wrote out a cheque and handed it to a co-conspirator ... On the second occasion accused No 1 involved a friend who happened to be a junior attorney ... His profession as an attorney required of him the utmost honesty. A breach thereof puts the crime in an even more serious light."[829]

The case of *Price* is a classic example of the way in which an attorney's trust account can be transformed into an instrumentality of money laundering. The syndicate in which Price was involved was organised extremely well: it had the capacity to steal cheques, clear them for payment, and then intercept and destroy the paid cheques when they were returned to the drawer. But the entire scheme turned upon the availability of his trust account through which to wash clean the money so acquired. In this sense, the case highlights the attractions which an attorney's trust account holds for money launderers and the dangerous temptations for attorneys which accompany the prospects of easy money.

The case of *Pillay*[830] arose out of a robbery by an armed gang, some of whom were police officers. The robbery netted a massive amount of R31 million. Pillay was one of nineteen accused facing charges of robbery with aggravating circumstances, He was convicted eventually as an accessory after the fact to robbery on the strength of his having facilitated the laundering of a portion of the proceeds of the robbery. Pillay did not participate in the robbery itself. However, a few months after the robbery he acted as the attorney for one of the robbers, a police sergeant by the name of Hanujayam Mayadevan, in the purchase of a night club for R1,2 million. Mayadevan paid the purchase price in cash, with money snatched in the robbery. The state alleged that Pillay was aware of the criminal provenance of the money and that he had helped to launder it, thereby incurring accessorial liability. He drafted two deeds of sale: the first reflected a purchase price of only R250 000 and did not identify any

[829] Cited by Farlam JA at Para 23.

[830] *Pillay & others v S* 2004 (1) All SA 61 (SCA) Para 60. See also Millard & Vergano (2013: 390) and Van der Westhuizen (2011: 29).

purchaser; the second recorded a purchase price of R420 000 and identified one Logan Chetty as purchaser. According to the court, Pillay's deflation of the price and evasion about the identity of the purchaser were "obviously consistent with an attempt to exclude any reference to Mayadevan and to conceal the large amount of money involved".[831] However, Pillay claimed that the actual purchase price of R1,2 million was to be paid by way of a deposit of R400 000 and three instalments, two of R250 000 each and one of R300 000, to settle the balance of R800 000. He averred that a deed of sale to this effect had been signed by the parties, but was unable to produce it.

A chartered accountant who performed an audit of Pillay's trust account revealed that he had received three cash payments in quick succession into said account, which he credited to the Embassy Night Club.[832] The three payments amounted to R420 000 which coincided with the purchase price in the second deed of sale. According to Pillay, he paid the R420 000 by way of trust cheques to the six members of the close corporation which owned the night club.[833] The remainder of the purchase price was paid by Mayadevan in cash instalments. However, these did not pass through Pillay's trust account as had the R420 000. The cash was delivered to his office, where the sellers were in attendance. The money was handed to the sellers who divided it immediately amongst themselves. All the instalments remained unreceipted. The court described this procedure as "bizarre".[834]

In the result, Pillay was adjudged to have been aware that the money paid by Mayadevan was part of the illegal proceeds of the robbery. What is more, Pillay himself guaranteed payment of the balance of R800 000 by signing an acknowledgment of debt for that amount in favour of the sellers. The court inferred that "he must have been extremely confident that the money would be forthcoming", and hence that he was "aware of its source".[835] The legal arrangements in terms of which Mayadevan was able to purchase the Embassy Night Club anonymously at the deflated price of R420 000 amounted to a scheme to launder R1,2 million emanating from the robbery. Pillay had used his trust account and his offices to implement this scheme, thereby assisting his client to replace a black asset with a legitimate one. The scheme was designed

---

[831] *Pillay & others v S* 2004 (1) All SA 61 (SCA) Para 60. Van der Westhuizen (2011: 29).

[832] The first amount was R249 050; the second was R169 850; and the third was R1 200.

[833] *Pillay & others v S* 2004 (1) All SA 61 (SCA) Para 46.

[834] *Pillay & others v S* 2004 (1) All SA 61 (SCA) Para 55.

[835] *Pillay & others v S* 2004 (1) All SA 61 (SCA) Para 69.

to help his client evade justice, leading to his conviction as an accessory after the fact to robbery and a sentence of five years' imprisonment. As in *Price*, here too we see an attorney, with malice aforethought, transforming his trust account from a guarantee of financial propriety into a mechanism of criminal impropriety.

In both *Price* and *Pillay* the attorneys were not charged with money laundering *per se*. The remainder of this section will consider three unreported cases in which lawyers did face or are facing charges as launderers. In the case of *Rossouw*,[836] money laundering was one of a number of charges brought against an attorney.[837] The charge related to Rossouw's alleged participation in the financial stratagems of a certain Eben Greyling, one of his clients.[838] The state's case against Rossouw was founded, *inter alia*, upon the following averments. Greyling ran the Gallagher Fund, an offshore investment fund operating out of Hong Kong. He sought to solicit investments from South Africans. Rossouw acceded to Greyling's request to have South African investors in the Gallagher Fund deposit their investments into his trust account. An amount of some R11 500 000 was deposited thus into Rossouw's trust account by local investors in terms of this arrangement. According to the state, these deposits were received fraudulently, not as *bona fide* investments, but as contributions to a pyramid scheme allegedly designed to enrich Greyling and Rossouw personally. There was also an attempt to legitimise the scheme by incorporating the Gallagher Fund as Gallagher Corporate (Pty) Ltd, in which Rossouw acted as intermediary between Greyling and the person who effected the conversion. The state alleged that both Greyling and Rossouw appropriated for themselves funds invested in the scheme.[839] Like all pyramid schemes, this one folded when it could no longer attract investments.

[836] *S v Rossouw*, unreported, case number: B1679/09, SHD163/09, Wynberg Regional Court.

[837] The money laundering charge was one of five different charges. The other four were fraud, contravention of Section 11(1) of the Bank Act 94 of 1990, contravention of Section 2(a) of the Financial Institutions (Protection of Funds) Act 28 of 2001 and contravention of Regulation 10(1)(c) of the Exchange Control Regulations as promulgated in terms of the Currency and Exchanges Act 9 of 1933. There was also a sixth default charge of conspiracy to commit the five main crimes.

[838] Greyling negotiated a plea bargain independently of Rossouw and accepted a sentence of eight years' imprisonment, three of which were suspended for five years. He also agreed to testify against Rossouw.

[839] Greyling apparently used the appropriated funds to buy an expensive property, a helicopter and two racing cars.

Rossouw tried to placate fearful investors by explaining that the delay in the repayment of their funds had been occasioned by a problem in Hong Kong.

The money laundering charge preferred against Rossouw on the strength of these allegations was formulated in terms of Section 5 of POCA. Put briefly, Section 5 criminalises the conduct of one person which is aimed at assisting another person to retain or enjoy the proceeds of that other's unlawful activities. In other words, the section renders criminal efforts by one person to launder the proceeds of the unlawful activities of another person. By relying upon Section 5 the state was alleging that Rossouw had assisted Greyling to retain and benefit from the proceeds of his fraudulent scheme by making his trust account available to launder said proceeds.

However, despite being charged, Rossouw was never tried. The state had prevaricated unduly in commencing with the prosecution, and Rossouw's attorney had scheduled an application for a permanent stay of prosecution. However, the state failed to file its opposition to the application timeously, and requested a further postponement. Naturally, the defence objected. The court brought proceedings to an end by striking the matter off the roll for unreasonable delay.[840]

In the case of *Hattingh*,[841] an attorney (who was also a conveyancer) faced a raft of 66 charges of fraud, theft and money laundering arising from a property scheme in which he purloined a total sum of R55 million from four prominent South African banks, namely, ABSA, Standard Bank, First National Bank and Nedbank.[842] The scheme included Hattingh's registering properties which he acquired in the names of his relatives, and registering two mortgage bonds from two different banks against the same property. The scheme was apparently so complex that in certain cases of double-bonded properties it was not possible to establish the identity of the second mortgagor. The charge of money laundering emanated from the fact that he had used his trust account as a conduit for the purloined funds, depositing them into the account when he first received them from the banks and then later withdrawing them for personal use. In other words, he had operated his trust account as a vehicle

---

[840]There remains the theoretical possibility that the state can request the matter to be enrolled again.

[841]*S v Hattingh* unreported, Bloemfontein Regional Court. Regrettably, the court papers pertaining to this case were not available, and the discussion of this case is based on information published in the media.

[842]See Stuurman www.publiceyenews.com.

through which to launder the proceeds of his unlawful activities. He has the distinction of being a self-interested launderer, having committed fraud and theft himself and then washing his loot through his trust account. Hattingh was convicted of all charges and sentenced to an effective 20 years behind bars, with the money laundering conviction carrying a suspended sentence of eight years' imprisonment.[843]

Then there is the case of the so-called "three amigos" which is pending before the KwaZulu-Natal High Court.[844] The "three amigos" are attorneys Nozibele Phindela, Jabulani Thusi and Ian Blose of the firm Kuboni & Shezi.[845] They and their firm have been charged with money laundering.[846] The charges relate to an amount of R1 million which the three allegedly laundered through the firm's trust account. The state avers that the R1 million was a kick-back paid by Uruguayan billionaire Gaston Savoi to the former KZN treasury head, Sipho Shabalala, for Savoi's company, Intaka Holdings, to be awarded government contracts to supply 20 water purification plants to medical facilities in KwaZulu-Natal.[847] The award to Intaka Holdings circumvented the usual procurement process governing the allotment of government contracts. The state alleges further that Savoi paid the R1 million into the trust account of Kuboni & Shezi, and the "three amigos" subsequently laundered the funds by disbursing them according to instructions received from Shabalala and his wife. The trial was scheduled to commence in December 2012, but Savoi took the matter to the Constitutional Court to have certain sections of POCA declared unconstitutional.[848] Savoi's challenge focused on having the definitions of "enterprise" and "pattern of racketeering activity" in Section 2(1) of POCA struck down as overbroad and void for vagueness. He also contended that Chapter 2 of POCA operates retrospectively, in violation of the rule of law and the right to a fair trial contained in Section 35 of the Constitution, and that Section 2(2) of POCA violates the right to a fair trial because it provides for admission of otherwise inadmissible evidence. Unfortunately, this matter did not discuss the involvement of the "three amigos" or the effect of the

[843]See Stuurman www.publiceyenews.com. and Broughton http://www.iol.co.za.

[844]As with the case of *Hattingh*, the case documents of this matter were not available and the ensuing discussion is based on media reports.

[845]There were sixteen accused in all, but the case has become known for the money laundering allegations against the three lawyers.

[846]See Peters http://www.iol.co.za.

[847]See Stuurman www.publiceyenews.com.

[848]*Savoi and Others v National Director of Public Prosecutions and Another* [2014] ZACC 5.

legislation on the legal profession. The further details of the involvement of the "three amigos" in this case remain sketchy. However, it goes well beyond the 'three amigos' themselves, apparently reaching into the upper echelons of the government of the province of KwaZulu-Natal. Regrettably, the true nature and extent of the scheme in which the "three amigos" became involved will, in all probability, not be made public during the trial. On 2 October 2012, the charges against the three attorneys, who have become known as the "three amigos", were withdrawn.[849]

In *S v Wei and Others,* a matter that is currently before the Western Cape High Court, it is alleged that Anthony Broadway, a defence attorney, is guilty of money laundering.[850] There are 30 accused and 590 charges in this matter. Broadway represented various clients who are his co-accused and who allegedly have been members of a criminal enterprise since 2002. He also allegedly assisted a co-accused, Frank Barends, in his financial affairs and received various sums of cash as fees from members of the enterprise. It is contended that he was at all relevant times aware that the members or employees or associates of the enterprise did not have any legal income to justify the amounts required to pay his fees.[851] He is thus the first attorney in South Africa to be charged for receiving tainted fees.

Broadway is facing charges also of racketeering[852] and with of contravening Section 2(1)(b), read with Sections 1, 2 and 3, of POCA[853] in that he had received or retained property whilst he knew that such property was derived from a pattern of racketeering activity.[854] He has been charged further with money laundering and offences relating to proceeds of unlawful activity by contravening Sections 4, 5, and 6 of POCA,[855] with a failure to comply with the provisions of FICA and with the failure to register with the FIC.[856] Other money laundering charges relate to the retrieval of money invested on behalf of Barends with a financial broker; an amount of R1,5 million paid

---

[849]See Oellerman www.news24.com.

[850]*S v Wei & Others*, pending case before the Western Cape High Court.

[851]*S v Wei & Others* Summary of facts Para E 27.

[852]This relates to receiving or retaining property on behalf of the enterprise.

[853]*S v Wei & Others* Summary of facts Para F3.

[854]Section 2(1)(b) of POCA.

[855]The charges here are money laundering and offences relating to the proceeds of unlawful activities.

[856]*S v Wei & Others* Summary of facts Para G 51, Count 566.

into his trust account for the benefit of Barends;[857] an amount of R425 058 paid from his trust account into the business account of a close corporation, Royal Albatross Investment 142 CC;[858] a cash cheque of R90 000 payable to him, which was cashed;[859] and an amount of R600 474,76 paid directly into his personal savings account.[860] It is not clear from the indictment, but one can presume safely that all these amounts are alleged to be the proceeds of unlawful activities, which supposedly were cleaned by Broadway.

His has been charged also with failure to submit STRs and CTRs to the FIC.[861] One of the counts alleges that Barends lent more than R1 million to one Johan Van der Berg and that Broadway, after he had requested the money via a letter of demand, facilitated the sale of Van der Bergs wife's house to Barends at a reduced price.[862] This is an example of a property scam to launder the R1 million in question.

It is not possible to draw any firm conclusions from the five cases discussed above and it would be patently unwise to attempt to do so. As intimated earlier, the paucity of cases may be interpreted optimistically or cynically. However, neither interpretation negates the need for sustained vigilance by attorneys, as gatekeepers, about the integrity of their accounts. If they demonstrate anything, the cases canvassed in this section confirm the persistent perils that attorneys have to negotiate in order to protect their accounts and businesses from criminal contamination. There is the real possibility that a crackdown on dirty money could result on a crackdown on the legal profession.[863] Anthony Broadway could be the first of many who find themselves in a situation where they have to face a judge or magistrate not from the counsel's bench, donned in their professional attire, but as an accused from the accused's booth.

3.9 Conclusion

It appears that the South African AML measures are more onerous than the FATF standards and the provisions contained in the international and

[857] *S v Wei & Others* Summary of facts Para G 52, Count 567.
[858] *S v Wei & Others* Summary of facts Count 519, 425.
[859] *S v Wei & Others* Summary of facts Para G 53 Count 573.
[860] *S v Wei & Others* Summary of facts Para G 53, Count 574.
[861] *S v Wei & Others* Summary of facts Para G 54 and 58.
[862] *S v Wei & Others* Summary of facts Para G 55.
[863] Hawkey (2011: 9).

regional instruments. There is no indication that the South Africa legislature or the legal profession has even considered amending the STR requirement for lawyers, despite the worldwide debate in the FATF and the development of the RBA, which does not include compulsory STRs for lawyers. The tainted fee issue has not received any consideration by the legal profession in South Africa thus far. At least the declaration of unconstitutionality of Section 45B of FICA has settled the issue of warrantless searches of law offices for now.[864]

It will be interesting to learn the outcome of the Wei matter, pending before the Western Cape High Court, regarding the questions of tainted fees and the non-submission of STRs.[865] The next chapter commences the comparative consideration of American and Canadian jurisprudence, with a focus on tainted funds as legal fees.

[864]A scenario which was predicted by Bester (2002: 29). Hawkey (2011: 9).

[865]*S v Wei & Others.*

4

THE PAYMENT OF LEGAL FEES WITH SUSPECTED TAINTED FUNDS

4.1 Introduction

This chapter contains a comparative study of US, Canadian and South African jurisprudence pertaining to the payment of legal fees with dirty money. In particular, it deals with the culpability of defence counsel for receiving a fee paid with money deriving from a criminal offence, and the forfeiture of fees paid to a lawyer by a client whose assets are targeted for forfeiture. The tainted fees[866] issue has a number of consequences for lawyers. The mere acceptance of tainted funds could be regarded as a crime and lawyers could be prosecuted. It has repercussions also for an accused person's right to legal representation and lawyers' right to exercise their chosen profession. The position in South Africa is that, in terms of both FICA and POCA, the payment of fees with tainted funds is a crime for both lawyers and clients. This chapter therefore investigates whether any lessons can be learned from the US and Canadian jurisprudence on this issue.

The US position will be surveyed first, and then the Canadian. The US, like South Africa, has a common law tradition, according to which the courts not only interpret the law, but also develop it and enlarge its meaning. As South Africa has a comparatively recent AML regime, there have been as yet few cases which have dealt with the impact of tainted fees on the legal

[866]It will be recalled from § 1.10 that "tainted fees" is shorthand for legal fees paid with dirty money.

profession.[867] The US, by contrast, was the first country to enact an AML law, one which has influenced the AML laws of many states around the world. Since the early 1970s, beginning with the decision of *California Bankers Association v Schultz*,[868] the US has developed a very considerable body of jurisprudence concerning the conduct of legal professionals in relation to its AML laws. Section 1957 of the Money Laundering Control Act (MLCA) of 1986 contains an important exemption for lawyers, excluding some of their fees.[869] The legal profession in the US has had to deal with the forfeiture of attorneys' fees and the possible prosecution of lawyers who represent launderers. These matters lie at the heart of this thesis, and it is useful therefore to understand how they have been dealt with in the US.

Canada was chosen as a comparator because it has dealt comprehensively with issues highlighted in this thesis. Canadian lawyers, like their American counterparts, aggressively resisted incursions into the independence of their profession and the right to counsel. Canada has developed principles governing tainted legal fees and fees paid out of seized assets. Unlike South Africa, the Canadian courts have built up a sizeable jurisprudence concerning the conduct of the legal profession in relation to Canadian money laundering laws. The Canadian legal profession challenged Canada's AML legislation over a period of fifteen years. It is instructive, therefore, for both South African lawyers and courts to understand how the US and Canadian legislation has been interpreted with respect to the abovementioned issues.

4.2 The Forfeiture and Criminalisation of Tainted Fees

4.2.1 The US Position

The US forfeiture statutes do not deal directly with money laundering, but have left a profound impact on the legal profession.[870] These statutes are concerned with the forfeiture of lawyers' fees. The main forfeiture statutes

---

[867] *S v Wei & Others.*

[868] *California Bankers Association v Shultz* 416 US 21 (1974).

[869] See Gaetke & Welling (1992: 1168), Richards (1999: 141) and Nelson (2009: 51).

[870] See Nelson (2009: 52), Gaetke & Welling (1992: 1176), Brickey (1986: 494), Brickey (1988: 48), Rudowsky (1987: 1965) and Winick (1989: 766).

are the Racketeer Influenced and Corrupt Organizations Act (RICO),[871] the Continuing Criminal Enterprise Act (CCE)[872] and the Comprehensive Forfeiture Act (CFA).[873] They do not contain any provisions that exempt attorneys' fees from forfeiture.[874]

The reason for the enactment of these forfeiture laws was to prevent an accused from dissipating and hiding tainted assets before conviction.[875] The CFA allowed the state to obtain restraining orders against accused persons in order to preserve the suspect property.[876] The assets of the accused may be attached before conviction.[877] The CFA also contains a "relation back clause" in terms of which the forfeited assets belong to the state as of the date on which the crime was committed.[878]

According to Section 1961(5) of RICO, a conviction requires that the state establish that an accused has exhibited a pattern of racketeering in two or more instances comprising a number of drug related and white collar crimes.[879] A number of other RICO provisions are particularly relevant in the context of money laundering. Section 1962 criminalises specific racketeering activities,[880] Section 1963 sanctions the forfeiture of the benefits of crime[881] and Section 1964 creates certain civil remedies that are available to both individuals and the

[871]See Sections 1961-1968 of RICO. See also Nelson (2009: 47), Richards (1999: 131), Brickey (1986: 484), Weinstein (1988: 369) and Winick (1989: 766).

[872]See Sections 848 *et seq* of the CCE. See also Nelson (2009: 47), Weinstein (1988: 369), Brickey (1986: 494) and Winick (1989: 766).

[873]21 USC 1984 Amending Section 1963 of RICO and Section 853 of the CFA. See also Nelson (2009: 49), Brickey (1986: 495), Rudowski (1988: 1968) and Winick (1989: 769).

[874]See Brickey (1986: 495) and Winick (1989: 770).

[875]See Gaetke & Welling (1992: 1176), Brickey (1986: 496) and Nelson (2009: 49).

[876]See Brickey (1986: 496) and Nelson (2009: 49).

[877]See Section 853(e) of the CFA and Section 1963(d) of RICO. See also Gaetke & Welling (1992: 1176) and Nelson (2009: 49).

[878]For a meaning of "Relation back" means: (law) the principle that an act done at a later time is deemed by law to have occurred at an earlier time. http://www.thefreedictionary.com. See Section 853(c) of the CFA and Section 1963(c) of RICO. See also Gaetke & Welling (1992: 1176), Nelson (2009: 49), Winick (1989: 770), Rudowski (1988: 1968) and Jacobs (1989: 337).

[879]Racketeering refers to criminal activity that is performed to benefit an organisation such as a crime syndicate. Examples of racketeering activity include extortion, money laundering, loan sharking, obstruction of justice and bribery. www.investopedia.com. Section 1961(1) of RICO. See also Van Jaarsveld (2011: 395).

[880]Section 1962 of RICO. See also Van Jaarsveld (2011: 395).

[881]Section 1963 of RICO and Section 853 of the CFA. See also Irvine & King (1987: 89), Gaetke & Welling (1992: 1176) and Van Jaarsveld (2011: 395).

state.[882] Section 848(c) of the CCE deals with a situation where the defendant receives a substantial income from a drug related enterprise together with five or more people.

Initially RICO forfeitures were instituted under Section 1963 of RICO and CCE drug forfeitures under Section 853 of the CFA.[883] The forfeiture provisions in the RICO and the CCE statutes are worded similarly and this resulted in Congress amending them in 2005 to provide that the CCE forfeiture under Section 853 of the CFA is the primary statute regarding federal criminal forfeiture.[884] Particularly important for the legal profession are the pre-trial restraining orders to preserve assets which are subject to forfeiture.[885] In terms of Sections 1963(d)(1)(A) of RICO, which is identical to Section 853(e)(1)(A) of the CFA,[886] the state may apply for a restraining order and the court may grant such an order if it is satisfied that there is a substantial probability that the state will be successful on "the issue of forfeiture and that a failure to grant such an order will result in the property being destroyed, removed from the jurisdiction of the court, or otherwise made unavailable for forfeiture".[887] It also must be proved to the court that a need exists "to preserve the availability of the property that outweighs the hardship on any party against whom the order is to be entered".[888]

Attorneys suffered the consequences of these sections in that they were used to forfeit attorneys' fees.[889] A remedy is available to attorneys in Section 853(n)(6) of the CCE, to the effect that if the attorney can prove that he was unaware that the property was subject to forfeiture under the section, the fees will not be forfeited.[890] If the attorney is successful in the application, the court order will be amended accordingly.

These statutes resulted in criminal lawyers forfeiting their fees and having

---

[882] Section 1964 of RICO. See also Van Jaarsveld (2011: 396).

[883] Sections 1961-1968 of RICO. See also Gaetke & Welling (1992: 1176).

[884] 28 USC Section 2461(c). Sections 1961-1968 of RICO. See also Gaetke & Welling (1992: 1176) and Winick (1989: 770).

[885] See Brickey (1986: 496) and Nelson (2009: 49).

[886] Section 1963A(d)(1) of RICO.

[887] Section 853(e)(1)(B)(i) of the CFA.

[888] Section 853(e)(1)(B)(ii) of the CFA.

[889] *United States v Monsanto* 491 US 600 (1989). *Caplin & Drysdale, Chartered, Petitioner v United States* 491 US 617 (1989).

[890] Section 853(n)(6B) of the CFA and Section 1963(a)(3)(c) of RICO. See also Brickey (1986: 498), Gaetke & Welling (1992: 1177), Winick (1989: 770) and Nelson (2009: 48).

to hand over money which they already had earned as a fee.[891] Even if an accused has hidden, commingled or diminished the dirty assets, the state is allowed to substitute such assets by confiscating clean assets belonging to the accused.[892] In the event of the accused transferring the assets to third parties, such as lawyers, they may be seized from such third parties.[893] This means that fees which the accused may have paid to his lawyer for his representation may be forfeited.[894] The only defence available to a lawyer is the so-called *bona fide* purchaser defence.[895] The onus is on the lawyer to prove that he was unaware that the property was subject to forfeiture. As a result lawyers, who defended accused persons who are subject to forfeiture orders, stood to lose their fees if they could not prove this defence.[896]

Certain provisions of the forfeiture statutes have been subject to challenges initiated by the legal profession in the cases of *United States v Monsanto*[897] and *Caplin & Drysdale*.[898] The reason for these challenges was the perception that the provisions in question infringe on the domain of attorney-client confidentiality, result in the forfeiture of legal fees, and violate an accused's Sixth Amendment right to legal representation. These cases are considered in detail below.

4.2.1.1 *United States v Monsanto*

In this matter, it was alleged that Peter Monsanto was involved in a large-scale heroin distribution enterprise.[899] He was indicted for alleged violations of racketeering laws, the creation of a continuing criminal enterprise, and tax and firearm offences.[900] It was averred further that he had accumulated three specified assets as a result of his narcotics trafficking, all of which were

[891] See Gaetke & Welling (1992: 1177), Nelson (2009: 55), Winick (1989: 770) and Brickey (1986: 497).

[892] See Section 853(p) of CFA and Section 1963(m) of RICO. See also Gaetke & Welling (1992: 1176).

[893] Section 853(c) of the CFA and Section 1963(c) of RICO. See also Brickey (1986: 498).

[894] See Gaetke & Welling (1992: 1176), Brickey (1986: 498) and Winick (1989: 772).

[895] Section 853 of the CFA. See also Gaetke & Welling (1992: 1177), Brickey (1986: 498) and Nelson (2009: 48).

[896] See Gaetke & Welling (1992: 1177) and Brickey (1986: 498).

[897] *United States v Monsanto* 491 US 600 (1989).

[898] *Caplin & Drysdale, Chartered, Petitioner v United States* 491 US 617 (1989). See also O'Brien (2008: 1).

[899] *United States v Monsanto* 491 US 600 (1989). See also Nelson (2009: 53) and Winick (1989: 772).

[900] See Nelson (2009: 53). *United States v Monsanto* 491 US 600 (1989) at 603.

subject to forfeiture under Section 853(e)(1)(A) of the CFA.[901] The District Court granted the *ex parte* motion for an order freezing the assets pending trial.[902] Monsanto raised various statutory arguments, claiming that the order interfered with his Sixth Amendment right to counsel of his choice.[903] He sought a declaratory order which would stipulate that if the assets were used to pay attorneys' fees, the third party transfer provision in Section 853(c) of the CFA would not be invoked to reclaim such payments if he were convicted and the assets forfeited.[904] This motion was denied by the District Court, but the Court of Appeals ordered that the restraining order be amended to allow him to pay attorneys' fees.[905] The matter then was appealed to the United States Supreme Court.

The Supreme Court, per White J,[906] found that no exemption from forfeiture exists in Section 853(a) of the CFA for assets that a defendant wishes to use to retain an attorney.[907] The Court stated that the language of Section 853(a) is plain and unambiguous.[908] It held that strong words were chosen by Congress to express its intent that forfeiture be mandatory. The Section states that upon conviction a person "shall forfeit ... any property" and that the sentencing court "shall order" a forfeiture.[909] There was no indication that the definition of property in the statute excluded attorneys' fees.[910]

The Supreme Court decided further that the restraining order did not the violate the respondent's right to counsel of choice as protected by the Sixth Amendment or the Due Process Clause of the Fifth Amendment.[911] It held that the federal drug forfeiture statute authorising a district court to enter a pre-trial order freezing assets in a defendant's possession, even where the

---

901 The assets comprised a home, an apartment and $35 000 in cash.

902 Section 853(e)(1)(A) of the CFA provides that a district court "may enter a restraining order or injunction or take any other action to preserve the availability of property ... for forfeiture..." *United States v Monsanto* 491 US 601. See also Nelson (2009: 53).

903 *United States v Monsanto* 491 US 600 (1989) at 604.

904 *United States v Monsanto* 491 US 600 (1989) at 604.

905 *United States v Monsanto* 491 US 600 (1989) at 604.

906 *United States v Monsanto* 491 US 600 (1989).

907 Section 853(a) of the CFA.

908 *United States v Monsanto* 491 US 600 (1989) at 607.

909 *United States v Monsanto* 491 US 600 (1989) at 607.

910 *United States v Monsanto* 491 US 6007 (1989) at 607.

911 *United States v Monsanto* 491 US 600 (1989) at 614.

defendant seeks to use those assets to pay an attorney, is permissible under the Constitution.[912] The court relied upon Section 853(c) which provides that:

> "All right, title, and interest in property described in subsection (a) of this section vests in the United States upon the commission of the act giving rise to forfeiture under this section. Any such property that is subsequently transferred to a person other than the defendant may be the subject of a special verdict of forfeiture and thereafter shall be ordered forfeited to the United States, unless the transferee establishes in a hearing pursuant to subsection (n) of this section that he is a *bona fide* purchaser for value of such property who at the time of purchase was reasonably without cause to believe that the property was subject to forfeiture under this section."[913]

The Supreme Court equated attorneys' fees to stock-brokers' fees, laundry bills or country club memberships, which also were not exempted from forfeiture.[914] It held that the District Court had the authority to issue a pre-trial restraining order against the assets, despite a defendant's right to counsel. It further held that this practice did not violate defendants' due process rights and that pre-trial restraining orders do not interfere arbitrarily with the right to retain counsel.[915]

4.2.1.2 *Caplin & Drysdale, Chartered, Petitioner v United States*

In *Caplin & Drysdale,*[916] a law firm sought payment for representing a client facing CCE charges. Christopher Reckmeyer was charged with running a massive drug importation and distribution scheme alleged to be a continuing criminal enterprise.[917] The state applied for an order to forfeit to

---

[912]*United States v Monsanto* 491 US. 600 (1989) at 614.

[913]Section 853(c) of the CFA. *United States v Monsanto* 491 US 600 (1989) at 613.

[914]*United States v Monsanto* 491 US 600 (1989) at 609. See also Nelson (2009: 53).

[915]*United States v Monsanto* 491 US 600 (1989) at 616. See also Nelson (2009: 54) and Gaetke & Welling (1992: 1177).

[916]*Caplin & Drysdale, Chartered, Petitioner v United States* 491 US 617 (1989). See also Nelson (2009: 54).

[917]*Caplin & Drysdale, Chartered, Petitioner v United States* 491 US 617 (1989) at 619.

it certain property that was acquired by Reckmeyer via drug-law violations.[918] The indictment sought forfeiture in terms of Section 853(a) of the CFA, of the specified assets that were in Reckmeyer's possession. A restraining order was granted by the District Court, which prohibited Reckmeyer from transferring any of the potentially forfeitable assets.[919] Despite the court order, he transferred $25 000 to the applicant, his lawyers.[920] He was represented by the applicant until after his indictment. He then applied to the District Court to amend the order to enable him to use some of the restrained assets to pay his lawyers' fees and he requested the Court to exempt such assets from post-conviction forfeiture.[921] However, before the Court could deliver its judgment, Reckmeyer entered into a plea bargain with the state in which he agreed to forfeit all of the specified assets.[922]

As a result of the agreement, the Court rejected his application, and thereafter ordered that virtually all of his assets be forfeited to the state.[923] The applicant then argued that assets used to pay an attorney are exempt from forfeiture under Section 853 of the CFA and, if they are not, that the statute's failure to provide an exemption renders the section unconstitutional.[924] It applied in terms of Section 853(n) of the CFA for an order to declare its third-party interest in the forfeited assets, which was granted in the District Court.[925] The decision, however, was overturned in the Court of Appeals, on the basis that there was no exception to the forfeiture requirement and that the statutory scheme was constitutional.[926]

On a further appeal, the US Supreme Court confirmed, in reference to its own earlier decision in *United States v Monsanto,*[927] that the discretion in Section 853(e) of the CFA, which authorises District Court judges to refuse to issue pre-trial restraining orders on potentially forfeitable assets, does not include a discretion to allow an accused to withhold assets to pay *bona fide*

[918] Section 853(a) of the CFA. *Caplin & Drysdale, Chartered, Petitioner v United States* 491 US 619 (1989).

[919] This was done in terms of Section 853(e)(1)(A) of the CFA. *Caplin & Drysdale, Chartered, Petitioner v United States* 491 US 617 (1989) at 619.

[920] *Caplin & Drysdale, Chartered, Petitioner v United States* 491 US 617 (1989) at 620.

[921] *Caplin & Drysdale, Chartered, Petitioner v United States* 491 US 617 (1989) at 621.

[922] *Caplin & Drysdale, Chartered, Petitioner v United States* 491 US 617 (1989) at 621.

[923] *Caplin & Drysdale, Chartered, Petitioner v United States* 491 US 617 (1989) at 621.

[924] *Caplin & Drysdale, Chartered, Petitioner v United States* 491 US 617 (1989) at 621.

[925] *Caplin & Drysdale, Chartered, Petitioner v United States* 491 US 617 (1989) at 621.

[926] *Caplin & Drysdale, Chartered, Petitioner v United States* 491 US 617 (1989) at 622.

[927] *United States v Monsanto*, 491 US 600 (1989) at 611-614.

attorneys' fees.[928] It also held that, in terms of Section 853(e) of the CFA, this discretion does not allow for non-restrained assets used for attorneys' fees to be forfeited subsequently under Section 853(c) of the CFA. Section 853(c) of the CFA provides for the recapture of forfeitable assets transferred to third parties, which in this case referred to attorneys' fees.[929]

The Court held that the CFA is not a burden on an accused's Sixth Amendment right to legal representation.[930] It stated that an accused cannot regard the spending of someone else's money as a Sixth Amendment right. This includes the payment of legal fees to an attorney.[931] It held further that the money in possession of a defendant is at that stage not rightfully his money.[932] The applicant's claim, that it is a Sixth Amendment right of a criminal defendant to pay attorneys' fees with assets which were forfeited to the state, was unsuccessful.[933] The Court found also that the forfeiture provisions do not disturb the balance of power between the state and the accused in a manner that is in conflict with the Due Process Clause of the Fifth Amendment.[934]

The Court acknowledged that forfeiture provisions are powerful weapons in the war on crime and that their impact can be devastating when used unjustly.[935] It noted further that due process claims alleging such abuses usually pertain to specific cases of prosecutorial misconduct.[936] The applicant in this case did not allege any prosecutorial misconduct.[937] The Court considered the applicant's claim that "the power available to prosecutors under the statute could be abused" to be somewhat far-fetched as there are "many tools available to prosecutors that could be abused in a manner that violates the rights of innocent persons".[938]

---

[928]*Caplin & Drysdale, Chartered, Petitioner v United States* 491 US 617 (1989) at 623.

[929]*Caplin & Drysdale, Chartered, Petitioner v United States* 491 US 617 (1989) at 623. See also Gaetke & Welling (1992: 1177) and Nelson (2009: 54).

[930]*Caplin & Drysdale, Chartered, Petitioner v United States* 491 US 617 (1989) at 626.

[931]*Caplin & Drysdale, Chartered, Petitioner v United States* 491 US 617 (1989) at 626. See also Nelson (2009: 55). *Laska v United States*, 82 F.2d 672, 677 (CA10 1936).

[932]*Caplin & Drysdale, Chartered, Petitioner v United States* 491 US 617 (1989) at 626. See also Nelson (2009: 55).

[933]See Gaetke & Welling (1992: 1176).

[934]*Caplin & Drysdale, Chartered, Petitioner v United States* 491 US 617 (1989) at 623. See also Nelson (2009: 54 & 76).

[935]*Caplin & Drysdale, Chartered, Petitioner v United States* 491 US 617 (1989) at 634.

[936]*Caplin & Drysdale, Chartered, Petitioner v United States* 491 US 617 (1989) at 634.

[937]*Caplin & Drysdale, Chartered, Petitioner v United States* 491 US 617 (1989) at 634.

[938]*Caplin & Drysdale, Chartered, Petitioner v United States* 491 US 617 (1989) at 634.

4.2.1.3 The Dissenting Judgment in *Monsanto* and *Caplin & Drysdale*[939]

In a dissenting minority judgment, Blackmun J argued that the majority did not take into account the devastating consequences that attorneys' fee forfeitures had on the integrity of the adversarial system of justice.[940] He confirmed that the majority rightfully acknowledged that nowhere in Section 853 of the CFA is there a provision referring expressly to the forfeiture of attorneys' fees and that there is no record that this was discussed by the legislature when drafting and passing the Act.[941] He held that the fact that "the legislative history and congressional debates are similarly silent on the use of forfeitable assets to pay stockbroker's fees, laundry bills, or country club memberships", means nothing.[942] According to Blackmun J, it cannot be believed that Congress was unaware that interference with the payment of attorneys' fees, unlike interference with these other expenditures, would raise Sixth Amendment concerns.[943] He agreed that Section 853(a) of the CFA is broad in language and is cast in mandatory terms, but disagreed with the majority's conclusion that the lack of an express exemption for attorneys' fees in Section 853(a) of the CFA makes the statute as a whole unambiguous.[944] He submitted that Congress also had a more traditional punitive goal in mind, which was to strip convicted criminals of all assets purchased with the proceeds of their criminal activities, particularly in the area of drug trafficking.[945]

The minority judgment, unlike the majority, discussed the effect of fee forfeitures on lawyers' right to practise their profession. Blackmun J submitted that fee forfeitures in the long run would decimate the private criminal-defence bar.[946] He considered that it could result in only the most idealistic

[939]Both cases were heard in the Supreme Court on the same day and by the same judges. Although Blackmun J's dissenting judgment is recorded in *Caplin & Drysdale*, it is applicable to both *Monsanto* and *Caplin & Drysdale*. See also Jacobs (1989: 336).

[940]*Caplin & Drysdale, Chartered, Petitioner v United States*. 491 US 617 (1989) at 635. Blackmun J delivered the minority judgment in which Brennan J, Marshall J and Stevens J concurred.

[941]*Caplin & Drysdale, Chartered, Petitioner v United States* 491 US 617 (1989) at 636. *United States v Monsanto* 491 US 608-609 (1989).

[942]*Caplin & Drysdale, Chartered, Petitioner v United States* 491 US 617 (1989) at 636. *United States v Monsanto* 491 US 600 (1989) at 608-609.

[943]*Caplin & Drysdale, Chartered, Petitioner v United States* 491 US 617 (1989) at 639. See also Jacobs (1989: 339)

[944]*Caplin & Drysdale, Chartered, Petitioner v United States* 491 US 617 (1989) at 637.

[945]*Caplin & Drysdale, Chartered, Petitioner v United States* 491 US 617 (1989) at 614.

[946]*Caplin & Drysdale, Chartered, Petitioner v United States* 491 US 617 (1989) at 646 & 650. See

and the least skilled young lawyers being attracted to the field of criminal practice.[947] He found that any attorney who is asked to represent the target of a drug or racketeering investigation would have to consider the possibility that the accused's assets could be forfeited.[948] He argued that the reluctance of an attorney to represent clients facing a forfeiture threat effectively strips the accused of the right to retain counsel.[949]

Blackmun J maintained that in dealing with reclaiming the assets under Section 853(c) of the CFA, a third-party transferee may keep assets if he was "reasonably without cause to believe that the property was subject to forfeiture".[950] However, he posited that although most legitimate service providers would meet these requirements for exemption, the situation for criminal defence attorneys was totally different.[951] Criminal lawyers would be unable to do their job without asking questions that would reveal the source of the accused's assets.[952] He concluded that pre-conviction forfeiture interferes with an accused's ability to secure counsel of choice and a fair trial.[953]

Blackmun J's position that fee forfeiture has a great impact on the right to counsel and a fair trial cannot be accepted fully. However, it is submitted that the long-term negative effects of the fee forfeiture practice on the right of lawyers to exercise their profession is a real possibility. The possible reluctance of law graduates to enter the sphere of criminal law practice could be one such long-term effect.

Correlative to the forfeiture issue is the question of whether the payment of legal fees with tainted funds should be regarded as a crime. The Money Laundering Control Act (MLCA) is the first US statute to deal directly with money laundering and was adopted to increase the government's ability to prosecute money launderers.[954] It creates two substantive money laundering

---

also Winick (1989: 781-782) and Orentlicher (1999: 1361).

[947]*Caplin & Drysdale, Chartered, Petitioner v United States* 491 US 617 (1989) at 651. See also Winick (1989: 781-782).

[948]*Caplin & Drysdale, Chartered, Petitioner v United States* 491 US 617 (1989) at 654.

[949]*Caplin & Drysdale, Chartered, Petitioner v United States* 491 US 617 (1989) at 654.

[950]*Caplin & Drysdale, Chartered, Petitioner v United States* 491 US 617 (1989) at 655.

[951]*Caplin & Drysdale, Chartered, Petitioner v United States* 491 US 617 (1989) at 655.

[952]*Caplin & Drysdale, Chartered, Petitioner v United States* 491 US 617 (1989) at 655.

[953]*Caplin & Drysdale, Chartered, Petitioner v United States* 491 US 617 (1989) at 655.

[954]Section 1956 and 1957 of the Money Laundering Control Act of 1986 (MLCA). See Nelson (2009: 49), Irvine & King (1988: 182), Richards (1999: 136), Weinstein (1988: 370) and Shuck (1996: 509).

offences and prohibits the splitting of currency transactions into amounts less than $10 000 in order to avoid reporting requirements.[955] It also provides for civil and criminal forfeiture of funds or property implicated in money laundering.[956] A person is prohibited from knowingly conducting a financial transaction with the proceeds of an unlawful activity or prohibited from transporting certain funds into or out of the US.[957] An accused will be convicted of the offence of money laundering if he had knowledge that the property involved in a transaction was derived from an unlawful activity. The forfeiture of the property to the US Government is regulated by this statute.[958] The MLCA supplemented the Bank Secrecy Act to compel financial institutions to report money laundering. The two substantive money laundering offences are included in Section 1956 and Section 1957,[959] both of which are particularly relevant for the legal profession and need to be examined separately.

4.2.1.4 Section 1956 of the MLCA

Section 1956 is divided into subsections (a) to (i) and further subdivided into three key parts relating to (1) financial transactions,[960] (2) international transportation[961] and (3) undercover sting operations.[962] Section 1956(a)(1) is most relevant to the legal profession and will be discussed in detail. It reads as follows:

> "Whoever, knowing that the property involved in a financial transaction represents the proceeds of some form of unlawful activity, conducts or attempts to conduct such a financial

[955]Sections 1956(a)(B)(ii) and Section 1957 of the MLCA. See also Irvine & King (1988: 182), Richards (1999: 136), Madinger (2012: 25), Shams (2004: 30) and Weinstein (1988: 370).

[956]See Irvine & King (1988: 182), Richards (1999: 136), Madinger (2012: 25), Weinstein (1988: 370), Shams (2004: 28) and Sultzer (1996: 159).

[957]Section 1956(a)(2)(B) of the MLCA 1986. See also Irvine & King (1988: 182).

[958]See Weinstein (1988: 373) and Irvine & King (1988: 183).

[959]See Richards (1999: 136), Doyle (2012: 1), Weinstein (1988: 373), Irvine & King (1988: 182), Sultzer (1996: 159) and Leslie (2014: 169).

[960]Section 1956(a)(1) of the MLCA. See also Madinger (2012: 25), (1999: 136), Doyle (2012: 1) and Sultzer (1996: 160).

[961]Section 1956(a)(2) of the MLCA. See also Madinger (2012: 25), (1999: 136), Doyle (2012: 1) and Sultzer (1996: 160).

[962]Section 1956(a)(3) of the MLCA. See also Madinger (2012: 25), (1999: 136), Doyle (2012: 1) and Sultzer (1996: 160).

transaction which in fact involves the proceeds of specified unlawful activity-

(A)(i) with the intent to promote the carrying on of specified unlawful activity; or

(ii) with intent to engage in conduct constituting a violation of Section 7201 or 7206 of the Internal Revenue Code of 1986; or

(B) knowing that the transaction is designed in whole or in part

(i) to conceal or disguise the nature, the location, the source, the ownership, or the control of the proceeds of specified unlawful activity; or

(ii) to avoid a transaction reporting requirement under State or Federal law, shall be sentenced to a fine of not more than $500,000 or twice the value of the property involved in the transaction, whichever is greater, or imprisonment for not more than twenty years, or both."

It is apparent that four kinds of money laundering are dealt with in Section 1956.[963] It prohibits anyone from conducting or attempting to conduct a financial transaction that involves the proceeds of specified unlawful activities[964] intending to promote the carrying on of specified unlawful activity[965] or intending to evade taxation,[966] or knowing that the transaction is intended to hide the laundering of the proceeds,[967] or knowing that the transaction is meant to avoid AML reporting requirements.[968] Thus, if any lawyer is suspected of assisting a client, knowing that a client is conducting or attempting to conduct a financial transaction involving the proceeds of unlawful activities, promoting or continuing the unlawful activity, or evading

[963]See Richards (1999: 138), Doyle (2012: 1) and Weinstein (1988: 370).

[964]Section 1956(a)(1) of the MLCA. See also Madinger (2012: 24), Richards (1999: 136), Doyle (2012: 1), Sultzer (1996: 160) and Irvine & King (1988: 182).

[965]Section 1956(a)1(A)(i) of the MLCA. See also Madinger (2012: 24), Richards (1999: 138), Doyle (2012: 1) and Irvine & King (1988: 182).

[966]Section 1956(a)1(A)(ii) of the MLCA. See also Madinger (2012: 24), Richards (1999: 138) and Doyle (2012: 1).

[967]Section (1956(a)1B)(i) of the MLCA. See also Nelson (2009: 56), Sultzer (1996: 161), Weinstein (1988: 374) and Irvine & King (1988: 183).

[968]Section 1956(a)1(B)(ii) of the MLCA. See also Weinstein (1988: 374) and Irvine & King (1988: 183).

the payment of taxes or concealing the proceeds or avoiding AML reporting requirements, that lawyer could be prosecuted.

Section 1956 is consonant with the United Nations Conventions and the EU Directives. It prohibits financial transactions where the source of the funds is specified unlawful activity.[969] In addition to federal crimes, foreign offences mentioned in the MLCA include schemes to defraud a foreign bank, drugs trafficking, robbery and extortion.[970] For a conviction it must be proved that an accused had knowledge that the property involved in a transaction was derived from an unlawful activity.[971] The accused is not required to have actual knowledge of the exact origin of the proceeds, the exact details of the underlying offence or even its nature; it is sufficient that he knew that the proceeds came from a criminal activity and constitute the proceeds of a predicate offence.[972] Turning a blind eye to reality will not be regarded as a lack of knowledge.[973] The knowledge required may be inferred from the surrounding facts that indicate a criminal activity. Lawyers thus can be prosecuted, and have been, if they knew that their clients used the proceeds of unlawful activity and were engaging them as legal representatives to conceal that unlawful activity.[974]

In his defence, a lawyer can argue that he did not intend to promote a criminal activity or was unaware that payment was designed to conceal the proceeds of a crime.[975] A person cannot be convicted for negligent involvement in a money laundering scheme. Under Section 1956, an accused can receive a

---

[969]Section 1956(c)(7) of the MLCA. See also Richards (1999: 137) also Weinstein (1988: 373).

[970]Section 1956(c)(7)(B)(i)–(iii) of the MLCA. See also Gaetke & Welling (1992: 1170), Sultzer (1996: 162) and Weinstein (1988: 370).

[971]Section 1956(a)(1) of the MLCA. See *US v Santos* 128 S.Ct. 2020 (2008). See also Van Jaarsveld (2011: 392) and Doyle (2012: 4).

[972]As explained in chapter two in the context of money laundering a predicate offence is a crime (such as theft, fraud, robbery) which produces the proceeds to be laundered and which found the charge of money laundering. See further Article 2(h) of UNCAC. See also Irvine & King (1988: 183), Weinstein (1988: 373) and Shams (2004: 30).

[973]See Van Jaarsveld (2011: 390), Richards (1999: 137), Madinger (2012: 27) and Sultzer (1996: 161).

[974]*United States v Velez* F.3d 875 (11th Cir. 2009), *United States v Abbel* 271, F.3d 1286 (11th Cir.2001), *United States v Reed* 167 F.3d 984 (6th Cir. 1999), *United States v Ross 190 F.3d 446 (6th Cir. 1999), In United States v Elso* 422 F.3d 1305 (11th Cir.2005). See also Nelson (2009: 58), Weinstein (1988: 374) and Richards (1999: 140).

[975]*United States v Velez no 05-20770-cr-cook* (2008), *United States v Velez* F.3d 875 (11th Cir . 2009). See also Weinstein (1988: 374).

20-year sentence, but the prosecution has to prove beyond a reasonable doubt that the accused had knowledge of the origin of the money. Section 1956 must be distinguished from Section 1957, which deals with transactions affecting an accused person's right to legal representation.

4.2.1.5 Section 1957 of the MLCA

Section 1957 of the MCLA contains an offence regarding engagement in monetary transactions involving property derived from specific unlawful activity.[976] This section at first did not contain an exemption for lawyers. It initially stated that:

> "whoever knowingly engages or attempts to engage in a monetary transaction in criminally derived property that is of a value greater than $10 000 and is derived from specific unlawful activity, shall be punishable."

In essence, Section 1957 deals with the receipt or disbursement of more than $10 000 in criminally derived property in a monetary transaction.[977] In contrast to Section 1956, there is no requirement that the funds be used for any additional criminal purpose nor is there a need that the accused have any intent to engage in another criminal transaction.[978] The purpose of Section 1957 is to keep dirty money out of banks and financial institutions.[979] It criminalises the mere receipt or disbursement of more than $10 000 in a monetary transaction involving criminally derived property. The section requires that a person have knowledge that the money was derived from a specific unlawful activity.[980] It puts lawyers in an unenviable position if they knew that their clients paid them with tainted money.

---

[976]See Madinger (2012: 34), Weinstein (1988: 373), Brickey (1988: 48), Gaetke & Welling (1992: 1168), Irvine & King (1988: 173), Orentlicher (1999: 1349) and Nelson (2009: 56).

[977]See Madinger (2012: 34), Irvine & King (1988: 183), Brickey (1988: 48) and Weinstein (1988: 373).

[978]See Madinger (2012: 34), Shams (2004: 31) and Weinstein (1988: 373).

[979]See Irvine & King (1988: 183) and Madinger (2012: 34).

[980]See Madinger (2012: 34), Gaetke & Welling (1992: 1168), Shams (2004: 31) and Weinstein (1988: 373).

The section contains a further requirement that there be conduct on the part of the accused to engage or attempt to engage in a monetary transaction.[981] The payment to a lawyer of his fee could qualify as a monetary transaction. In addition to the fact that the property must be derived from a specific unlawful activity,[982] initially three objective jurisdictional facts must exist: the monetary transaction must affect interstate commerce; the offence(s) must occur in the US; and the accused must be a citizen of the US.[983]

A "monetary transaction", as originally defined in Section 1957(f)(1), reads as follows:

> "The term 'monetary transaction' means the deposit, withdrawal, transfer or exchange, in or affecting interstate or foreign commerce, of funds or monetary instrument (as defined for the purposes of subchapter II of chapter 53 of title 31) by, through, or to a financial institution (as defined in section 5312 of title 31)."

A monetary transaction includes any type of transaction that one can carry out in a bank.[984] Section 1957 has a wider impact for the lawyers than Section 1956. Whereas the latter specifies a number of crimes, the former only refers to one type of offence,[985] the acceptance of tainted funds of a value of more than $10 000.[986] In terms of Section 1957, the prosecution does not have to prove any of the intention requirements referred to in Section 1956.[987] The state only has to prove that the lawyer had knowledge that the funds were tainted and paid by his client in a monetary transaction. Section 1957 prescribes a lesser penalty than Section 1956. The sentence for a violation of Section 1957 can be a maximum fine of $ 250 000 or imprisonment for no more than 10 years or both.[988] Instead of the prescribed fine, the court may opt for a fine of up to to twice the amount "of the criminally derived property involved in the

[981]See Gaetke & Welling (1992: 1168).
[982]See Gaetke & Welling (1992: 1169) and Jacobs (1989: 310). Section 1957(f)(3) of the MLCA 1986 refers to Section 1956(c)(7) of the MLCA 1986.
[983]See Gaetke & Welling (1992: 1168).
[984]See Madinger (2012: 34) and Jacobs (1989: 311).
[985]See Richards (1999: 140).
[986]See Richards (1999: 140) and Gaetke & Welling (1992: 1168).
[987]See Richards (1999: 140) and Shams (2004: 31).
[988]Section 1957(b)(1) of the MLCA.

transaction".[989] For violating Section 1956, an accused can receive "a fine of not more than $500,000 or twice the value of the property involved in the transaction, whichever is greater, or imprisonment for not more than twenty years, or both".[990] The reason for the lesser penalty for violating Section 1957 is that the mental elements required for this offence are less stringent in that the prosecution does not have to show that the accused knew where the money originated. A prosecution for money laundering under Section 1957 may take place only where the sum of money at issue exceeds $10 000. By implication, the acceptance of an amount less than $10 000 will not be punishable under Section 1957.

The penalty in Section 1957 was a novel type when introduced in 1986. It was the first time that heavy criminal penalties could be imposed on persons who knowingly provide services and goods in exchange for dirty money, without having the intention to promote the original criminal activity.[991] It was particularly troublesome for lawyers who faced possible criminal conviction if the state could prove that they were implicated in some form of monetary transaction of more than $10 000 involving the proceeds obtained from a criminal activity.[992] The original Section 1957 could have applied to criminal lawyers who deposit fees when they know that their clients have generated the money from crime.[993] This possibility gave rise to numerous objections and the fundamental argument was that the Sixth Amendment right to legal representation was affected. As a result of this criticism, in 1988 an amendment was made to the definition of a monetary transaction to exclude some lawyers' fees.[994] The amended subsection 1957(f)(1) now reads (with the change highlighted and underlined):

> "As used in this section—
>
> the term "monetary transaction" means the deposit, withdrawal, transfer, or exchange, in or affecting interstate or foreign commerce, of funds or a monetary instrument (as defined in section 1956(c)

[989] Section 1957(b)(2) of the MLCA.

[990] Section 1956(B)(ii) of the MLCA.

[991] See Gaetke & Welling (1992: 1170) and Shams (2004: 31).

[992] See Irvine & King (1988: 185), Brickey (1988: 48) and Shams (2004: 31).

[993] See Gaetke & Welling (1992: 1168), Irvine & King (1988: 185) and Weinstein (1988: 374).

[994] See Gaetke & Welling (1992: 1168), Richards (1999: 141) and Nelson (2009: 51).

> (5) of this title) by, through, or to a financial institution (as defined in section 1956 of this title), including any transaction that would be a financial transaction under section 1956(c)(4)(B) of this title, **but such term does not include any transaction necessary to preserve a person's right to representation as guaranteed by the sixth amendment to the Constitution.**"[995]

This is an important exemption. It does not give an accused a right to spend stolen money or the proceeds of crime, but it exempts lawyers from prosecution should they represent criminals who pay them with tainted funds.[996] Obviously, criminals or lawyers should not be allowed to abuse this exemption by using the payment of unnecessarily high fees in order to clean ill-gotten gains.[997] Fee payments should not be a scam to hide the tainted property or money.[998] This exemption is applicable even if lawyers gain knowledge of the tainted funds from confidential attorney-client communication and from the lawyers' own efforts in the cause of representation.[999] The knowledge needs to have existed before the representation.[1000] The relevant time for determining the lawyer's knowledge is the time of the financial transaction and not when the fees are received.[1001] Lawyers are exempted only when clients are indicted.[1002] Any dispute regarding the exemption should be determined by the trial courts or a court of appeal. Lawyers can be prosecuted for concealment under Section 1956 together with a Section 1957 charge.[1003] In the US, it is highly unlikely that a lawyer will be prosecuted only for being paid with tainted funds, because of the 1988 amendment to Section 1957 of the MLCA.

---

[995] Section 1957(f)(1) of the MLCA. See also Gaetke & Welling (1992: 1168) and Nelson (2009: 51). Emphasis added.

[996] See Jacobs (1989: 314).

[997] See Nelson (2009: 51) and Weinstein (1988: 374).

[998] See Nelson (2009: 51) and Weinstein (1988: 369).

[999] See Gaetke & Welling (1992: 1172) and Nelson (2009: 51).

[1000] See Gaetke & Welling (1992: 1172) and Nelson (2009: 51).

[1001] See Gaetke & Welling (1992: 1172) and Nelson (2009: 51).

[1002] See Gaetke & Welling (1992: 1173) and Nelson (2009: 56).

[1003] See Nelson (2009: 56). *United States v Velez no 05-20770-cr-cook* (2008). *United States v Velez* F.3d 875 (11th Cir. 2009). Weinstein (1988: 374).

4.2.2 The Canadian Position

In Canada the forfeiture of attorneys' fees is regulated by the Criminal Code.[1004] The Criminal Code contains two important definitions: "designated offence" and "proceeds of crime". A "designated offence" is defined as:

> "(a) any offence that may be prosecuted as an indictable offence under this or any other Act of Parliament, other than an indictable offence prescribed by regulation, or
> (b) a conspiracy or an attempt to commit, being an accessory after the fact in relation to, or any counselling in relation to, an offence referred to in paragraph a." [1005]

"Proceeds of crime" is defined as:

> "any property, benefit or advantage, within or outside Canada, obtained or derived directly or indirectly as a result of
> (a) the commission in Canada of a designated offence, or
> (b) an act or omission anywhere that, if it had occurred in Canada, would have constituted a designated offence."[1006]

These definitions are extensive and include any proceeds derived from the commission of a designated offence.[1007] In addition, they cover all proceeds which originated inside Canada as well as proceeds obtained outside Canada from offences which, if committed in Canada, would have qualifies as designated offences.[1008] These provisions are applicable also to those individuals who move illegally obtained assets from other countries into Canada.[1009] Such assets, in the event of arriving in Canada, could be forfeited or placed under a restraining order.[1010]

[1004]The Criminal Code codifies most criminal offences and procedures in Canada. Its official long title is "An Act Respecting the Criminal Law" (R.S.C. 1985, c. C-46, as amended). See also Carter *et al* (2008: 43).

[1005]Section 462.3(1) of the Criminal Code. See also Murphy (2004: 64), Beare (1997: 1440), Rose (1995: 46) and Ryder (2012: 145).

[1006]Section 462.3(1) of the Criminal Code. See also Tapley (2004: 37), McBride (1995: 2), Murphy (2004: 65), Pitman (1998: 247), Rose (1995: 47) and Ryder (2012: 145).

[1007]See McBride (1995: 3), Rose (1995: 47) and Pitman (1998: 255).

[1008]See McBride (1995: 3) and Pitman (1998: 255).

[1009]See McBride (1995: 3) and Pitman (1998: 255).

[1010]See McBride (1995: 3), Brucker (1997: 680) and Pitman (1998: 255).

Money laundering is criminalised in Section 462.31(1) of the Criminal Code. It reads:

> "Everyone commits an offence who uses, transfers the possession of, sends or delivers to any person or place, transports, transmits, alters, disposes of or otherwise deals with, in any manner and by any means, any property or any proceeds of any property with intent to conceal or convert that property or those proceeds, knowing or believing that all or a part of that property or of those proceeds was obtained or derived directly or indirectly as a result of
> (a) the commission in Canada of a designated offence; or
> (b) an act or omission anywhere that, if it had occurred in Canada, would have constituted a designated offence." [1011]

This definition of money laundering accords with the UN Conventions.[1012] In terms of Section 462.31(1), an offence is committed when a person deals with any property or with any proceeds of property in any manner and by any means with intent to conceal or convert it whilst knowing that it has an illegal origin.[1013] Not only is it illegal to be in possession of the proceeds derived from criminal activities, but the proceeds of the illegal activities also could be forfeited to the state.[1014] There is, however, a knowledge requirement in that the individual must know that the property or proceeds was obtained in whole or in part, directly or indirectly, as the result of criminal conduct.[1015] The punishment for a person who is found guilty of an offence under Section 462.31(1) of the Criminal Code is a term of imprisonment not exceeding ten years.[1016]

These provisions are applicable also to lawyers should they participate in using or converting property or proceeds whilst they know that it originated

---

[1011] See also McBride (1995: 3), Murphy (2000: 286), Murphy (2004: 65), Kroeker (1995: 865), Tapley (2004: 37, 40), Brucker (1997: 680), Wilbern (2008: 18), Nelson (2009: 87) and Rose (1995: 47).

[1012] Article 3(b)(i) of the Vienna Convention and Articles 6(a)(i), (a)(ii) and 6(b)(i) and (ii) of UNCTOC.

[1013] See McBride (1995: 3), Brucker (1997: 680) and Wilbern (2008: 18).

[1014] Section 462.37(2) of the Criminal Code. See also McBride (1995: 3), Wilbern (2008: 18), Tapley (2004: 40) and Rose (1995: 50).

[1015] See McBride (1995: 4), Brucker (1997: 680) and Wilbern (2008: 18).

[1016] Section 462.31(2)(a) of the Criminal Code. See also Wilbern (2008: 18).

from illegal activity and they may be prosecuted under the Criminal Code.[1017] Legal fees found to be the proceeds of unlawful activity could be forfeited thus.

The definition of money laundering in the Criminal Code has been retained in the Proceeds of Crime (Money Laundering) and Terrorist Financing Act (PCMLTFA) which makes express reference to Section 462.31 of the Criminal Code.[1018]

The acceptance of tainted fees could result in the prosecution of lawyers, if they knew that the money was the proceeds of crime. An exemption, however, is granted by section 462.32(1) of the Criminal Code to lawyers in in relation to the special search warrant available to the prosecution where there is a reasonable belief that there is property which is the proceeds of crime[1019] and an application for a restraining order is made against such property.[1020] The special warrant forms part of the arsenal of the police and the Attorney General and permits the freezing of the property of an accused through a restraining order prior to conviction.[1021] The accused is then divested of any property that he derived as a result of engaging in an illegal enterprise.[1022] Ultimately, such property could be forfeited to the state[1023] and it could include money in a lawyer's trust account.[1024]

Certain requirements must be met before a Section 462.32(1) special search warrant may be obtained. There must be a reasonable belief that the property is hidden and not in plain view. The property must be the proceeds of crime and a designated offence must have been committed in relation to that property.[1025] Accompanying an application for a special search warrant is usually a request from the Attorney General for a restraining order against the property.[1026] Such an order is intended to thwart the disposal before trial of the

[1017]See Schneider (2004: 65) and Wilbern (2008: 18 & 24-28).

[1018]The Proceeds of Crime (Money Laundering) and Terrorist Financing Act, S.C. 2000, c.17 (PCMLTFA). In the definition clause reference is made to the definition of money laundering as contained in the Criminal Code.

[1019]Section 462.32 of the Criminal Code. See also McBride (1995: 4).

[1020]Section 462.33 of the Criminal Code. See also McBride (1995: 4) and Brucker (1997: 682).

[1021]Section 462.33 of the Criminal Code. See also (McBride 1995: 4-5) and Rose (1995: 47).

[1022]See McBride (1995: 5) and Tapley (2004: 40).

[1023]Section 462.37 of the Criminal Code. See also McBride (1995: 7).

[1024]See Rose (1995: 48).

[1025]See McBride (1995: 4) and Rose (1995: 48).

[1026]Section 462.33 of the Criminal Code. See also McBride (1995: 5).

property by the accused.[1027] This type of application is particularly useful in respect of property which cannot be seized physically, such as money in bank accounts and interests in businesses or real estate.[1028]

The Attorney General must provide an appropriate undertaking in respect of damages or costs or both in relation to the issuance and execution of the warrant and the forfeiture of the proceeds of crime.[1029] This security for costs must be filed before the warrant is issued by the judge. This requirement initially resulted in reluctance on the Attorney General's part to use this type of application.[1030]

However, as intimated above, the Criminal Code provides that in certain circumstances the person who has been charged, but not convicted of a crime yet, has the right to use the alleged proceeds of crime to pay his reasonable legal expenses.[1031] Before the application for legal expenses is made, there must be a restraining order against the property. Although a lawyer could be prosecuted for being in receipt of tainted funds, the release of legal expenses out of the proceeds of property under restraint supersedes such prosecution. There is currently no indication that Canada is pursuing the prosecution of lawyers whose fees are paid with tainted money.[1032]

4.2.2.1 The Legal Fees Exemption

Section 462.34 of the Criminal Code regulates the release of legal expenses under certain circumstances to any person who has an interest in the property seized and who applies for a review of a special warrant and restraining order. Such a person may obtain an order to examine and have returned some or all of the property that was seized. Section 462.34(4)(c)(ii) allows for an

---

[1027]See McBride (1995: 5).

[1028]See McBride (1995: 5).

[1029]Section 462.32(6) and Section 462.33(7) of the Criminal Code. See also Beare (1992: 1442), Murphy (2000: 286), McBride (1995: 5) and Rose (1995: 49).

[1030]The Attorney General preferred to use a Section 487 warrant which was easier to obtain than a Section 462.32 warrant. The advantages initially were that the exemption for legal fees was allowed only in terms of a Section 462.32 warrant. See also Rose (1995: 49).

[1031]Section 462.34(4)(c)(ii) of the Criminal Code. See also Murphy (2000: 289), Brucker (1997: 680) and Beare (1992: 1444).

[1032]This is in direct opposition to South Africa with the prosecution of Anthony Broadway in the Western Cape High Court.

application for the release of money for legal expenses before a forfeiture is granted.[1033] The Section reads:

> "On an application made to a judge under paragraph (1)(*a*) in respect of any property and after hearing the applicant and the Attorney General and any other person to whom notice was given pursuant to paragraph (2)(*b*), the judge may order that the property or a part thereof be returned to the applicant or, in the case of a restraint order made under subsection 462.33(3), revoke the order, vary the order to exclude the property or any interest in the property or part thereof from the application of the order or make the order subject to such reasonable conditions as the judge thinks fit, ...
> (*c*) for the purpose of ...
> (ii) *meeting the reasonable business and legal expenses of a person* referred to in subparagraph (i)."[1034]

A judge may release property or money under the seizure or restraint order or revoke or vary the order for the purpose of meeting the reasonable business and legal expenses of a person.[1035] Initially, it was uncertain whether this legal fees exemption is allowed only under Section 462.34(4)(c)(ii) or whether it is available also under other sections of the Criminal Code or other legislation.[1036] Applications for the release of legal expenses when property was seized in terms a search warrant under the Narcotic Control Act or in terms of a Section 487 Criminal Code warrant were not allowed.[1037] However,

[1033]See Brucker (1997: 679), Beare (1992: 1444) and Kroeker (1995: 868).

[1034]Section 462.34(4)(c)(ii) of the Criminal Code. Emphasis added.

[1035]Section 462.34(4)(c)(ii) of the Criminal Code. See also *R v Gagnon* (1993) 80 C.C.C. (3d). *Wilson v R* (1991) 68 C.C.C. (3d) 569. See also Brucker (1997: 680), Kroeker (1995: 868) and Murphy (2000: 289).

[1036]*Wilson v R* (1991) 68 C.C.C. (3d) 569), *R v Gagnon* (1993) 80 C.C.C. (3d) and *R. v. Sterling* 1992 1704 (BCSC).

[1037]A Section 487 warrant: See *R v Gaudreu* (1994) 4628 (SK CA), *Giles v Canada* (1991) 63 C.C.C. (3d) 18, *R v Felix* [1993] B.C.J. No. 1870 B.C.S.C, *R v Chen* [1995] O.J. 4846 (Ont. Gen. Div.). On a NCA warrantless search: See *R v Galas* (1990) 57 C.C.C. (3d) 353. On a NCA search warrant: *Wilson v R* (1991) 68 C.C.C. (3d) (569), *R v Chen,* [1995] O.J. 4846 (Ont. Gen. Div.), *R v Galas* (1990) 57 C.C.C. (3d) 353. See also McBride (1995: 16) and Rose (1995: 102).

this matter has been resolved with the enactment of Section 32 of Bill C-17, which inserted a new Section 462.341 after Section 462.34, which reads:

> "Subsection 462.34(2), paragraph 462.34(4)(*c*) and subsections 462.34(5), (5.1) and (5.2) apply, with any modifications that the circumstances require, to a person who has an interest in money or bank-notes that are seized under this Act or the *Controlled Drugs and Substances Act* and in respect of which proceedings may be taken under subsection 462.37(1) or (2.01) or 462.38(2)."[1038]

This amendment covers situations where money or bank notes are seized in terms of the Controlled Drugs and Substances Act or any other section of the Criminal Code and allows for applications to be lodged in terms of Section 462.34(4)(c)(ii) of the Criminal Code for the release of legal expenses.[1039]

4.2.2.2 Entitlement to Legal Expenses

The application for the release of the money for legal expenses is regarded as a two-stage process.[1040] It must be determined, firstly, whether the accused is entitled to the release of the fees and, secondly, whether the legal expenses are reasonable.[1041] The first stage of this approach is described as a *Rowbotham* hearing.[1042] It is the procedure to determine whether the applicant is entitled to a portion of the seized or restrained property for payment of his legal fees under Section 462.34(4)(c)(ii).[1043] In *R v Rowbotham*, it was established that Section 7 and Section 11(d) of the Canadian Charter[1044] require that state-

[1038]Section 362.341 of the Criminal Code. See also Brucker (1997: 682) and McBride (1995: 17).

[1039]In *R v Kalenuik* 2004 Can LII 1999 (ONSC), the money of the accused was seized under the Drugs Act, but he was allowed to bring the application for legally expenses in terms of Section 462.34(4)(c)(ii). In *R v Murtaza* & *Murtaza* 2011 (ONSC) 7577, search warrants were executed in the seizure of a total of 116 kg of heroin in terms of Section 487 of the Criminal Code and Section 11 of the Controlled Drugs and Substances Act. The application was allowed in terms of Section 462.34(4)(c)(ii) of the Criminal Code.

[1040]See Brucker (1997: 680).

[1041]*R v Lortie* (1985) 21 C.C.C. (3d) 436 and *R v Clymore* (1992), 74 C.C.C. (3d) 217 (B.C.S.C.). See also Brucker (1997: 681).

[1042]The name derives from *R v Rowbotham* (1987) 41 C.C.C. (3d) 1 (Ont. C.A.). See also Brucker (1997: 680) and Rose (1995: 102).

[1043]See Brucker (1997: 681).

[1044]The Canadian Charter of Rights and Freedoms.

funded counsel be provided in exceptional circumstances where the accused wants, but cannot afford, a lawyer and his representation by counsel is essential to a fair trial. It is a requirement that a judge be satisfied that the applicant has no other assets or means available and that no other person appears to be the lawful owner of or lawfully entitled to the property. This has been interpreted to mean that an applicant would have to show "complete impecuniosity".[1045] The court should consider also the unrestrained and unseized assets of an accused before making a ruling about legal fees.[1046] The onus is on an accused during such an application to provide the court with the information to prove on a balance of probabilities that he needs the money to pay his reasonable legal expenses and that he lacks other sufficient assets.[1047] The applicant's entitlement to reasonable expenses must be based on evidence under oath and he could be subjected to cross-examination.[1048]

Canadian case law is ambivalent about whether applications for legal aid assistance should be made before an application for legal expenses, or thereafter. The "no other assets" notion has been interpreted to include the possibility of legal aid funding. There are decisions which require that an accused first apply for legal aid before an application for the release of funds in terms of Section 462.34(4)(c)(ii) can be made,[1049] and there are others which state that it is not necessary for an application for legal aid to be made before a Section 462.34(4)(c)(ii) application.[1050] It is submitted that an accused should not be required to apply for legal aid before a Section 462.34(4)(c)(ii) application is made. At that stage the money has not been forfeited yet and it has not been decided yet whether he is guilty or not.

[1045]*R v Lortie* (1985) 21 C.C.C. (3d) 436.

[1046]*R v Clymore* (1992) 74 C.C.C.(3d) 217 (B.C.S.C.). See also Brucker (1997: 681).

[1047]See Brucker (1997: 681).

[1048]*R v Morra* (1992) 77 C.C.C. (3d) 380 (Ont. C t.Gen. Div.). In *Wilson v R* (1993) 15 O.R. (3d) 645. See also Brucker (1997: 681).

[1049]There exists a divide in the relevant jurisprudence as to whether a Section 462.34(4)(c)(ii) applicant is required to first to seek legal aid funding and this request must be denied, before an application for legal expenses may be made. In *R v Allen* [2004] O.J. No. 3423 (S.C.J.) (QL), *R v Kalenuik* (2004) CAN LII 19299 (ONSC), *R v Cheng* [2011] O.J. No. 3415 (S.C.J.)(QL) and *R v Murtaza & Murtaza* 2011 ONSC [36], the courts held that the applicant must apply for a legal aid. The Section 462.34(4)(c)(ii) was denied because the person might have qualified for legal aid.

[1050]In *R v Battista* [2008] O.J. No. 3053 (S.C.J.) (QL), *R v Comrie* [2007] O.J. No. 4502 (S.C.J.) (QL), *R v Ro* [2006] O.J. No. 3347 (S.C.J.) (QL), *R v Bedi* [2004] O.J. No. 5825 (S.C.J.)(QL) and *R v Gader* [2001] S.J. No.105 (Q.B.)(QL), the courts held that it is not necessary to apply for legal aid. The Section 462.34(4)(c)(ii) application of the Criminal Code was allowed despite no legal aid application.

4.2.2.3 Reasonableness of Legal Expenses

The second stage of the process for the release of legal expenses is the enquiry as to the reasonableness thereof. In determining the reasonableness of the legal expenses, the application to the court must be *in camera* and the court must "take into account the legal aid tariff of the province".[1051] The court, however, is not bound by the legal aid tariff.[1052] To determine the reasonableness, the Attorney General may "make representations as to what would constitute the reasonableness of the expenses, other than legal expenses";[1053] and what "would constitute reasonable legal expenses referred to in subparagraph (4)(c)(ii)".[1054] The taxing of the legal fees is allowed under Section 462.34(5)(2).

4.2.2.4 Fine in lieu of Forfeiture

In Canada, fees that were paid to a lawyer before forfeiture was granted, will not be forfeited to the state. Instead, the question arose as to whether an accused should be punished more harshly because some of the monies, transferred to his lawyer, are no longer available for a possible fine. One negative consequence of the release of legal expenses for an accused concerns his sentence. An accused who was allowed to have money released for legal expenses might receive a higher fine or a longer period of imprisonment, if convicted. It is possible that, when the court orders the seized property to be forfeited to the state, the whole or a large part thereof has been transferred to his lawyer and is no longer available for forfeiture.[1055] The accused can be requested then to pay a fine equal to the amount of the value of the property that could have been forfeited, including the amount that was released for his legal expenses. If the accused is unable to pay a fine in terms of Section 462.37(4) of the Criminal Code, the court may impose a jail term.[1056] In such a case, an accused could spend a longer period in prison, simply because his legal expenses were released to his lawyer.[1057] The accused and his counsel are

---

[1051]Section 462.34(5) of the Criminal Code. See also *R v Murray* 2004 (SKQD) 66 Para 19.

[1052]See Brucker (1997: 682).

[1053]Section 462.34(5)(a) of the Criminal Code.

[1054]Section 462.34(5)(b) of the Criminal Code.

[1055]See Krane (2010: 74).

[1056]Section 462.37(4) of the Criminal Code. See also Rose (1995: 50) and McBride (1995: 8).

[1057]This situation arose in *R v Pawlyk* (1991) 72 Man. R. (2d) 1. See also Brucker (1997: 683), Beare (1992: 1442) and McBride (1996: 8).

thus faced with a dilemma before deciding to bring a Section 462.34(4)(c)(ii) application. If they bring a successful application for legal expenses and the property is forfeited later to the state, the accused could face the possibility of a longer term of imprisonment or a more substantial fine.

The issue, whether a fine should be imposed or not, has resulted also in a difference of opinion in the courts. In *R v Gagnon,*[1058] the accused was charged with trafficking in cocaine and possession of stolen property, in the form of a log skidder. Gagnon used the log skidder in a logging contract and earned $1 500 which he used to pay his bail on the possession charge. He later signed over the bail bond of $1 500 to his lawyer. After his conviction, the state sought to seize the $1 500 as proceeds of crime. Alternatively, the state, in terms of Section 462.37(3) of the Criminal Code, requested that a fine of $1 500 be imposed on him *in lieu* of forfeiture of the amount. The Court had to decide whether an order in terms of Section 462.37(3) of the Criminal Code should be made.

The Court denied the motion of the state and held that the monies had been assigned irrevocably to the accused's lawyer before the state gave notice of its intention to seize them. The Court found that being in possession of stolen property amounts to possession of proceeds of crime and that the accused could be fined pursuant to Section 462.37(3). The accused spent the proceeds of crime on legal fees and if the state had seized these funds before they had been assigned to the lawyer, the accused could have applied under Section 462.34(4)(c)(ii) of the Criminal Code to use the money to pay legal fees.

The Court ultimately held that it was not going to impose a fine for the following reasons. Firstly, the "substantive crime underlying the forfeiture motion was at the low end of the scale".[1059] Secondly, the accused likely could have obtained "permission of the court to have these proceeds of crime spent on lawyers' fees".[1060] It is unfair to require a person to spend additional time in jail simply because he elected to spend his money on legal fees. Lawyers should not be charged with the responsibility of defending accused persons and then running the risk of having their fees forfeited to the state. Thirdly, because of the lengthy jail terms already imposed upon the accused and the forfeiture of property already suffered, the "imposition of the fine here would be excessively punitive".[1061]

[1058] *R v Gagnon* 10 (1993) 80 C.C.C. (3d) 508.
[1059] *R v Gagnon* 10 (1993) 80 C.C.C. (3d) 508.
[1060] *R v Gagnon* 10 (1993) 80 C.C.C. (3d) 508.
[1061] *R v Gagnon* 10 (1993) 80 C.C.C. (3d) 508.

However, in *Wilson et al v The Queen*, a different approach was followed.[1062] It was held that Section 462.34 of the Criminal Code recognises the right of accused to have assistance of counsel when charged with an enterprise crime offence.[1063] Although the Court elected not to impose a fine *in lieu* of the forfeiture order, it held that even if an assignment of funds in favour of defence counsel is upheld and monies are turned over to the lawyer, the amount of the legal fees is deemed still to be proceeds of crime and the accused could be subject still to a fine *in lieu* of forfeiture of the specific funds.

In Canada the focus is less on whether it is a crime for attorneys to be paid a tainted fee than on the release of legal fees where property is under forfeiture orders. The concern is with whether the release of legal expenses will result in a possible higher sentence for a convicted person. In terms of Section 462.31(1) of the Criminal Code, whenever a person handles property or the proceeds thereof with the intention of camouflaging its illegal origin, that person is guilty of an offence.[1064] Although lawyers could have been prosecuted under this section for being paid with tainted fees, this did not happen. There is, however, an exemption for the release of legal fees.[1065]

The Proceeds of Crime (Money Laundering) and Terrorist Financing Act (PCMLTFA) was enacted in Canada in 2000 and the Regulations implementing certain provisions of the Act came into force in November 2001.[1066] The legislation did not refer to the forfeiture of attorneys' fees and did not criminalise the payment of fees with tainted funds. The litigation initiated by the legal profession against this legislation focused on exempting lawyers from the force of the Act and its Regulations.[1067] The court challenges did not mention attorneys' fee forfeitures or tainted fees as a crime. The issue was whether the legislation threatened the independence of the bar and attorney-client confidentiality, and created a conflict between lawyers' duties to their clients and their obligation to report confidential information to the government.[1068] Neither in the main AML

[1062] *Wilson v R* (1991) 68 CCC (3d) (569).

[1063] *Wilson v R* (1991) 68 CCC (3d) (569). See also Brucker (1997: 679) and Nelson (2009: 89).

[1064] Section 462.31(1) of the Criminal Code.

[1065] Section 462.34(4)(c)(ii) of the Criminal Code allows for the release of fees before a forfeiture order is granted.

[1066] See also Macdonald (2010: 144), Carter *et al* (2008: 57) and Gallant (2009: 211).

[1067] The Act and the Regulations is collectively referred to as the "Regime" or "Canadian regime". See Also Terry (2010: 3 & 34), Paton (2010: 171), Macdonald (2010: 144) and Gallant (2009: 211).

[1068] Although the phrases used in Canada are "solicitor-client privilege" and "solicitor-confidentiality", in this study, for purposes of consistency, "attorney-client privilege" and

legislation, nor in the court challenges that spanned 15 years, was the question of tainted fees as a crime an issue.[1069] It is thus evident that in Canada it is not a crime to be paid with tainted fees.

4.2.3 The South African Position

The acceptance of tainted legal fees as a crime was discussed in detail in § 3.2 above, but it will be revisited here briefly for the sake of completeness. The definition of the proceeds of unlawful activity contained in POCA[1070] criminalises the acceptance of tainted fees. It includes the scenario where a lawyer knows that his fees originated from the unlawful activities of his client, but he continues with the representation. Where a lawyer enters, as a result of his representation, into an agreement with his client and it has the consequence of making available the proceeds of crime to his client, the lawyer will also be committing a crime.[1071] Should a lawyer acquire or be found to be in possession of proceeds which he knows to have unlawful origins, he will be guilty of a crime.[1072] On conviction of a money laundering offence under Section 2, 4, 5 or 6 of POCA, a lawyer may receive as punishment a maximum fine of R100 million or imprisonment for a period not exceeding 30 years.

Under FICA, tainted fees will fall into the category of an activity which has the effect of concealing the proceeds of an unlawful activity, which is regarded as a crime.[1073] Thus, when a lawyer is paid with funds which originated from crime, he is committing an offence. The maximum penalties for such a transgression is 15 years' imprisonment or a fine of R10 million.[1074] This presents a huge problem for lawyers. When a lawyer is requested to represent an accused person on money laundering charges, and his fee is paid, he well may be committing an offence in terms of both FICA and POCA.

"attorney-client confidentiality" will be used. See also Gallant (2009: 211) and Macdonald (2010: 144).

[1069] *Law Society of British Columbia v Canada* 2001 BCSC 1593. *Federation of Law Societies of Canada v Canada* 2011 (BCSC) 1270, *Federation of Law Societies of Canada v Canada* 2013 (BCCA) 147 and *Canada (Attorney General) v Federation of Law Societies of Canada* 2015 SCC 7.

[1070] Section 4 of POCA.

[1071] Section 5 of POCA.

[1072] Section 6 of POCA.

[1073] Section 1(1) of FICA.

[1074] Section 68 of FICA. See also Hamman & Koen (2012: 76), Burdette (2010: 21) and Millard & Vergano (2013: 402).

Lawyers have an ethical duty to defend even the admittedly guilty, and information given by clients could be subject to attorney-client confidentiality and legal profession privilege. Thus, if a lawyer fulfils his duty toward his client in money laundering matters, he could go to jail for it. Surely, a situation whereby the mere acceptance of a tainted fee is criminalised cannot be accepted. The declaration of tainted fees as a crime by the South African legislature was a quite drastic step.

Neither FICA nor POCA provides for an exemption from prosecution for lawyers if tainted money is received as fees and the right to legal representation is at risk of being compromised. As mentioned earlier, a South African lawyer, Anthony Broadway, has been charged in the Western Cape High court with money laundering. One of the charges relates to the payment of fees with tainted funds. Broadway's prosecution could be the forerunner to a trend of prosecuting South African lawyers for this type of crime.[1075]

4.2.4 Comparative Commentary

In comparing the South African approach to tainted fees with that of the US and Canada, a number of trends may be observed. The US, Canada and South Africa all introduced legislation to curb money laundering as part of their international obligations. In all three jurisdictions the effect of the legislation was that lawyers could be prosecuted when they were paid with funds with a suspected unlawful origin. The difference amongst the three countries was the response to the legislation. The US and Canadian legal professions responded by voicing their opposition to and dissatisfaction with the legislation. This discontent resulted in the amendment of the legislation in the US and the favourable interpretation of the legislation for lawyers in Canada. South Africa's legal profession did not voice its concern to any extent that could have resulted in amendments to the AML legislation. Apart from submitting articles to and voicing their discontent in legal journals such as the *De Rebus*, no efforts were made to challenge the legislation in court. Ironically, the international obligation to enact domestic laws to criminalise the offence of money laundering, does not impose a duty on countries to criminalise the payment of legal fees with tainted funds.

The US legislation allows for the forfeiture of legal fees; and in the event that a fee has been paid and a forfeiture order is granted afterwards, lawyers

[1075] *S v Wei & Others.*

will have to pay back the money. Canadian legislation also includes forfeiture provisions, but they are not applied against attorneys' fees.[1076] Whereas the US employs the forfeiture provisions against attorneys' fees, Canada allows for the release of money under forfeiture orders to cover the legal expenses of an accused. Canada has developed a system which secures attorneys' fees, despite the fact that the property of the accused is subject to a forfeiture application or a forfeiture order. Although the provisions of RICO and the CFA were utilised in the US to forfeit the fees of lawyers, they were never utilised to prosecute attorneys, which fees were paid with tainted funds. In Canada, the fact that tainted fees are not illegal excludes the possibility of attorneys being prosecuted for accepting such fees. In South Africa, however, attorneys face the very real possibility of prosecution.

Both *Caplin & Drysdale* and *Monsanto* confirmed the constitutional validity of the forfeiture provisions in the US. Even though the Canadian provisions theoretically could have been utilised for the prosecution of lawyers, they were applied to benefit accused persons and lawyers by allowing the release of money for legal expenses. In fact, the Canadian provisions are more favourable to lawyers than the US provisions. Evidently, both Canada and the US regard the right to a fair trial and the right to legal representation as very important. In Canada the focus is on whether an accused is entitled to the release of the legal expenses and the reasonableness of the expenses. Canadian case law tends to focus also on the possibility of a more severe sentence or a more substantial fine where money has been transferred to a lawyer and a forfeiture order subsequently is granted. There is no indication that the state in Canada intends claiming the money from a convicted person or that the lawyer may forfeit his fee. Section 462.34(4)(c)(ii) of the Criminal Code has wording similar to Sections 26 and 44 of POCA, allowing funds to be released for legal expenses. The South African and Canadian positions favour the accused and his attorney more than does the US, at least as far as the release of legal expenses is concerned. Regrettably, Section 1 of FICA and Sections 4, 5 and 6 of POCA continue to regard the receipt of a tainted fee as a crime.

In the US, the provisions of RICO and the CFA which dealt with the forfeiture of attorneys' fees were disputed in court. The litigation focused on whether the forfeiture of attorneys' fees infringed on the right to legal representation. What is more, Section 1957(f)(1) of the MLCA exempts lawyers from prosecution if

[1076] Section 462.34 of the Criminal Code.

a tainted fee payment was made to ensure a client's Sixth Amendment right to counsel. This exemption clause in the MLCA was invoked successfully also to stop the prosecution of a lawyer who was charged with the offence of money laundering for vetting the fees of a colleague.[1077] Regrettably, this exemption from prosecution is not available to lawyers in South Africa and Canada.

However, in Canada lawyers are not being prosecuted for being paid a tainted fee. If this situation should ever occur, one presumes that the Federation of Law Societies of Canada (FLSC) likely will approach the courts to declare the prosecution unconstitutional. In the various matters where the FLSC challenged the AML legislation for infringing on attorney-client confidentiality and the independence of the profession, the tainted fee was not raised even as an issue.

For South African lawyers, the possibility of the release of legal expenses granted to lawyers in terms of POCA is encouraging. [1078] However, South African legislation, on the one hand, allows for the release of legal expenses from property about to be forfeited and, on the other hand, regards the payment of legal fees with tainted funds as a crime. The main difference between South Africa and Canada regarding the release of funds for legal expenses is that South Africa requires that an applicant declare under oath a list of his assets and liabilities, whereas Canada does not. Unfortunately for the legal profession in South Africa, neither the Law Societies of South Africa (LSSA) nor the legislature has regarded the issue of tainted fees as particularly serious. There was no outcry from the organised profession to lobby for any changes in the legislation and no attempt by the profession to challenge the legislation in court.

In South Africa, the criminalisation of tainted fees will have an effect not only on lawyers, but also on the accused persons. They have the right to remain silent, the right not to be compelled to make a confession and a privilege against self-incrimination. They are presumed to be innocent, although they factually could be guilty and are entitled to receive a fair trial. Lawyers are in a position to ensure that this happens and to give effect to the right to legal representation. If the receipt of tainted funds remains a crime, lawyers could decide over time to stop defending criminals. The effect can be that an accused person is unable to secure counsel of his choice.

[1077] *United States v Velez no 05-20770-cr-cook* (2008) and *United States v Velez* F.3d 875 (11th Cir. 2009).

[1078] Sections 26 and 44 of POCA.

It is clear from the above that the South African legislature did not give the issue of tainted fees the attention that it deserves. There is no evidence that lawyers who represent criminals are guilty of cleaning money on a large scale. On the contrary, this study reveals that there is a paucity of cases where attorneys have been charged with the offence of money laundering.

There are a number of lessons that can be learned from the US and from Canada. Although these countries have incorporated forfeiture provisions in their legislation, they contain special protection for lawyers. In the US, the legal profession is exempted from prosecution especially where a client's right to legal representation is concerned. Both the US and Canada have not prosecuted lawyers merely for being paid with tainted funds. The US has amended its AML legislation to include specific provisions to exempt attorneys from prosecution. In Canada, tainted fees are not regarded as a matter of concern. In fact, in the Canadian case of *R v Gagnon* it was stated that the American situation is an unfortunate one. The matter of tainted fees has not been mentioned even in the fifteen years of litigation between the Law Societies of Canada and the Attorney General.

In comparison to the US and Canada, it is evident that South Africa erred in drafting legislation which declared it a crime simply for lawyers to receive tainted fees. Lawyers in the US have the luxury that certain exemptions apply to tainted fees, which South African and Canadian attorneys do not enjoy. Although Canadian attorneys are not exempted in legislation from prosecution, their attorneys are not prosecuted merely for accepting tainted fees. South African attorneys thus are more vulnerable than their US and Canadian counterparts to prosecution as money launderers in respect of the receipt of tainted fees. It is submitted that there is no justification to regard the mere receipt of tainted fees a crime and that the South African legislation which authorises this is unconstitutional.

As can be seen from the indictment of attorney Anthony Broadway, the position of lawyers in South Africa is precarious compared to their counterparts in the US and Canada. If an overzealous prosecuting authority decides to prosecute more South African attorneys for being paid with funds that are tainted, a situation could arise where a high number of lawyers could end up as accused in South African criminal courts. The issue probably will be highlighted only and receive wider attention and media coverage should the trial of attorney Anthony Broadway proceed and should he be convicted for being paid with dirty money.

It is not being advocated that attorneys who are guilty of criminal conduct not be prosecuted. However, such liability should not be extended to the attorney simply for accepting tainted fees. The examination of the US and Canadian jurisdictions do not support the South African notion that the payment of fees with suspected tainted funds should be regarded as a crime for lawyers. Therefore, it is submitted that the mere receipt of tainted money as legal fees should be decriminalised and that POCA and FICA should be amended accordingly.

4.3 Tainted Fees and the Right to Legal Representation

4.3.1 The US Position

The debate regarding tainted fees and legal representation raged in the US since the 1980s,[1079] when RICO and CCE forfeiture of fees first had an impact on the right to counsel. The issue was settled finally in the cases of *Caplin & Drysdale* and *Monsanto* with the finding that forfeiture of fees does not infringe upon the right to counsel. These cases did not resolve the issue of whether the mere acceptance of tainted funds infringe upon the right to counsel. Indeed, under Section 1956 and Section 1957 of the MLCA there is the theoretical possibility that lawyers can be convicted of money laundering merely because their fees were paid with dirty money.

Section 1956(a)(1)(B)(ii) of the MLCA contains the intention element pertaining to the person who knowingly conceals the proceeds of unlawful activity. It makes very vulnerable lawyers who receive a tarnished payment, knowing that it derives from a crime, and who, by accepting it as fees, conceal its criminal origin. Furthermore, Section 1956(a)(2)(B)(i) of the MLCA is applicable to lawyers who, for example, assist in importing the proceeds of a crime from a foreign country. In such a case, the lawyer could be indicted. However, as noted earlier, in 1988 an exemption for lawyers was granted by the promulgation of Section 1957(f)(1) of the MLCA to exclude a monetary transaction where the right to counsel is at issue. It effectively exempts lawyers from prosecution should they represent criminals who pay their fees with tainted money.

The constitutionality of Section 1956 and Section 1957 of the MLCA has not been challenged as yet and lawyers remain in the unenviable position that

---

[1079]See Winick (1989: 766) and Brickey (1986: 494).

they can be prosecuted where they represent a client who pays them with dirty money, despite the exemption in Section 1957(f)(1). An analysis of *United States v Velez* is essential to illustrate how the proverbial sword still is hanging over lawyers who represent certain types of accused persons.[1080]

The case concerns the indictment of attorney Ben Kuehne on money laundering charges,[1081] and highlights the dangers facing lawyers involved with the receipt of tainted fees. Besides being a popular Miami criminal lawyer, Kuehne is also a prominent member of the Democratic Party and served on Al Gore's legal team during the US presidential election of 2000, when the US Supreme Court controversially ordered a halt to the recount of votes in Florida and awarded the presidency to George W Bush.[1082] Kuehne's indictment came in February 2008. A former Medellin drug lord, Fabio Ochoa-Vasquez, had been extradited to the US in 2001 to stand trial for conspiring to smuggle to the US about thirty tons of cocaine per month between 1997 and 1999.[1083] He was convicted in 2003.

Kuehne was engaged in 2001 by Ochoa-Vasquez's American lawyer, Roy Black, to determine whether the money Black was receiving from his client as fees was clean.[1084] Kuehne had two co-accused, Gloria Florez Velez and Oscar Saldarriaga Ochoa, Ochoa-Vasquez's former accountant and Colombian attorney respectively. Together they drafted six opinions, each of which pronounced the fee source to which it related to be untainted.[1085] Between January 2002 and April 2003, the family of Ochoa-Vasquez deposited a total of $5 289 762,67 into Kuehne's trust account by means of wire transfers. Kuehne subsequently disbursed all the funds (except a little more than $50 000 which was withheld as a retainer fee) to Ochoa-Vasquez's lawyers. He was paid $197 300 for the work he performed in vetting the fees.

[1080]*United States v Velez no 05-20770-cr-cook* (2008) and *United States v Velez* F.3d 875 (11th Cir. 2009).

[1081]Kuehne was indicted under, *inter alia*, Section 1956(a)(1)(B)(i), for knowingly concealing the proceeds of unlawful activity and Section 1956(a)(2)(B)(i), for importing these proceeds from a foreign country, specifically Colombia, as well as Section 1957, for engaging in monetary transactions constituting criminally derived property. See also Healy *et al* (2009: 807), Nelson (2009: 56), Podgor (2010: 195) and Slater (2008: 1).

[1082]For an incisive account and analysis of the election debacle of 2000, see Bugliosi (2001).

[1083]See Healy *et al* (2009: 807), Nelson (2009: 56) and Podgor (2010: 196).

[1084]See Nelson (2009: 57) and Healy *et al* (2009: 807).

[1085]See Podgor (2010: 195) and Healy *et al* (2009: 807).

Kuehne was charged under Section 1957 of the MLCA. According to the indictment, Roy Black paid Kuehne approximately $200 000 to vet about $5 000 000 in fees originating from Colombia before Ochoa-Vasquez was convicted.[1086] It was alleged that Kuehne, along with his co-accused, knowingly falsified documents and facilitated a series of wire transfers to the US via the Black Market Peso Exchange,[1087] whilst they knew that the funds were the proceeds of drug trafficking.

On 22 December 2008, District Judge Cooke granted Kuehne's motion to dismiss the Section 1957 charge, because of the Section 1957(f)(1) Sixth Amendment exemption. The government appealed.[1088] The matter came before the US Court of Appeal for the 11th Circuit.[1089] The state argued that the exemption in Section 1957(f)(1) had been nullified because, shortly after the statute was promulgated, the Supreme Court held in *Caplin & Drysdale*[1090] that the Sixth Amendment does not protect the right to counsel where an accused used criminally derived proceeds for legal fees.[1091] Kuehne and his co-accused argued that they were protected by this exemption and applied for the charge under Section 1957 to be dismissed. Kuehne argued that he did not know that the funds were tainted.

The Court accepted the submission of Kuehne and his co-accused and ruled accordingly in November 2009.[1092] The Court found that *Caplin & Drysdale* addressed a different statute, and that that statute had no bearing on Section 1957(f)(1) of the MLCA. It held that *Caplin & Drysdale* addressed the constitutionality of Section 853 of the CFA, a federal statute, which does not contain an exemption as does Section 1957 of the MLCA.[1093]

The Court of Appeal agreed with Judge Cooke that Kuehne could not be prosecuted because the funds were for legitimate legal services.[1094] It held

---

[1086]See Healy *et al* (2009: 807) and Nelson (2009: 57).

[1087]For an explanation of the operation of the Black Market Peso Exchange see http://money.howstuffworks.com/money-laundering2.htm.

[1088]*United Sates v Velez* No.09-10199 D.C Docket no. 05-20770-CR-MGC. 2009. See also Nelson (2009: 58) and Healy *et al* (2009: 807).

[1089]*United States v Velez* F.3d 875 (11th Cir. 2009) at 5.

[1090]*Caplin & Drysdale v United States* 491 US. 617 (1989) at 617 & 626.

[1091]*United States v Velez* No. 05-20770-CR-Cooke/Bandstra.2008 WL. 540909 (S.D FLA Dec.30.2008). See also Slater (2008: 1).

[1092]See Podgor (2010: 196). See also *United States v Velez* F.3d 875 (11th Cir. 2009) at 9.

[1093]*United States v Velez* F.3d 875 (11th Cir. 2009) at 5.

[1094]*United States v Velez* F.3d 875 (11th Cir. 2009) at 9.

that representation as guaranteed by the Sixth Amendment refers to the type of representation. It is not the transaction that must be guaranteed but the representation itself. It therefore confirmed the decision of the District Court that the accused are not subject to criminal prosecution under Section 1957. It held that the plain language of Section 1957(f)(1) clearly exempts criminally derived proceeds used to secure legal representation to which an accused is entitled under the Sixth Amendment.[1095] The judgment was delivered on 26 October 2009.[1096] After the ruling of the 11th Circuit, the state dismissed the case against Kuehne.[1097]

The constitutionality of Sections 1956 and 1957 was not challenged by Kuehne's lawyers, but Section 1957(f)(1) was utilised to stop his prosecution.[1098] This was the first indictment under the federal money laundering statutes of an attorney for vetting, or performing due diligence on, another lawyer's legal fees. It is regarded as a key case for determining the extent to which *Monsanto* and *Caplin & Drysdale*[1099] can be used by prosecutors to extend liability to practitioners. The indictment of Kuehne, a well-respected lawyer renowned among his colleagues for his ethical and professional behaviour, shocked the US legal community. It was seen also as a re-ignition of the "war between the government and the criminal defence bar which raged at the time of *Monsanto* and *Caplin & Drysdale*" in the 1980s.[1100]

Although he was cleared, Kuehne had been under indictment for two years and had to cope with the stresses and strains and the expense of defending himself against the charges. He was charged even though Ochoa-Vasquez, who had supplied the allegedly tainted funds, was not his client. He had been hired by Ochoa-Vasquez's lawyers for the sole purpose of ascertaining whether they were being paid with dirty money, and he was indicted even though his investigations had verified that the money was clean. He had been charged under Section 1957 of the MLCA even though the section contains a proviso which exempts attorneys from prosecution who are paid with tainted money

---

[1095]*United States v Velez* F.3d 875 (11th Cir. 2009) at 9.

[1096]*United States v Velez* F.3d 875 (11th Cir. 2009).

[1097]See Podgor (2010: 196). See also government motion to dismiss third superseding indictment with prejudice, *United States v Kuehne*, US S.D. Fl., Case No. 0520770-Cr-Cook, available at http://lawprofessors.typepad.com/filess/kuehne=dismossal-order.pdf. [Accessed 21 March 2014].

[1098]See Healy *et al* (2009: 807).

[1099]*Caplin & Drysdale, Chartered*, 491 US 617 (1989).

[1100]Nelson (2009: 56-57).

when giving effect to a client's constitutional right to legal representation. The point is that, like Kuehne, all South African attorneys face a plurality of perils in exercising their professional responsibilities of providing paid representation to clients. They, too, could become ready targets of criminal prosecution if they are paid with funds which turn out to be tainted.

4.3.2 The Canadian Position

It will be recalled that neither in the Criminal Code nor in the PCMLTFA is mention made of tainted fees as a crime. Because of its not being an issue, the discussion in Canada did not confront the question of how tainted fees may affect an accused person's right to legal representation. However, in the case of *R v Gagnon,* a comparison was made between the Canadian position and the US position. It was noted that the intention of the Canadian legislature, with the promulgation of Section 362.34(4)(c)(ii) of the Criminal Code, was to mitigate some of the unfortunate results seen in the US when the courts considered the proceeds of crime legislation.[1101] The Court in *R v Gagnon* characterised lawyers' fees as a "special type of expenditure linked to a constitutionally protected right".[1102] Because of Canada's liberal approach to releasing legal expenses, and since Canada is not prosecuting lawyers for the mere receipt of tainted funds, there is no effect to speak of that tainted fees has on the right to legal representation.

4.3.3 The South African Position

The right to legal representation is entrenched in the South African constitution.[1103] Such entrenchment seeks to ensure that an accused person receives a fair trial. An accused person has a number of rights enumerated in the Constitution. They include the right to remain silent, the right to be presumed innocent, the right not to give self-incriminating evidence, and the right not to be forced to make a confession.[1104] These rights mean almost nothing without the intervention of a lawyer. An accused person may know his rights, but he may not know how to exercise them. For example, when he is

[1101] *R v Gagnon* 10 (1993) 80 C.C.C. (3d) 508.

[1102] *R v Gagnon* 10 (1993) 80 C.C.C. (3d) 508.

[1103] Section 35(2) and 35(3) of the Constitution of 1996.

[1104] Section 35(1) of the Constitution of 1996.

required to make a statement to the police, he may not know when the content of the statement would contain incriminatory information.

Lawyers are essential to ensure that an accused person's rights are recognised and respected by the police and the courts. The problem is that by declaring the mere receipt of tainted fees a crime, South Africa has saddled lawyers with difficult decisions. The challenge for the practitioner is whether to accept the fees and risk becoming part of a money laundering scheme or whether to refuse a brief. These decisions ultimately affect an accused person's constitutional right to legal representation and to prevent lawyers from accepting tainted fee payments could violate that right.[1105]

A lawyer's reluctance to take on matters when he knows that he likely is committing a crime is understandable. The lawyer may realise that he may be charged and convicted and could be incarcerated. If one lawyer refuses and all the lawyers in an area likewise refuse to assist an accused person, he will be without counsel to represent him. In the end, a refusal by practitioners to render legal services could nullify an accused person's right to legal representation in South Africa. There is thus a risk that the right to legal representation could be in danger for an accused person who wishes to employ counsel and pay his legal fees with tainted money.[1106]

4.3.4 Comparative Commentary

The issue of whether the criminalisation of tainted fees has an impact on the right to legal representation is comprehended differently in the three jurisdictions. It enjoys more prominence in the US than in Canada and South Africa. In the US, it has been considered in relation to the forfeiture of attorneys' fees and in relation to the prosecution of lawyers under Section 1957 of the MLCA. Although the courts in *Caplin & Drysdale* and *Monsanto* did not consider the effect that the criminalisation tainted fees had on the right to counsel, the principles extracted from the judgments matter. Canada does not consider the acceptance of tainted fees as a crime and therefore had no debate about the effect thereof on the right to legal representation. As intimated earlier, this issue has not been considered in any real depth in South Africa as yet.

[1105]See Bussenius (2004: 30).

[1106]See discussion of this issue in §3.2.3 above.

In the US, the debate regarding the right to legal representation initially did not focus on tainted fees, but on the forfeiture of fees. The concern was whether the possibility of losing a fee is sufficient to warrant a lawyer not taking on certain matters and thereby affecting the right to counsel. As submitted earlier, the courts correctly considered that the forfeiture of fees would not deter a lawyer from taking on a case. However, the threat of incarceration surely would be enough to deter a lawyer from taking on a matter which entails this possibility.

With the enactment of Section 1957 of the MLCA in 1986, the debate regarding tainted fees as a crime and its effect on the right to legal representation gained momentum. The section had the effect that a lawyer would commit a crime merely by accepting tainted fees to represent his client. This was regarded as unacceptable for the legal profession. It cannot be expected from a lawyer to give effect to an accused person's right to legal representation whilst himself being exposed to a possible criminal conviction. The problem was resolved with the insertion of the Section 1957(f)(1) exemption into the MLCA. Unfortunately, South African and Canadian legislation does not have such an exemption protecting lawyers from prosecution where there is a nexus to the right to legal representation.

Valuable lessons may be taken from the experiences of the US, in particular how it dealt with the amendment of Section 1957 of the MLCA. Despite the existence of several enactments aimed at dissuading US lawyers from facilitating money laundering, the AML legislation leaves the constitutional right to legal representation intact. The application of the AML measures in the US demonstrates an attempt to balance the combating of lawyer-facilitated money laundering with the constitutional right to legal representation.

An exemption similar to that contained in Section 1957 of the MLCA should be incorporated into South African legislation. It is suggested that the legislature seriously consider inserting such an exemption for attorneys in POCA and FICA to ensure that the right to legal representation is not infringed. Alternatively, the LSSA could bring a court application to request an amendment to POCA and FICA or to stop the prosecution of Broadway on the charge of receiving tainted fees.[1107]

[1107] *United States v Velez* F.3d 875 (11th Cir. 2009) at 9.

4.4 The Effect of Tainted Fees on Lawyers Exercising their Profession

4.4.1 The US Position

The US position regarding tainted fees and their impact on the right of lawyers to practise their profession is summarised amply by Blackmun J in his minority judgment in *Monsanto* and *Caplin & Drysdale.* Although his judgment dealt with the effect of fee forfeitures on lawyers' right to exercise their profession, it is applicable equally to lawyers being paid with tainted funds. It will be recalled that Blackmun J was of the opinion that fee forfeitures in the long run would destroy the private criminal defence bar.[1108] His view that only the most idealistic and the least skilled young lawyers would be attracted to the field of criminal practice can apply also to lawyers being prosecuted for tainted fees.[1109]

The impact on lawyers exercising their profession is much greater when a lawyer faces a possible criminal conviction than a possible forfeiture of legal fees. The majority opinion in *Caplin & Drysdale* that the forfeiture of fees would not prompt someone reconsider the exercise of his profession is acceptable. However, a lawyer who faces possible incarceration for being paid with dirty money almost certainly will reconsider being a criminal defence practitioner. Apart from the minority judgment of Blackmun J in the abovementioned cases, this aspect of the tainted fees issue has not been canvassed in any detail in the US. However, given the exemption for lawyers contained in Section 1957(f)(1) of the MLCA, it is understandable that the matter is not contentious.

4.4.2 The Canadian Position

The effect of tainted fees on the right to exercise a profession also has not been debated in Canada. However, in *R v Gagnon*[1110] it was considered to be the professional duty of a lawyer to represent a client to the best of his abilities even if that means that the lawyer is not paid for all of the time spent on that

---

[1108] *Caplin & Drysdale, Chartered, Petitioner v United States.* 491 US 617 (1989) at 646 & 650. See also Winick (1989: 781-782) and Orentlicher (1999: 1361).

[1109] *Caplin & Drysdale, Chartered, Petitioner v United States.* 491 US 617 (1989) at 651. See also Winick (1989: 781-782).

[1110] *R v Gagnon* 10 (1993) 80 C.C.C. (3d) 508 Para 18.

client's case. The Court also found that lawyers are human and if they are not paid for all of the work that they have done they may stop doing the things for which they are not paid.[1111] Interestingly, Veit J also referred to the US Supreme Court decisions in *Caplin & Drysdale* and *Monsanto* and noted that, contrary to the US position, Canada allows "moneys to be spent by an accused person for such expenses as reasonable living expenses, reasonable business expenses and lawyers' fees".[1112] Veit J also posed the question: "What lawyer would undertake the defence of an accused person if fees paid by the accused could eventually be recovered by the state?"[1113] The obvious answer to the question is that the lawyer would not represent the client. By extrapolation, the danger of being convicted of a crime for accepting tainted fees would render the lawyer even more unwilling to undertake the defence of an accused.

The Court also remarked that an accused person will not have the benefit of a full constitutional defence if the lawyers' fees are not released. [1114] Veit J posed the following question:

> "What accused would then have the benefit of the constitutional right to a full defence, given the dual problems of finding a lawyer who will act under those conditions and of serving time in addition to the sentence imposed for the substantive crime if the lawyers' fees are not repaid to the state as proceeds of crime?"[1115]

She remarked that it would be difficult to find a lawyer to represent a client if there is a chance that the lawyer could lose his fee. The Court made it clear that the reluctance of a lawyer to represent an accused person is understandable if he will not be paid. Obviously, a lawyer will be much more reluctant if there is a possibility that he will go to jail for representing a certain type of accused.

Although the issue has not been dealt with expressly in Canada, it is highly unlikely that the Canadian legal profession and courts will tolerate a situation where the criminalisation of tainted fees negatively affects the right of lawyers to practise their profession.

[1111] *R v Gagnon* 10 (1993) 80 C.C.C. (3d) 508 Para 19.
[1112] *R v Gagnon* 10 (1993) 80 C.C.C. (3d) 508 Para 21.
[1113] *R v Gagnon* 10 (1993) 80 C.C.C. (3d) 508 Para 22.
[1114] *R v Gagnon* 10 (1993) 80 C.C.C. (3d) 508 Para 22.
[1115] *R v Gagnon* 10 (1993) 80 C.C.C. (3d) 508 Para 22.

4.4.3 The South African Position

Although the consequences of tainted fees as a crime have not been confronted yet in South Africa, one of the inevitable consequences is that it will influence lawyers not to do criminal work. The current position in South Africa is that lawyers who represent criminals and who are then paid with tarnished funds can be prosecuted on the strength of the provisions in POCA and FICA. This definitely will influence a young lawyer's decision to practise criminal law. If young lawyers are discouraged from doing criminal work, the right to earn a living and to exercise a chosen profession will be affected. Such a development would be in direct opposition to Section 22 of the Constitution which states that everyone is entitled to earn a living from his profession.[1116]

The case against Anthony Broadway could foreground the question of the effect of tainted fees on a lawyer's right to practise his profession. Should the prosecution be successful, the legal profession will be confronted with the possibility of its members being convicted of a crime for the mere receipt of tainted fees. Such a result could be a catalyst for law graduates to abandon any desire or intention to become criminal defence practitioners.

4.4.4 Comparative Commentary

Since the payment of fees with dirty funds is not regarded as a crime in both the US and in Canada, the question of the effect of tainted fees on the right of lawyers to exercise their profession has not been considered seriously. However, the effect of the forfeiture of fees on the right to practise law as a profession has been discussed by Blackmun J in *Caplin & Drysdale* and *Monsanto.*[1117]

It will be recalled that Blackmun J regarded the possibility of fee forfeiture as sufficient reason for young attorneys to decide not to join the criminal defence bar. This sentiment is debatable. However, it is submitted that the criminalisation of tainted fees definitely will influence some to decide not to practise criminal law. A South African law graduate, fresh to the profession, does not know what his sphere of specialisation in law will be. This decision follows later, once experience has been gained. If, however, a lawyer decided to specialise in criminal litigation after finishing his period of articles, it is a

[1116]Section 22 of the Constitution of 1996.

[1117]*Caplin & Drysdale, Chartered, Petitioner v United States.* 491 US 617 (1989) at 651.

choice made with the knowledge that another branch of the profession could have been chosen, such as corporate law, tax law, civil litigation, insurance or liquidations. To declare the mere receipt of tainted fees a crime, is to make such a lawyer decide either to continue with criminal litigation, knowing that he likely will commit a crime, or change his chosen speciality.

In such a situation, a lawyer's right to practise his chosen field of law has been infringed. As Blackmun J stated, it is possible that "the criminal defence bar could be decimated" by young lawyers choosing not to do criminal work. The criminalisation of tainted fees has a dual effect: it affects an accused person's right to legal representation and a lawyer's right to exercise his profession.

In South Africa, it is a crime for a lawyer to accept tainted fees. It is arguable, therefore, that the right of South African criminal lawyers to practise their profession already has been compromised.

5

REPORTS AND RECORDS

5.1 Introduction

This chapter continues the comparative work commenced in chapter 4. It considers the South African position in relation to the US and Canada as regards STRs, CTRs and government access to confidential client information in possession of lawyers.

In South Africa, Section 29 of FICA makes it mandatory for a lawyer to report suspicious and unusual transactions of his clients to the FIC.[1118] Section 28 of FICA provides that as soon as a lawyer comes into possession of cash that exceeds R24 999,99 he must report it to the FIC. Apart from their reporting obligations, lawyers have a duty to verify the identity of clients and keep detailed client records.[1119] The failure to file a CTR in terms of Section 28 and an STR in terms Section 29 of FICA are criminalised in Sections 51 and 52 of FICA respectively. Fortunately for South African lawyers, Section 45B of FICA has been declared unconstitutional in the case of *Estate Agency Affairs Board v Auction Alliance*.[1120] If the declaration did not happen, lawyers' offices could have been subjected to warrantless searches and lawyers could have become providers of evidence against their clients. The obligation to file STRs and CTRs means that lawyers have to report their clients and not inform them that such a report has been made, or face prosecution. The lawyer is left in an unenviable position: choose between your duties towards your client or your obligation to obey the law.

[1118]See discussion of Section 29 of FICA in§ 3.2.

[1119]Kilbourn (2008: 18.3).

[1120]*Estate Agency Affairs Board v Auction Alliance* 2014 (4) BCLR 373 (CC).

Lawyers in the US faced the same dilemma. Although the US received a report of non-compliance from the FATF regarding customer due diligence, monitoring and the filing of STRs, the legal profession vehemently opposed the filing of STRs and do not apply the NTO rule. US lawyers played a crucial role in developing the RBA of the FATF and, represented by the American Bar Association (ABA), have put their experience with the US AML legislation to good use by being involved actively in the FATF deliberations and policy making. US activism has benefited lawyers in other jurisdictions by tempering the FATF's desire to subject them to the same, stringent due diligence and reporting obligations as financial institutions and other DNFBPs.[1121]

The Canadian legal profession, since the inception of Canada's main AML statute, the PCMLTFA, has embarked on a litigation crusade to prevent STRs and CTRs being applicable to its members.[1122] Part of its opposition to the legislation was to ensure that its lawyers are not subjected to stringent reporting requirements and are not required to collect confidential client information which could be used by the prosecution.

Canada's PCMLTFA was enacted in 2000 and the Regulations implementing certain provisions of the Act came into force in November 2001.[1123] The litigation against the legislation commenced with injunction proceedings in 2001, then it went to the Supreme Court of British Columbia in 2011, thereafter to the British Columbia Court of Appeal in 2013,[1124] and the matter was settled finally in the Supreme Court of Canada in 2015.[1125] The courage of the Canadian legal profession in challenging the PCMLTFA is to be admired. Immediately after the promulgation of the statute, the Federation of Law Societies of Canada (FLSC) instituted proceedings seeking to exempt lawyers

---

[1121]See FATF Third Mutual Evaluation Report on Anti-Money Laundering and Combating the Financing of Terrorism (2006). See also Healy *et al* (2009: 799), Terry (2010: 36), Shepherd (2009: 624), Kazmerski (2011: 93) and Cummings & Stepnowsky (2011: 19).

[1122]See Terry (2010: 3), Paton (2010: 171) and Macdonald (2010: 144). See also Federation of Law Societies of Canada (FLSC) and the Canadian Bar Association (CBA), Money Laundering Chronology of events (April 2003). [Hereinafter referred to as: Canada Chronology].

[1123]The Proceeds of Crime (Money Laundering) Act (2001) (PCMLTFA), See also Macdonald (2010: 144) and Gallant (2009: 211).

[1124]*Law Society of British Columbia v Canada* 2001 (BCSC) 1593; *Federation of Law Societies of Canada v Canada* 2011 (BCSC) 1270 and *Federation of Law Societies of Canada v Canada* 2013 (BCCA) 147.

[1125]*Canada (Attorney General) v Federation of Law Societies of Canada* 2015 SCC 7.

from the force of the Act and its Regulations.[1126] The FLSC's court challenges focused on whether the legislation threatened the independence of the bar, undermined attorney-client confidentiality, and created a conflict between lawyers' duties to their clients and their obligation to report confidential information to the government.[1127] Unlike South Africa, the Canadian courts have built up a sizeable jurisprudence concerning the conduct of the legal profession in relation to Canada's money laundering laws and it is beneficial for both South African lawyers and courts to understand this jurisprudence.

5.2 Suspicious Transaction Reporting

5.2.1 The US Position

The contentious issue of the filing of STRs in the US was handled by the ABA. In February 2002, the ABA established a Task Force on Gatekeeper Regulation and the Profession (Gatekeeper Task Force), to tackle matters surfacing from the Gatekeeper Initiative.[1128] The term "gatekeeper" was first used when lawyers were referred to as such in the Moscow Communiqué.[1129] Lawyers were regarded as gatekeepers to the international financial system. The term used in the Communiqué resulted in the formation of the Gatekeeper Initiative, which is an effort by governments to recruit the support of gatekeepers, such as lawyers, to combat money laundering and terrorist financing.[1130] It was the mission of the Gatekeeper Initiative to respond to the proposals of the DOJ, the Treasury, the Congress, the FATF, and other stakeholders that will affect the attorney-client relationship in the framework of AML enforcement.[1131] The Gatekeeper Task Force performs four functions: It "(a) reviews and evaluates ABA policy and rules regarding the ability of attorneys to disclose client activity ABA information; (b) works to develop positions on the gatekeeper initiative issue; (c) develops educational programs

[1126]See Terry (2010: 3 & 34), Paton (2010: 171), Macdonald (2010: 144) and Gallant (2009: 211).
[1127]See Gallant (2009: 211) and Macdonald (2010: 144).
[1128]See Shepherd (2010: 89), Castilla (2011: 18), Shepherd (2012: 34), Cummings & Stepnowsky (2011: 18) and Gregory (2004: 38).
[1129]Paragraph 32 of the Moscow Communiqué (1999).
[1130]Shepherd (2009: 611)
[1131]See Shepherd (2010: 89), Cummings & Stepnowsky (2011: 18) and Healy *et al* (2009: 797).

for legal professionals and law students; and (d) organises resource materials to allow lawyers to comply with their AML responsibilities". [1132]

The ABA and the American College of Trust and Estate Counsel (ACTEC) participated from 2004 in FATF meetings with the private sector and certain DNFBPs.[1133] The ABA always has opposed the mandatory imposition of due diligence, record keeping and suspicious activity reporting by attorneys.[1134] The FATF *Lawyer Guidance* is a collaborative effort by the private sector, the FATF, and FATF member states to encourage the adoption of a risk-based guidance for lawyers and to educate them about the risks of money laundering and terrorist financing.[1135] The US and its lawyers played a pivotal role in the drafting of the RBA of the FATF.[1136]

The controlling body of the ABA is called the House of Delegates. The control and administration of the ABA is vested in this House, which is also the policy-making body of the association. The House meets twice every year, during the ABA's annual and mid-year meetings. The Gatekeeper Task Force has been instrumental in the adoption of two ABA House of Delegates resolutions on Gatekeeper Initiative issues: House of Delegates Resolution 104, adopted in 2003; and House of Delegates Resolution 300, adopted in 2008.[1137]

5.2.1.1 House of Delegates Resolution 104 of 2003

A recommendation and report were submitted to the House of Delegates on the Gatekeeper Initiative by the Gatekeeper Task Force in February 2003.[1138] The recommendation opposed any law or regulation that would compel lawyers to disclose privileged or confidential information to government

---

[1132]See Shepherd (2010: 89) and Cummings & Stepnowsky (2011: 50).

[1133]Meetings were held in Paris 2004, Brussels 2005, Amsterdam 2006, London 2007, Berne 2007, Paris 2008, London 2008, Ottawa 2008. See Shepherd (2010) for a detailed discussion of these meetings. See also Healy *et a*l (2009: 798) and Cummings & Stepnowsky (2011: 19).

[1134]See Cummings & Stepnowsky (2011: 18), Gregory (2004: 41) and Kazmerski (2011: 94).

[1135]See Healy *et al* (2009: 799), Kazmerski (2011: 94) and Terry (2010: 15).

[1136]See Shepherd (2010: 92), Terry (2010:16) and Kazmerski (2011:94). The 2007 December meeting in Bern, Switzerland was attended by representatives from the Gatekeeper Task Force and the American College of Trust and Estate Counsel.

[1137]See Shepherd (2010: 90), Terry (2010: 39), Cummings & Stepnowsky (2011: 19) and Terry (2010: 37).

[1138]See Shepherd (2010: 90), Castilla (2011: 19), Healy *et al* (2009: 796), Cummings & Stepnowsky (2011: 19) and Terry (2010: 37).

officials based on "suspicious" activity of clients or otherwise compromise the attorney-client relationship or independence of the bar.[1139] It suggested that model rules of professional responsibility be reviewed as they relate to the obligation of lawyers to maintain client confidence.[1140] The report that accompanied the recommendation urged bar associations and law schools to undertake educational efforts on money laundering risks and concerns.[1141] It examined the role of lawyers in the US and government efforts to combat money laundering. It analysed the legal and ethical dilemmas arising from any mandatory reporting obligation which could reveal the information of clients that involves a suspicion of money laundering, and discussed the existing legal and ethical requirements to minimise the risk of lawyer-facilitated money laundering.[1142] The 2003 recommendation was adopted by the House of Delegates as Resolution 104.

5.2.1.2 House of Delegates Resolution 300 of 2008

Resolution 300 was drafted in 2008 by the ABA Gatekeeper Task Force which submitted a report and recommendation to the House of Delegates. In August 2008, at the ABA annual general meeting held in New York City, the House of Delegates adopted the Resolution in opposition to federal legislation that would bring lawyers involved in the corporate formation process under the Bank Secrecy Act regulations.[1143] It opposed measures that would impose obligations on lawyers to undertake extensive due diligence and determine beneficial ownership when they assist clients in incorporating non-public business entities and trusts.[1144] This was a response to federal legislation which proposed that those who form "unincorporated business entities, trusts, partnerships, and other organizational structures are required to document, verify, and make available to law enforcement authorities the record and

[1139]See Shepherd (2010: 90), Castilla (2011: 19), Healy *et al* (2009: 796), Shepherd (2012: 35) and Cummings & Stepnowsky (2011: 19).

[1140]See Shepherd (2010: 90).

[1141]See Shepherd (2010: 90) and Gregory (2004: 43).

[1142]See Shepherd (2010: 90).

[1143]The House of Delegates is the ABA's policy making body. See Healy *et al* (2009: 795, 797), Shepherd (2010: 90) and Castilla (2011: 19).

[1144]House of Delegates Resolution 300 at 17. See also Cummings & Stepnowsky (2011: 19), Shepherd (2010: 90) and Healy *et al* (2009: 797).

beneficial ownership of these business entities".[1145] The Resolution advocates that state and local bar associations, with the assistance of the Gatekeeper Initiative, develop a voluntary risk-based guidance for legal professionals.[1146]

The ABA realised that it needed to exhibit leadership to ensure that a risk-based guidance not imposed by government is developed for US lawyers.[1147] The concern also was that mandatory reporting obligations placed on lawyers regarding their clients' activities could result in rules-based guidance criminal penalties.[1148] The fact that there was no development of a rules-based guidance for US lawyers based on the FATF *Lawyer Guidance*, prompted a concern that "Congress would enact legislation designed to impose a rules-based system on US lawyers".[1149] Since the adoption of Resolution 300, the Gatekeeper Task Force has developed the Good Practices Guidance, obtained endorsements of the Guidance from various ABA sections and bar associations and participated in lawyer educational programmes on AML risks.[1150]

5.2.1.3 The Good Practices Guidance

The FATF encourages the development of good practices for legal professionals.[1151] In adhering to its request to develop good practices, the Gatekeeper Task Force, together with representatives from ABA sections and other bar associations, developed a voluntary Good Practices Guidance for lawyers to detect and combat money laundering and terrorist financing.[1152] The Good Practices Guidance, dated 23 April 2010, incorporates the FATF's risk-based approach to customer due diligence, but excludes any ethical obligation to file STRs.[1153] When the Gatekeeper Initiative was established, its focus was

---

[1145] House of Delegates Resolution 300 at 3.

[1146] House of Delegates Resolution 300 at 2. See also Healy *et al* (2009: 797) and Cummings & Stepnowsky (2011: 26).

[1147] See Shepherd (2010: 90) and Healy *et al* (2009: 798).

[1148] See Healy *et al* (2009: 796) and Terry (2010: 57).

[1149] The Voluntary Good Practices Guidance for Lawyers to Detect and Combat Money Laundering and Terrorist Financing (Good Practices Guidance) 8. See also Castilla (2011: 19), Healy *et a*l (2009: 798) and Cummings & Stepnowsky (2011: 19).

[1150] The Voluntary Good Practices Guidance for Lawyers to Detect and Combat Money Laundering and Terrorist Financing (Good Practices Guidance) 3.

[1151] See Healy *et al* (2009: 801) and Terry (2010: 47).

[1152] See Shepherd (2010: 96) and Castilla (2011: 20).

[1153] See Cummings & Stepnowsky (2011: 20).

on federal AML policy. The most important issue was the filing of STRs and the accompanying NTO rule.[1154] The Good Practices Guidance gives practical and understandable guidance to the legal profession in the US. Since there are immense differences across practices in US law firms, the Good Practices Guidance is essentially a resource that lawyers can use in developing their own voluntary RBA.[1155] The main purpose of the Good Practices Guidance is to encourage and empower lawyers to develop and implement voluntary but effective RBAs that are consistent with the FATF's *Lawyer Guidance*. The idea is that the implementation of the Good Practices Guidance will render federal regulation of the legal profession unnecessary.[1156]

The first part of the Good Practices Guidance includes an overview of the mechanics of money laundering and terrorist financing. This is meant to assist practitioners in acquiring an enhanced understanding of these concepts.[1157] It is followed by a description of the RBA and identification of the lawyers who are subject to the *Lawyer Guidance*.[1158] The specified activities which are described in the *Lawyer Guidance* and in the FATF Recommendations are mentioned also in this part.[1159] Thereafter, the Good Practices Guidance lists and analyses the risk categories and the risk variables. It concludes with a suggested protocol for client intake and assessment.[1160] It also emphasises the importance of continuing legal education in the area of money laundering and terrorist financing.[1161] The Good Practices Guidance essentially simplifies the *Lawyer Guidance* for practitioners.[1162] It includes practise pointers, that is, hypothetical factual scenarios to provide guidance and insights to practitioners.[1163] The Good Practices Guidance is seen as one of the factors

---

[1154]See Shepherd (2010: 90) and Kazmerski (2011: 89 & 91).

[1155]See Shepherd (2010: 96) and Cummings & Stepnowsky (2011: 20).

[1156]See Shepherd (2010: 96), Shepherd (2012: 37) and Cummings & Stepnowsky (2011: 19).

[1157]See Shepherd (2010: 97), Shepherd (2012: 37) and Cummings & Stepnowsky (2011: 209).

[1158]See Shepherd (2010: 97) and Shepherd (2012: 37). The Good Practice Guidance also highlights the various risk factors as contained in the FATF *Lawyer Guidance* of 2008.

[1159]See Shepherd (2010: 97), Shepherd (2012: 37) and Kazmerski (2011: 95).

[1160]See Shepherd (2010: 97), Shepherd (2012: 37) and Cummings & Stepnowsky (2011: 20).

1161See Shepherd (2010: 97), Shepherd (2012: 37) and Cummings & Stepnowsky (2011: 27).

[1162]See Shepherd (2010: 97) and Shepherd (2012: 37). FATF *Lawyer Guidance* is regarded as a complex document. See discussion in §2.4.4 above.

[1163]See Shepherd (2010: 97), Shepherd (2012: 38) and Cummings & Stepnowsky (2011: 20).

that could influence Congress not to enact legislation imposing a rules-based system on US lawyers.[1164]

The FATF mutual evaluation of the US took place in 2005-2006. The FATF's report rated the US as non-compliant with its Recommendations and its lawyers were listed as non-compliant in the areas of customer due diligence, monitoring of customers and filing of suspicious activity reports.[1165] Ironically, this negative assessment arises from the fact that lawyers in the US are not required to comply with the AML gatekeeper regulations regarding customer due diligence, record keeping and suspicious activity reporting.[1166] The position of US lawyers is thus much more favourable than their South African counterparts as regards the filing of STRs.

5.2.2 The Canadian Position

The STR issue was dealt with swiftly by the legal profession of Canada. As already intimated, the Canadian AML and CFT regime is founded upon the PCMLTFA of 2000. The legislative purpose of the Act is to enable authorities to detect and deter money laundering, to facilitate the investigation and prosecution of money laundering offences, to enhance law enforcement, and to assist Canada in fulfilling its international commitments to participate in the global battle against money laundering.[1167] The legislation further creates the Financial Transactions and Reports Analysis Centre of Canada (FINTRAC) and empowers it to gather information concerning money laundering, including suspicious transactions, and to share it with domestic and international law enforcement agencies.[1168] The provisions of the Act and its accompanying Regulations were viewed by the legal profession as infringing upon attorney-client confidentiality and the fundamental independence of Canadian lawyers.[1169] The parts of the legislation that affected lawyers most

---

[1164]See Shepherd (2010: 98), Shepherd (2012: 37) and Cummings & Stepnowsky (2011: 26).

[1165]See FATF (2006) "Third Mutual Evaluation" Report. See also Cummings & Stepnowsky (2011: 15), Healy *et al* (2009: 799), Terry (2010: 36) and Shepherd (2009: 624).

[1166]See Cummings & Stepnowsky (2011: 14) and Shepherd (2010: 90).

[1167]Section 3 of the PCMLTFA. See also *Law Society of British Columbia v Canada* 2001 BCSC 1593 Para 5.

[1168]Section 41 of the PMLTFA. See also Carter *et al* (2008: 58), Gallant (2013: 8), Priestley (2009: 15), Terry (2010: 34) and Paton (2010: 174). *Law Society of British Columbia v Canada* 2001 BCSC 1593 Para 6.

[1169]See Priestley (2009: 11), Paton (2010: 172), Terry (2010: 34) and MacDonald (2010: 144).

were the provisions on STRs,[1170] CDD,[1171] and the NTO rule.[1172] Section 7 of the PCMLTFA makes STRs mandatory:

> "Every person or entity shall report to [FINTRAC], in the prescribed form and manner, every financial transaction that occurs in the course of their activities and in respect of which there are reasonable grounds to suspect that the transaction is related to the commission of a money laundering offence."[1173]

In terms of Section 10 of the Regulations, it is required that a STR referred to in Section 7 must be sent to the FINTRAC within 30 days after the person or entity:

> "first detects a fact respecting a transaction that constitutes reasonable grounds to suspect that the transaction is related to the commission of a money laundering offence."[1174]

This meant that when a lawyer deals with a client and had a suspicion that the client was busy with a transaction related to a money laundering offence, he had to file a report with FINTRAC.[1175] The lawyer then is prohibited from disclosing to the client that a STR has been made, under the NTO clause in Section 8.[1176] Attorney-client privilege receives protection in Section 11 of the Act, which allows lawyers not to disclose any communication that is subject to attorney-client privilege. The scope of this privilege, however, is not defined.[1177] A contravention of Section 7 of the Act may result in a fine of up to $2 000 000

[1170]Section 7 of the PCMLTFA. See also Terry (2010: 34), MacDonald (2010: 144) and Gallant (2013: 8).

[1171]Section 6 of the PCMLTFA. See also MacDonald (2010: 144) and Gallant (2013: 8).

[1172]Section 8 of the PCMLTFA. See also Gallant (2013: 9).

[1173]Section 7 of the PCMLTFA. See also *Law Society of British Columbia v Canada* 2001 BCSC 1593, MacDonald (2010:144), Gallant (2013: 8) and Murphy (2000: 293).

[1174]Section 10 of the PCMLTFA. See also *Law Society of British Columbia v Canada* 2001 BCSC 1593. Para 16.

[1175]Section 7 of the PCMLTFA.

[1176]Section 7 and Section 8 of the PCMLTFA. See also *Law Society of British Columbia v Canada* 2001 BCSC 1593 Para 17.

[1177]Section 11 of the Regulations of the PCMLTFA. See also *Law Society of British Columbia v Canada* 2001 BCSC 1593 Para 18 and Gallant (2013: 9).

and imprisonment for up to five years,[1178] and a breach of Section 8, the NTO clause, could result in imprisonment for up to two years.[1179]

Not all the provisions of the PCMLTFA came into operation simultaneously.[1180] On 28 October 2001 certain sections of Part 1 came into operation.[1181] Although lawyers were not named specifically in Part 1, they were referred to therein by implication. For example, Section 5(i) refers to persons engaged in a business, profession or activity described in the Regulations made under Section 73(1)(a). Also, Section 5(j) mentions persons engaged in a business or profession described in regulations made under Section 73(1)(b), while carrying out the activities described in the regulations. In terms of Sections 73(1)(a) and (b) it was left to the Governor to issue the Regulations as to which professions were covered by Section 5(i) and Section 5(j).[1182] According to Section 5 of the Regulations, subsequently issued by the Governor, lawyers are subject to Part 1 of the Act. The Regulation provides as follows:

> "Every legal counsel is subject to Part I of the Act when they engage in any of the following activities on behalf of any person or entity, including the giving of instructions on behalf of any person or entity in respect of those activities:
> (a) receiving or paying funds, other than those received or paid in respect of professional fees, disbursements, expenses or bail;
> (b) purchasing or selling securities, real property or business assets or entities; and
> (c) transferring funds or securities by any means."[1183]

If all of the provisions of the PCMLTFA and the Regulations were implemented, lawyers would have been required to file STRs and to report any client transaction exceeding $10 000 cash.[1184] In other words, lawyers

---

[1178]Section 75 of the PCMLTFA.

[1179]Section 76 of the PCMLTFA. See also *Law Society of British Columbia v Canada* 2001 BCSC 1593 Para 19.

[1180]See Paton (2010: 174).

[1181]Sections 5, 7, 8, 10 and 11 of Part 1 of the PCMLTFA. *Law Society of British Columbia v Canada* 2001 BCSC 1593 Para 9. See also Ryder (2012: 131).

[1182]Section 73(1) of the PCMLTFA.

[1183]Section 5 of the Regulations of the PCMLTFA.

[1184]Paton (2010: 172), Priestley (2009: 15) and Gallant (2013: 10).

would have been required to act as clandestine agents of the state by gathering information about their clients and submitting it to FINTRAC.[1185] These Regulations came into operation on 8 November 2001, prompting the litigation instituted by the Law Societies to prevent their operation.[1186] In November 2001, the British Columbia Supreme Court, in *Law Society of British Columbia v Attorney General (Canada,)* granted an interdict relieving lawyers of the duty to file STRs as required by the Act and the Regulations.[1187]

The Court also declared the Regulations to be *ultra vires* and of no force and effect[1188] until the other constitutional issues regarding the verification of the identity of clients, the keeping of records of clients and the third party access to client records, were resolved.[1189] Allan J, the presiding officer, read down Sections 5(i), 5(j), 62 and 63 of the PCMLTFA so as to exclude legal counsel from "persons and entities" referred to in those Sections. [1190] Section 5 of the Regulations was regarded as being *ultra vires,* and Section 5 of the Regulations and Sections 64 and 17 were found to be inconsistent with the Constitution, invalid and of no force and effect.

The Court concluded that the applicant (as well as lawyers and clients, and indeed the administration of justice) may suffer irreparable harm unless lawyers were exempted from filing STRs pending a determination of the constitutional issues.[1191] It held further that the potential harm identified to lawyers was serious compared to the potential harm of an exemption to the government.[1192] The harm to the government by exempting lawyers until the merits of the issues were settled was minimal. It stated that the PCMLTFA "itself does not impose a reporting duty on legal counsel [and] by exempting lawyers from the Regulations, the Act remained intact and applicable to all other persons and entities described" therein.[1193]

[1185]See Macdonald (2010: 1441) and Gallant (2013: 10).

[1186]*Law Society of British Columbia v Canada* 2001 BCSC 1593. See also Macdonald (2010:145), Priestley (2009: 11), Paton (2010: 172) and Terry (2010: 34).

[1187]*Law Society of v British Columbia v Canada* 2001 BSCC 1593. See also Paton (2010: 177) and Gallant (2013: 10).

[1188]Paton (2010: 78).

[1189]*Law Society of British Columbia v Canada* 2001 BCSC 1593.

[1190]Sections 5(i) and 5(j) of the PCMLTFA. See also Canada Chronology, Paton (2010: 174) and Priestley (2009: 11).

[1191]*Law Society of British Columbia v Canada* 2001 BCSC 1593 Para 84.

[1192]*Law Society of British Columbia v Canada* 2001 BCSC 1593 Para 103.

[1193]*Law Society of British Columbia v Canada* 2001 BCSC 1593 Para 103.

The Court noted that even without the obligations imposed by this legislation, lawyers are subject to codes of conduct and ethical obligations imposed by their Law Societies, as well as to the provisions of the Criminal Code.[1194] These existing obligations mean that lawyers cannot engage in money laundering schemes or be party to any transactions with clients that conceal or convert property or proceeds that they believe to involve money laundering.[1195] What is more, the exemption of lawyers would not undermine the legislative scheme.[1196]

An appeal to the British Columbia Appeal Court against the exemption failed, and an application to the Supreme Court of Canada to argue against the exemption was dismissed also.[1197] This was a victory for lawyers in Canada, because it effectively exempted lawyers from filing any STRs until the constitutionality of the legislation had been determined.[1198] Lawyers thus were not required to collect information about their clients for onward transmission to FINTRAC.

After the 2001 judgment, the FLSC, on behalf of provincial and territorial law societies, brought applications in courts across the country for a declaration that Sections 62 to 64 of the PCMLTFA were unconstitutional and of no force or effect to the extent that they applied to legal counsel. Courts in Alberta, Ontario, Saskatchewan and Nova Scotia followed the British Columbia decision.[1199] On 14 May 2002, the FLSC and the Attorney General signed an agreement for a test case in the British Columbia Supreme Court to resolve the constitutionality of the PCMLTFA. The agreement gave national recognition to the decision by Allan J in the British Columbia Court.[1200] The effect was that all Canadian lawyers and Quebec notaries were exempt from Part 1 of the PCMLTFA until the constitutional challenge was heard in the British Columbia Supreme Court and the merits of the case had been decided. The case commenced in 2003.

Meanwhile on 20 March 2003, the Canadian government repealed several regulations subjecting lawyers to the recording and reporting requirements

[1194]Section 462.31 of the Criminal Code.

[1195]*Law Society of British Columbia v Canada* 2001 BCSC 1593 Para 105.

[1196]*Law Society of British Columbia v Canada* 2001 BCSC 1593 Para 106.

[1197]*Law Society of British Columbia v Canada* 2002 BCCA 49. See also Priestley (2009: 13.) and MacDonald (2010: 143-144).

[1198]See Canada Chronology.

[1199]See Canada Chronology, MacDonald (2010: 144) and Paton (2010: 177).

[1200]See Canada Chronology.

of Part 1 of the PCMLTFA.[1201] The repeal completely exempted lawyers from filing STRs in respect of their clients under Part 1 of the PCMLFA.[1202] On 15 April 2003, the British Columbia Supreme Court ordered the adjournment of the constitutional challenge by consent until 1 November 2004.[1203] In June 2004, the hearing set for 1 November 2004 was adjourned to 31 October 2005.[1204] On 13 May 2005, the British Columbia Supreme Court postponed the matter *sine die,* subject to the following conditions:

> "1. That if a new set of regulations affecting legal counsel is enacted pursuant to the Proceeds of Crime Act by the Federal Government without the consent of the Federation, that the coming into force of those regulations would be deferred in accordance with the May 2002 Agreement between the Federation and the Attorney General of Canada;
> 2. That the Attorney General of Canada agrees to interlocutory injunctions exempting legal counsel and legal firms from the application of the Act and its Regulations should it become necessary to maintain the status quo at any stage of the proceedings; and
> 3. That the Federation and the Attorney General have an unrestricted right to re-set the petition for hearing." [1205]

The amendment to the PCMLTFA in December 2006 exempted lawyers from filing STRs. The Act was amended by the insertion of Section 10(1), which provided that Sections 7 and 9 (the reporting obligations) do not apply to legal counsel and legal firms when they are providing legal services. The STR matter did not feature again in the various other matters between the FLSC and the Attorney General.[1206]

[1201]See Canada Gazette Part II, Extra Vol. 137. No 2 Sor/2003=102 March 2003 Regulations amending certain Regulations made under PCMLTFA.

[1202]See Macdonald (2010: 145).

[1203]See Paton (2010: 178) and Canada Chronology.

[1204]See Canada Chronology.

[1205]See Paton (2010: 178).

[1206]*Federation of Law Societies of Canada v Canada* 2011 BCSC 1270, *Federation of Law Societies of Canada v Canada* 2013 BCCA 147 and *Canada (Attorney General) v Federation of Law Societies of Canada* 2015 SCC 7.

5.2.3 The South African Position

The South African position regarding STRs has been discussed in detail in Chapter 3, but will be referred to briefly here again. The non-submission of STRs and the tipping-off a client are criminalised in FICA.[1207] Lawyers are threatened with punishment of imprisonment not exceeding 15 years or the imposition of a fine not exceeding R10 million.[1208] The criminalisation of the failure to submit STRs has not been challenged by South African lawyers or any other accountable institutions, despite the fact that lawyers receive confidential information from clients virtually on a daily basis.

The compulsory filing of STR places a lawyer in a difficult position. The lawyer is required to report the client even if he merely suspects that the client is busy with illegal conduct. Section 37 of FICA does protect the common-law legal professional privilege. However, the privilege does not encompass all confidential information conveyed to a lawyer. When a lawyer receives suspicious information which will not qualify for protection under the legal professional privilege, he is obliged to submit that information to the FIC. In *S v Boesman,* the Court held that it was undesirable and against public policy that attorneys should testify against their clients.[1209] It is suggested, however, that an attorney eventually would have to testify against a client if he had submitted an STR and the client subsequently is prosecuted.

A lawyer, who is consulted by an accused person, charged with a money laundering offence theoretically can be committing a crime, if the lawyer suspects that the client committed an offence and the lawyer fails to file an STR.

5.2.4 Comparative Commentary

When the three jurisdictions are compared, South African lawyers seem to be receiving the short end of the stick once again. Both US and Canadian lawyers have received substantial proactive support from their law societies to oppose the requirements to file STRs. In the US, the ABA was instrumental in developing the FATF's RBA to ensure that there is no compulsion on lawyers to file STRs. In Canada, the FLSC initiated a litigation crusade against the

---

[1207] Section 29(3) of FICA.

[1208] Section 68 of FICA. See also Hamman & Koen (2012: 77).

[1209] *S v Boesman* 1990 (2) SACR 389 (E).

compulsory filing of STRs and succeeded. In South Africa nothing substantial to oppose the legislation has been done by the law societies.

As a result of the ABA's efforts, compulsory STRs are not included in the FATF *Lawyer Guidance* and are not part of the RBA. The ABA also drafted resolutions which opposed any law or regulation that would compel lawyers to disclose any suspicious activity of their clients. It has developed a voluntary Good Practices Guidance to assist lawyers and to prevent mandatory reporting. The ABA has protected its lawyers despite the fact that the FATF has given the US a non-compliance report regarding the filing of STRs. As a result, lawyers in the US are fortunate that they do not have to file any STRs.

Soon after their AML legislation was promulgated, the FLSC instituted injunction proceedings which ultimately exempted lawyers from reporting any suspicious activity of their clients. Canadian lawyers do not have to file any STRs when they provide legal services.

It is unfortunate that the South African legislature and the law societies did not take cognisance of the developments in Canada and the US regarding the compulsory filing of STRs for lawyers. It is disconcerting that South African lawyers and their representative bodies have failed to grasp the possible negative effects of compulsory STRs on attorney-client confidentiality and legal professional privilege. Whereas the Canadian and US professional bodies vehemently opposed compulsory STRs for lawyers, South African lawyers and bodies were noticeably quiet on this issue. FICA was enacted in 2001 and amended in 2008, but no court challenges or major objections have been lodged against the legislation. The only hint of opposition to the legislation was seen in 2008 when a representative of the LSSA addressed a Parliamentary portfolio committee on the FICA Amendment Bill. The LSSA emphasised the point that lawyers have a duty to advance the interests of their clients fearlessly and must assist the courts in upholding the law. It underlined the professional independence of lawyers. It submitted that it did not wish to shield lawyers from being held accountable in the performance of their professional duties, but that there was a need to protect clients and the independence of the legal profession.[1210]

The inaction of South African lawyers is curious. Could it be that they are so embroiled in their everyday chase to earn fees or so consumed by the day-to-day running of legal practices, that the possible prosecution of failing to submit an STR was not seen as an especially important concern? Is the fact

[1210]Van der Westhuizen (2008: 18).

that lawyers have not been prosecuted for failing to file STRs perhaps the reason for South African lawyers' *laissez-faire* attitude? Will the prosecution of lawyers serve as a wake-up call which could provoke South African lawyers to voice their dissatisfaction with STRs and challenge the offending parts of the legislation? Only time will tell whether and when the above questions will be answered.

There are certain lessons that can be learnt from the Canadian and US positions. The South African legal profession should act swiftly when confronted with legislation that has dire consequences for lawyers by approaching the courts, if necessary, to interdict its operation. The LSSA should its voice opinion against dubious legislation more vociferously and draft model rules of practice to circumvent unnecessary legislative intrusion into the legal profession. If pressure is not put on government to amend this type of legislation, lawyers could be prosecuted on a huge scale. It is recommended that Section 29 of FICA be amended to exempt lawyers as accountable institutions from the filing of STRs. Such an amendment would place them in a position akin to that of lawyers in the US and in Canada.

5.3 Cash Transaction Reporting

5.3.1 The US Position

Cash transaction reporting in the US is regulated by the Bank Secrecy Act (BSA) and the Internal Revenue Code (IRC). The BSA, promulgated in 1970, focuses on the regulation and prevention of money laundering.[1211] Initially, the concern was with financial institutions, on which record-keeping and reporting requirements were imposed.[1212] The main purpose of these requirements was to maintain and provide evidence in criminal, tax and other proceedings.[1213] The universally accepted KYC provision was one of the principles initiated by the BSA. [1214] The KYC principle required financial

[1211]The official title of the BSA is the Currency and Foreign Transaction Reporting Act of 1970, See also Shams (2004: 17), Irvine & King: (1988: 172, 174), Sultzer (1996: 152), Ryder (2012: 41) and Leslie (2014: 11).

[1212]See Shams (2004: 18), Gregory (2003: 27), Richards (1999: 133) and Madinger (2012: 24).

[1213]See Shams (2004: 18), Van Jaarsveld (2011: 383) and Irvine & King (1988: 175).

[1214]See Shams (2004: 18), Richards (1999: 135) and Shuck (1996: 510).

institutions to maintain records of the identity of each and every account holder.[1215] It was required further that domestic transactions involving the transfer of currency in excess of $10 000 had to be reported to the treasury department, the so-called Currency Transaction Report (CTR).[1216] In addition, the transportation of monetary instruments into or out of the US, where the amount of the instruments exceeded $10 000, had to be reported.[1217]

In *California Bankers Association v Schultz*, a class action was brought against the government, challenging the constitutionality of the reporting requirements of the BSA, but the challenge failed.[1218] A bank was prohibited from informing anyone involved in the transaction that a CTR was made.[1219] This can be regarded as the forerunner of the NTO clause. Information pertaining to customers who are "engaged in or reasonably suspected of engaging in terrorist acts or money laundering", however, could be shared with other financial institutions.[1220] The division of a large currency transaction into a number of smaller ones to avoid reporting and money laundering itself were not regarded initially as criminal offences.[1221] This loophole was exploited by individuals who structured certain transactions in such a way that the financial institutions would not be required to file a CTR.[1222] Financial institutions could not refuse to file a CTR based on a client's right to privacy. The decision of *United States v Miller* confirmed that bank customers had no privacy in

[1215]Section 5326 of the BSA. Records of certain domestic coin and currency transactions. See also Richards (1999: 135).

[1216]Section 5313(a) of the BSA and Section 6050I of the IRC. See also Gregory (2003: 27), Irvine & King (1988: 172 & 175), Madinger (2012: 24), Sultzer (1996: 153) and Leslie (2014: 12).

[1217]Section 5332 of the BSA. See also Irvine & King (1988: 175) and Sultzer (1996: 153).

[1218]*California Bankers Association v Shultz* 416 US 21 (1974). See also Madinger (2012: 24), Richards (1999: 131,135), Irvine & King (1988: 175) and Leslie (2014: 12).

[1219]Section 5318(g)(2) of the BSA. See also Van Jaarsveld (2011: 384).

1220See Van Jaarsveld (2011: 386).

[1221]See Richards (1999: 131), Shams (2004: 18), Madinger (2012: 24) and Gregory (2003: 27).

[1222]The judgments of the federal appellate courts dealing with individuals were inconsistent. In *United States v Cook* 745 F. 2d 1311, 1315 (10th Cir 1984), *United States v Puerto* 730 F. 2d 627, 633 (11th Cir 1984), *United States v Tobon-Builles* 706F2d. 1092, 1101 (11th Cir 1983), and *United States v Thompson* 603 F 2d. 1202, 1203-1204 (5th Cir 1979) individuals were held liable in terms of the BSA for money laundering because of structuring activities. However, in *United States v Varbei* 780 F.2d 758, 762 (9th Cir 1986) and *United States v Anzalone* 766 F. 2d. 676. 682 (1st Cir 1989) individuals were not held criminally liable for money laundering activities. See also Irvine & King (1988: 173), Richards (1999: 134) and Madinger (2012: 24).

the commercial records in possession of financial institutions.[1223] Although the BSA did not refer explicitly to lawyers in the process of combating money laundering, it initiated the KYC principle and the CTR requirement which could be extended later to lawyers by the IRC.[1224]

As noted above, the IRC also refers to the reporting of cash payments and provides that lawyers must report certain details about their clients.[1225] The relevant section of the IRC is Section 6050-I. In terms of this section, anyone who has received more than $10 000 cash in a business transaction, must disclose the name, address and the identity number of the payer.[1226]

Section 6050-I stipulates that:

> "Any person
> (1) who is engaged in a trade or business, and
> (2) who, in the course of such trade or business, receives more than $10,000 in cash in 1 transaction (or 2 or more related transactions), shall make the return described in subsection (b) with respect to such transaction (or related transactions) at such time as the Secretary may by regulations prescribe."[1227]

Lawyers fall under the umbrella terms, "trade or businesses", and are required to comply with this Section.[1228] Specifically they are required to complete a return, designated Form 8300, and submit it to the Internal Revenue Service. The return must include the cash payer's name and other identifying information.[1229]

Compliance with Section 6050-I could place lawyers in a position where they violate attorney-client confidentiality as they have to divulge certain information about their clients. It may threaten an accused's Sixth Amendment rights when lawyers tick the box where a large amount of cash

---

1223 *United Sates v Miller* 425 US 435 1976. See also Richards (1999: 135).

1224 See Richards (1999: 135).

1225 See Gregory (2003: 42) and Richards (1999: 182).

1226 See Allen (1997: 795), Gregory (2003: 42), Richards (1999: 182) and Shuck (1996: 509).

1227 See Gregory (2003: 42), Richards (1999: 182), Madinger (2012: 61), Christensen (2006: 311) and Migala (1996: 509).

1228 See Podgor (2010: 192), Gregory (2004: 42), Brickey (1988: 48), Gaetke & Welling (1992: 1173), Madinger (2012: 62) and Christensen (2006: 311).

1229 See Christensen (2006: 311), Podgor (2010: 192), Gregory (2004: 30 & 42), Richards (1999: 182), Madinger (2012: 62), Gaetke & Welling (1992: 1173) and Allen (1997: 796).

seems suspicious.[1230] It could undermine also an accused's Fifth Amendment right if disclosing information about the accused would violate his right not to be incriminated.[1231] Be that as it may, Section 6050-I requires the legal profession in the US to furnish the IRS with certain information about its clients.[1232] The US Supreme Court has not dealt with this issue yet. Therefore this section discusses only the Federal Court cases in which Section 6050-I was challenged.

United States v Goldberger & Dubin PC is one such case in which the reporting duty of law firms under Section 6050-I of the IRC came under scrutiny.[1233] Attorneys Fischetti, Pomerantz & Russo received cash fees in excess of $10 000 from two individuals.[1234] Both the clients were advised of the reporting requirements of Section 6050-I, but they requested that their attorneys not disclose their identities.[1235] Meanwhile the attorneys' firm of Goldberger and Dubin PC received similar cash fees in excess of $10 000 from each of three individuals.[1236] This firm duly filed a Form 8300, disclosing that the cash fee payment in each case was received, but excluding the identity of the persons who made the payments.[1237] The IRS then issued summonses directing the firm to appear and produce information identifying the payers.[1238] The respondents refused to comply and the state then applied to the District Court to order compliance.[1239] The two clients of Fischetti, Pomerantz & Russoi, identified as John Doe No 1 and John Doe No 2, were granted leave to intervene in the proceedings.[1240] Because the District Court ordered that the respondents comply with the IRS summonses and provide the payer

---

[1230]See Allen (1997: 803), Madinger (2012: 62) and Gaetke & Welling (1992: 1174).

[1231]See Allen (1997: 803) and Gregory (2004: 42).

[1232]See Brickey (1988: 48), Christensen (2006: 311), Podgor (2010: 192), Gregory (2004: 42) and Gaetke & Welling (1992: 1173).

[1233]*United States v Goldberger & Dubin PC* 935 F2d 501 (1991) at 502. See also Allen (1997: 817), Madinger (2012: 62), Gregory (2004: 42), Gaetke & Welling (1992: 1174) and Shuck (1996: 516).

[1234]*United States v Goldberger & Dubin PC* 935 F2d 501 (1991) at 502.

[1235]*United States v Goldberger & Dubin PC* 935 F2d 501 (1991) at 502.

[1236]*United States v Goldberger & Dubin PC* 935 F2d 501 (1991) at 502.

[1237]*United States v Goldberger & Dubin PC* 935 F2d 501 (1991) at 502.

[1238]*United States v Goldberger & Dubin PC* 935 F2d 501 (1991) at 502. See Allen (1997: 818).

[1239]*United States v Goldberger & Dubin PC* 935 F2d 501 (1991) at 502.

[1240]*United States v Goldberger & Dubin PC* 935 F2d 501 (1991) at 502.

information, the parties appealed the decision to the US Court of Appeals, Second Circuit.[1241]

The Court of Appeals held that the record-keeping and reporting provisions of the BSA were based upon congressional findings that they "have a high degree of usefulness in criminal, tax, and regulatory investigations or proceedings".[1242] It noted that when Congress expanded the reporting requirements in Section 6050-I to cash transactions in excess of $10 000, extensive lobbying efforts to exempt attorneys from the reach of this amendment were made, but they were unsuccessful.

The Court observed that the constitutional challenges in relation to the Fourth and Fifth Amendments had been rejected consistently in cases under the BSA.[1243] It held that the appellants' principal constitutional argument, that Section 6050-I deprives them of their Sixth Amendment right to counsel, is equally without merit.[1244] It stated that Section 6050-I stops far short of the forfeiture statutes that were at issue in *Caplin & Drysdale* and *Monsanto*,[1245] where it was concluded that the forfeiture of seized assets of an accused to pay his attorneys did not to violate the Sixth Amendment.[1246] The Court found that disclosure can be avoided easily under Section 6050-I, if payment is made to lawyers in some manner other than cash.[1247] The client had made a decision about how counsel was to be paid and the appellants had not given a legitimate reason why a mode of payment other than cash could not have been used. The Court then held that Section 6050-I passes constitutional muster.[1248]

The appellants' contention that Section 6050-I conflicts with the traditional doctrine of attorney-client privilege was rejected also.[1249] The Court held that "there is no evidence whatever herein, that the identification in Form 8300 of

---

[1241] *United States v Goldberger & Dubin PC* 935 F2d 501 (1991) at 501 7 504.

[1242] *United States v Goldberger & Dubin PC* 935 F2d 501(1991) at 501 & 504.

[1243] The court referred to decisions of the same court as well as the Supreme Court. See *United States v Miller* 425 US 435 and *California Bankers* 416 US at 44-75, 94.

[1244] *Wheat v United States*, 486 US 153, 159, 108 S.Ct. 1692, 100 L.Ed.2d 140 (1988), where the Court stated: "We have further recognized that the purpose of providing assistance of counsel simply to ensure that criminal defendants receive a fair trial."

[1245] *Caplin & Drysdale, Chartered v United States*, 491 US 617 (1989) and *United States v Monsanto*, 491 US 600 (1989).

[1246] See Madinger (2012: 62).

[1247] See Madinger (2012: 62).

[1248] *United States v Goldberger & Dubin PC* 935 F2d 501 (1991) at 505. See Allen (1997: 820).

[1249] *United States v Goldberger & Dubin PC* 935 F2d 501 (1991) at 502.

respondents' clients who make substantial cash fee payments is a disclosure of privileged information".[1250] It stated that a client should not be allowed to claim the attorney-client privilege, either directly or through his attorney, for the purpose of concealing his own on-going or contemplated fraud.[1251] It decided that IRS summons authority exists not for the purpose of accusing lawyers, but to inquire into the details of the payer.[1252]

In *United States v Gertner*, the same issue cropped up again.[1253] Attorneys Gertner and Newman represented a client during 1991 and 1992. The client paid for their legal services in cash,[1254] making four payments of $2 500, $17 260, $15 000 and $25 000.[1255] In compliance with Section 6050-I, the attorneys reported this matter on four separate Forms 8300,[1256] but they did not disclose the identity of the client. They reasoned that to disclose the identity would violate attorney-client confidentiality.[1257] The IRS then summoned Gertner and Newman to appear in court with certain records and information. It specifically wanted the name, address, occupation and social security number of the client. [1258] Gertner and Newman refused to comply with the summonses. They requested direction from the Committee on Professional Ethics of the Massachusetts Bar Association, which recommended that they refuse to divulge the requested information, unless there is a court order. The state then petitioned the Court for the district of Massachusetts to enforce the summonses. The Court demanded that Gertner and Newman offer evidence in opposition to the state's petition. The attorneys complied with the request and the court held that attorney-client privilege protects client identity because disclosure could implicate the client in the criminal activity for which he has sought legal advice.[1259]

[1250]*United States v Goldberger & Dubin PC* 935 F2d 501 (1991) at 505.

[1251]See *United States v Rosenstein*, 474 F.2d 705, 715 (2d Cir.1973); In re Special September 1978 Grand Jury, 640 F.2d 49, 62-63 (7th Cir.1980).

[1252]*United States v Goldberger & Dubin PC* 935 F2d 501 (1991) at 504.

[1253]*United States v. Gertner* 873 F. Supp. 729 (D. Mass. 1995). See also Allen (1997: 795).

[1254]*United States v. Gertner* 873 F. Supp. 729 (D. Mass. 1995). See also Allen (1997: 795).

[1255]*United States v. Gertner* 873 F. Supp. 729 (D. Mass. 1995). See also Allen (1997: 796).

[1256]*United States v. Gertner* 873 F. Supp. 729 (D. Mass. 1995). See also also Allen (1997: 796).

[1257]*United States v. Gertner* 873 F. Supp. 729 (D. Mass. 1995). See also Allen (1997: 796).

[1258]*United States v. Gertner* 873 F. Supp. 729 (D. Mass. 1995). See also Allen (1997: 796).

[1259]*United States v. Gertner* 873 F. Supp. 729 (D. Mass. 1995).

Then the matter went on appeal at the instance of the government to the United States Court of Appeals, First Circuit.[1260] The Court of Appeals agreed with the District Court's finding that the summonses were not drafted to probe the tax liability of the attorneys, but for the clandestine purpose of investigating their unnamed client.[1261] It thus seems that should the release of the payer's details have the effect of incriminating a client, lawyers legitimately could refuse to submit the information.

However, in *United States v Blackman*, heard in the US Court of Appeals, Ninth Circuit, the opposite was held.[1262] The Court found that the report made in terms of Section 6050-I does not conflict with traditional attorney-client privilege.[1263] It declared that the attorney-client privilege does not protect client and fee information even when disclosure would implicate the payer. It held that the privilege only protects client and fee information when disclosure would convey information that is tantamount to a confidential communication between attorney and client.[1264]

In the matter of *United States v Leventhal,* the Court of Appeals, Eleventh Circuit, also rejected the argument of a law firm because the clients already were under indictment for drug related offences.[1265] The prosecutors knew the client's identity and the Court acknowledged that the client only needs to pay his lawyer in some way other than cash to avoid the disclosure requirements of Section 6050-I.[1266]

The abovementioned cases indicate that the information requested from attorneys under Section 6050-I of the IRC is limited to details of clients who effect cash payments to the offices of lawyers. Should compliance with the section entail divulging information that warrants protection under legal professional privilege, lawyers will be entitled to withhold details of clients. Until Congress amends Section 6050-I of the IRC to exclude attorneys or the Supreme Court creates an exemption for attorneys, they are caught between potentially violating federal law and breaching attorney-client privilege.[1267]

[1260] *United States v. Gertner* 873 F. Supp. 729 (D. Mass. 1995).

[1261] *United States v. Gertner* 873 F. Supp. 729 (D. Mass. 1995).

[1262] *United States v. Gertner* 873 F. Supp. 729 (D. Mass. 1995). See also Allen (1997: 798).

[1263] *United States v. Gertner* 873 F. Supp. 729 (D. Mass. 1995). See also Allen (1997: 798).

[1264] *United States v Blackman* 72 F. 3d 1418 (9th Cir.1995) Para 23.

[1265] *United States v Leventhal* 961 F.2d 936 (11th Cir.1992). See also Allen (1997: 818).

[1266] *United States v Leventhal* 961 F.2d 936 (11th Cir.1992). See also Allen (1997: 818).

[1267] See Allen (1997: 820) and Migala (1996: 509).

5.3.2 The Canadian Position

FINTRAC, Canada's Financial Intelligence Unit, is the agency responsible for the collection, analysis, assessment and disclosure of financial information and intelligence.[1268] In terms of Guideline 3.2 of FINTRAC, a reporting entity has to send a large cash transaction report to FINTRAC if an amount of $10,000 or more in cash in the course of a single transaction is received.[1269] Each such transaction must be sent to FINTRAC separately. This report must be submitted within 15 calendar days of the transaction.

As discussed previously, when the Regulations to the PCMLTFA came into operation on the 8 November 2001, the FLSC obtained an interdict against its operation in relation to lawyers.[1270] Had the FLSC failed with its application, lawyers would have been put in a situation where they had to report any client transaction exceeding $10 000 in cash.[1271] The order of the British Columbia Supreme Court in November 2001 excused lawyers from filing CTRs as required by the Act and the Regulations.[1272] As a result of the amendment to the PCMLTFA in December 2006, lawyers were exempted not only from STRs, but also from CTRs.

To its credit the FLSC, in its efforts to prevent lawyers being compelled to file STRs and CTRs, did not rely only upon litigation.[1273] After the 2001 injunction, the FLSC decided to introduce its own rules to circumvent lawyer-facilitated money laundering.[1274] The No-Cash Rule, introduced in October 2004,[1275] meant that each Law Society had to implement rules which preclude lawyers from receiving cash amounts of more than $7 500,[1276] except for

---

[1268]FINTRAC www.fintrac-canafe.gc.ca. [

[1269]FINTRAC www.fintrac-canafe.gc.ca. See also Ryder (2012: 148).

[1270]*Law Society of British Columbia v Canada* 2001 BCSC 1593. See also Macdonald (2010: 145), Priestley (2009: 11), Paton (2010: 172) and Terry (2010: 34).

[1271]Paton (2010: 172); Priestley (2009: 15); Gallant (2013: 10).

[1272]*Law Society of British Columbia v Canada* 2001 BSCC 1593. See also Paton (2010: 177) and Gallant (2013: 10).

[1273]See Paton (2010: 181), Gallant (2009: 215), Terry (2010: 42), McDonald (2010: 145), Woolley (2013: 2) and Priestley (2009: 17).

[1274]Model Rules to Fight Money Laundering and Terrorist Financing.

[1275]See Paton (2010: 181), Priestley (2009: 17) and Terry (2010: 42).

[1276]See Gallant (2013: 11), (Woolley (2013: 2), Paton (2010: 181), Terry (2010: 42), McDonald (2010: 145), Priestley (2009: 17.) and Lawrence & van Houten (2013: 1).

the purposes of receiving payment of legal fees.[1277] It is also a requirement that should a lawyer receive a cash payment for his legal fees and later an amount needs to be refunded to the client, any such refund in excess of $1 000 must be paid in cash.[1278] The adoption of the No-Cash Rule rendered it totally unnecessary for lawyers to report cash transactions involving $10 000 or more to any government institution.[1279] A transgression of this rule entails disciplinary sanction from the appropriate Law Society.

In 2006, the PCMLTFA was amended further by the insertion of Section 10(1). The insertion exempted lawyers from filing CTRs when they are providing legal services.[1280] This addition to the legislation was a response to the Law Societies' adoption of the No-Cash Rule.[1281]

It was acknowledged by the British Columbia Court of Appeal in 2013 that the FLSC, by adopting the No-Cash Rule, had put sufficient measures in place to combat lawyer-facilitated money laundering and terrorist financing.[1282] The Court stated that compliance with these rules is ensured by the FLSC conducting annual audits and requesting reports.[1283] It noted that a significant difference between the PCMLTFA and information disclosed to Law Societies is that the latter is subject to an obligation that it will not be disclosed to others. This at least ensures that attorney-client confidentiality will be protected.

The No-Cash Rule was a clear indication that the Canadian Law Societies were taking their responsibility to combat lawyer-facilitated money laundering seriously.[1284] Although Canadian lawyers are exempted from submitting CTRs to FINTRAC, they must heed the no-cash requirement of the FLSC, or face disciplinary sanctions.

1277 See Paton (2010: 181), Woolley (2013: 2), Lawrence & van Houten (2013: 1) and Terry (2010: 42).

1278 *Federation of Law Societies of Canada v Canada* 2013 BCCA 147 Para 19. See also Woolley (2013: 2).

1279 See Gallant (2009: 215), Gallant (2013: 11), Paton (2010: 181), McDonald (2010: 145), Woolley (2013: 2) and Priestley (2009: 17).

1280 Section 10(1) of the PCMLTFA reads:

> "Sections 7 and 9 do not apply to persons or entities referred to in paragraph 5(i) or (j) who are, as the case may be, legal counsel or legal firms, when they are providing legal services."

1281 No-Cash Rule of the FLSC (2004).

1282 *Federation of Law Societies of Canada v Canada* 2013 BCCA 147 Para 148. See also Lawrence & van Houten (2013: 1).

1283 *Federation of Law Societies of Canada v Canada* 2013 BCCA 147 Para 23.

1284 See Gallant (2013: 11), Paton (2010: 181), McDonald (2010: 145), Woolley (2013: 2.

5.3.3 The South African Position

In South Africa, lawyers are required to submit to the FIC a CTR in respect of all cash transactions, which include payments to and receipts from a client, that exceed R24 999-99.[1285] The obligation includes single as well as multiple transactions.[1286] The failure to file such a report is criminalised and could result in the imposition of a fine of up to R10 million or a term of imprisonment of up to 15 years.[1287] There is currently no indication that the CTR requirement will be amended by the legislature in the near future.

Although it can be appreciated that the government intended CTRs as a weapon to prevent the cleaning of cash from illegal origins, the FICA requirement seems harsh. If someone pays a lawyer with cash of R25 000 or more, it does not matter that the client can provide an explanation for having the cash, a report must be filed with the FIC and if it is not filed the lawyer is committing a crime. However, there could be a logical explanation for a person paying with cash. South Africa has a vibrant informal economy in which vendors sell their goods at various stalls outside the formal shopping centres and in informal trading areas. Their only means of transacting is cash, both for accepting and making payments, especially if they do not have banking accounts. Also, a client could withdraw the money from a financial institution and come to the lawyer with a legitimate cash payment. What if such a client is oblivious of the fact that he could have asked his bank to make an electronic fee transfer or that he could have done so himself?

It seems that the legislature regards the mere payment of R25 000 or more in cash as being suspicious and therefore a CTR must be filed. The LSSA does not prescribe to lawyers anything about cash payments by clients and there is no prohibition when lawyers are paid in cash. Disturbing for lawyers is the fact that the failure to file a CTR is criminalised.

[1285]Regulation 22B of the Regulations to FICA. See also Hamman & Koen (2012: 73), Henning & Ebersohn (2001: 124) and Millard & Vergano (2013: 399).

[1286]This amounts to an attempt to prevent smurfing or structuring. See also Hamman & Koen (2012: 73).

[1287]Sections 51 and 68 of FICA.

5.3.4 Comparative Commentary

The CTR regime in South Africa has more stringent requirements than in the US and Canada. In the US, in terms of the BSA, it is required that domestic currency transactions that exceed $10 000 be reported to the Treasury Department. However, it must be noted that this requirement applies to financial institutions and not to lawyers. Under Section 6050-I of the IRC, any cash payments in excess of $10 000 should be reported to the IRS, with the details of the payer to be included in such report. It is submitted that should the disclosure of client information have the effect of furnishing information that warrants protection under attorney-client confidentiality or legal professional privilege, attorneys probably will not be compelled to furnish the information.

In Canada, the FLSC was successful in securing exemption for attorneys from the obligation to submit CTRs to FINTRAC for transactions involving cash in excess of $10 000. However, the FLSC has introduced the so called no-cash rule to prevent their lawyers from receiving cash payments in excess of $7 500.

South African lawyers are the worst off, because the failure to file a CTR is a crime and they could face prosecution for such failure. By contrast, in the US the Treasury Department or the IRS will subpoena lawyers to court to explain why a CTR was not made that included all the details of the payer, but lawyers will not be prosecuted for a failure to comply with the provisions of the BSA or the IRC. It is not regarded as a crime for lawyers not to file a CTR. The requirement in Section 6050-I of the IRC is that lawyers provide the details of the payer to the IRS. If the details are not provided, the IRS will conduct its own investigation against the client. The purpose of the IRS summons is not to accuse a person, but to commence an inquiry. In South Africa, the mere failure to report a transaction, and not the omission to furnish the particulars of the payer, is criminalised.

As mentioned previously, the LSSA does not prescribe to lawyers that they should not accept cash payment from clients, as Canada's FLSC does. The magnitude of South Africa's informal economy does not make it viable to put a prohibition on clients paying cash to lawyers. The LSSA should be requested to draft a rule to guide South African lawyers not to accept cash payment above a certain amount. The prohibition on accepting cash in excess of R24 999,99 can stand, as long as the non-submission of a CTR ceases to be a crime. Instead, a rule could be drafted to make it a disciplinary offence if cash above the agreed threshold is received by a practitioner in either his business or trust account. Such a payment could be verified by the chartered accountant who performs the annual audit on the trust account of an attorney. The transgression of such a rule could result in a fine or other administrative penalty for a lawyer, but it should not be a crime.

It seems that the drafters of the South African legislation were over-zealous, confronting lawyers with the threat of prosecution for not filing CTRs and STRs.

5.4 Third Party Access to Client Records

5.4.1 The US Position

The US position regarding third party access to confidential attorney-client is structured by Model Rule 1.6 of the ABA and the Fourth Amendment to the US Constitution. Model Rule 1.6 covers the confidentiality of information specifically in relation to the attorney-client relationship. All such information is privileged and a lawyer may not reveal any of it if it pertains to the representation of a client. Waiver of such privilege can occur only with the client's informed consent.[1288]

Lawyers are always in possession of client details and are expected not to divulge the information to third parties. The information may be revealed only where the lawyer reasonably believes that it is necessary to prevent death or substantial bodily harm,[1289] to prevent the client from committing a crime or fraud that could cause injury to someone else's finances or property,[1290] or to mitigate or rectify injury to someone else's finances or property whilst the client is utilising a lawyer's services.[1291] The information could be revealed also to provide advice about compliance with Model Rule 1.6, to establish a defence for a lawyer in the case of a dispute between lawyer and client,[1292] to defend a criminal charge or a civil claim,[1293] or to comply with a court order.[1294] In

[1288]Model Rule 1.6(a).

[1289]Model Rule 1.6(b)(1).

[1290]Model Rule 1.6(b)(2).

[1291]Model Rule 1.6(b)(3).

[1292]Model Rule 1.6(b)(4).

[1293]Model Rule 1.6(b)(5).

[1294]Model Rule 1.6(b)(6).

addition, information could be revealed if it will resolve a conflict of interest when a lawyer leaves his employment or changes occur in the composition of a legal firm, as long as the revealed information does not compromise the attorney-client privilege.[1295] In terms of Model Rule 1.6(c): "A lawyer shall make reasonable efforts to prevent the inadvertent or unauthorized disclosure of, or unauthorized access to, information relating to the representation of a client."

The Fourth Amendment provides protection to law offices against warrantless searches and seizures. It reads:

> "The right of the people to be secure in their persons, houses, papers and effects, against unreasonable searches and seizures, shall not be violated, and no Warrants shall issue, but upon probable cause, supported by Oath or affirmation, and particularly describing the place to be searched, and the persons or things to be seized."

Information contained in lawyers' files about confidential attorney-client discussions falls within the ambit of the Fourth Amendment. A duly authorised warrant, issued by a judicial officer, is required before a search of lawyers' office and a seizure of confidential information will be justified.

The Fourth Amendment seeks to prevent "unreasonable searches and seizures". In *Katz v US,* the Supreme Court established that a search and seizure is unreasonable if it violates the target's reasonable expectation of privacy in the object of the search and seizure.[1296] The test for the existence of a reasonable expectation of privacy is two-fold: firstly, the target of the search or seizure must have a subjective expectation of privacy; secondly, society must recognise that expectation as objectively reasonable.[1297]

It is submitted that lawyers necessarily have a reasonable expectation of privacy in respect of confidential client information and that this expectation meets the requirements of the two-legged test. In other words, the offices of US lawyers cannot be raided by a state agency without prior judicial authorisation in the form of a valid warrant based on probable cause. Certainly, warrantless searches and seizures to obtain client information that could help the prosecution are anathema in terms of the Fourth Amendment.

[1295]Model Rule 1.6(b)(7).

[1296]In *Katz v United States* 389 US 347(1967).

[1297]This two-requirement test was confirmed in *Kyllo v US* 533 US 27 (2001)190 f3D 1041.

5.4.2 The Canadian Position

The question of access to attorneys' files and offices was probably the main reason for the constitutional litigation pursued by the FLSC from 2001 to 2015. Various issues had lawyers up in arms. They had to verify the identity of clients by way of very stringent customer due diligence exercises. They had to keep detailed client records. And they had to grant access to FINTRAC to inspect their files, which inspection could be warrantless. What is more, Section 74 of the PCMLTFA included a penalty clause which stated that every person who or entity that knowingly contravenes a number of Sections or the Regulations is guilty of an offence.[1298] The punishment prescribed for a contravention and a summary conviction was a fine of not more than $50 000 or imprisonment of not more than six months or both.[1299] The sentence for a conviction on an indictment was a fine of not more than $500 000 or imprisonment of not more than five years or both.[1300] These threats to their lawyers formed the basis of the FLSC's bid to have Sections 62 to 65 of the PCMLTFA declared unconstitutional.

In June 2005, the Department of Finance issued a consultation paper which included proposals about amendments to the provisions of the PCMLTFA regarding FINTRAC's authority to examine the records of a client in possession of his lawyer.

The recommendations in the consultation paper included a reference to the case of *Lavallee, Rackel & Heintz* wherein the Supreme Court of Canada had set out stringent requirements that should be followed to protect attorney-client privilege when the police seize documents from law offices under search warrants.[1301] According to the consultation paper: "The proposed amendments would ensure that the compliance provisions under the PCMLTFA allowing FINTRAC to examine documents are consistent with these principles."[1302]

The FLSC, in responding to the consultation paper in September 2005, confirmed the need to address this issue and supported the Department of

---

[1298] Sections 6, 6.1, 9.1 to 9.3, 9.4(2), 9.5 to 9.7 or 11.1, 12(1) or (4) or 36(1), 37, 55(1) or (2), 57 or 62(2), 63.1(2) or 64(3) or the Regulations to the PCMLTFA.

[1299] Section 74(a) of the PCMLTFA.

[1300] Section 74(b) of the PCMLTFA. See also *Federation of Law Societies of Canada v Canada* 2011 BCSC 1270 Para 90.

[1301] *Lavallee, Rackel & Heintz v Canada* [2002] 3 SCR 209.

[1302] Department of Finance's June 2005 Consultation Paper Enhancing Canada's Anti-Money Laundering and Anti-Terrorist Financing Regime Consultation Paper June 2005, Para 6.17 at 44.

Finance's proposal to amend Sections 62 to 65 of the PCMLTFA in such a manner that they conform to the principles established by the *Lavallee* decision. The FLSC urged the government to ensure that attorney-client privilege is protected in the amendments to the PCMLTFA.[1303]

However, the Regulations which came into operation on 30 December 2008 effectively authorised warrantless searches of law offices and did not include the recommendations of the Department of Finance and the FLSC.[1304]

Section 62 of the PCMLTFA dealt with the contentious issues of third party access to client records,[1305] the entering of premises,[1306] the use of computers to examine data,[1307] the reproducing of records,[1308] and the use of any copying equipment.[1309] It was required that records should be made available to FINTRAC within 30 days after a request was made to examine them.[1310] This meant that lawyers should grant access to a third party to enter their offices and allow them to examine confidential, private client records. The PCMLTFA authorised FINTRAC to examine the client records of lawyers.[1311]

On 27 September 2011, the British Columbia Supreme Court held that Sections 62 to 64 of the PCMLTFA were unconstitutional.[1312] This was endorsed on appeal in 2013,[1313] and the Supreme Court of Canada confirmed the invalidity of the sections in February 2015.[1314] The Supreme Court stated that warrantless searches, such as those permitted under the PCMLTFA, were unreasonable.[1315] It found that the search powers in Sections 62, 63 and 63.1, when applied to lawyers, coupled with the insufficient safeguard of attorney-client privilege in Section 64, constitute a very substantial limitation of the

---

[1303]The FLSC Submission in response to the Department of Finances' Consultation Paper: 30 September 2005.

[1304]See Priestley (2009: 23).

[1305]Section 62(1) of the PCMLTFA.

[1306]Section 62(1)(a) of the PCMLTFA.

[1307]Section 62(1)(b) of the PCMLTFA.

[1308]Section 62(1)(c) of the PCMLTFA.

[1309]Section 62(1) of the PCMLTFA.

[1310]Section 62 of the PCMLTFA.

[1311]Section 62 of the PCMLTFA.

[1312]*Law Society of British Columbia v Canada* 2001 BCSC 1593. See also Chong (2013: 1) and Priestley (2009: 11).

[1313]*Federation of Law Societies of Canada v Canada* 2013 BCCA 147.

[1314]*Canada (Attorney General) v Federation of Law Societies of Canada*, 2015 SCC 7. See also Marrocco & Furniss (2013: 1).

[1315]*Canada (Attorney General) v Federation of Law Societies of Canada* 2015 SCC 7 Para 56.

right to be free of unreasonable searches and seizures guaranteed by Section 8 of the *Charter*.[1316] The Court read Sections 63 and 63.1 down to exclude lawyers from the scope of their operation.[1317] It declared that Section 64 was of no force or effect and that Sections 62 and 63.1 should be read down so that they exclude documents in the possession of lawyers or their offices.[1318] It was held that the duties that were imposed on lawyers by the state were in conflict with the interest of their clients and that compliance with such duties would turn lawyers into state instruments.[1319]

The Supreme Court of Canada's sentiment echoes that expressed in the 2011 judgment of Gerow J, who referred with approval to the following statement by Lebel J in *Maranda:*[1320]

> "[I]t is important that lawyers, who are bound by stringent ethical codes not have their offices turned into archives for the use of the prosecution."[1321]

Gerow J considered that to impose the recording and related obligations contained in PCMLTFA on legal counsel and legal firms would achieve precisely the result that Lebel J warned against.[1322]

The Supreme Court stated that "the lawyer's duty of commitment to the client's cause" requires constitutional protection against governmental intrusion,[1323] and that "the lawyer's duty of commitment to the client's cause" should be regarded as a principle of fundamental justice.[1324] The decision of the Court in February 2015 brings to an end a fifteen-year period of litigation between the FLSC and the Attorney General of Canada. It is a victory that

---

1316 *Canada (Attorney General) v Federation of Law Societies of Canada* 2015 SCC 7 Para 57.

1317 *Canada (Attorney General) v Federation of Law Societies of Canada* 2015 SCC 7 Para 63. This confirms the judgments of the courts a quo in *Federation of Law Societies of Canada v Canada* 2011 BCSC 1270 Para 229. Confirmed in *Federation of Law Societies of Canada v Canada v Canada* 2013. See also Chong (2013: 1).

1318 *Canada (Attorney General) v Federation of Law Societies of Canada* 2015 SCC 7 Para 67.

1319 *Canada (Attorney General) v Federation of Law Societies of Canada* 2015 SCC Para 77.

1320 *Federation of Law Societies of Canada v Canada* 2011 BCSC 1270 Para 143. *Maranda v Richer*, 2003 SCC 67 (CanLII), [2003] 3 S.C.R. 193 Para 37.

1321 *Maranda v Richer*, 2003 SCC 67 (CanLII), [2003] 3 S.C.R. 193 Para 37.

1322 *Federation of Law Societies of Canada v Canada 2011* BCSC 1270 Para 144. See also Chong (2013: 1).

1323 *Canada (Attorney General) v Federation of Law Societies of Canada* 2015 SCC Para 83.

1324 *Canada (Attorney General) v Federation of Law Societies of Canada* 2015 SCC Para 84.

must be savoured by Canadian lawyers. It has been settled definitively that the premises of lawyers will be not be entered,[1325] their records not examined,[1326] data on their computers not accessed,[1327] their records not reproduced,[1328] and their copying equipment not used by third parties such as FINTRAC,[1329] without a warrant duly authorised by a competent court. This brings certainty to the position in Canada regarding third party access to client records in lawyers' offices.

5.4.3 The South African Position[1330]

The object of FICA was to complement POCA by introducing mechanisms and measures aimed at preventing and combating money laundering activities. The legislation places the responsibility for detecting potentially illegal activities on accountable institutions, such as lawyers.[1331] The FIC was established to receive and analyse CTRs and STRs and to implement the mechanisms set out in FICA and POCA. [1332] FICA required lawyers to report confidential client information[1333] and it authorised the FIC and the LSSA to examine a lawyer's client records by way of a warrantless search.[1334]

However, in *Estate Agency Affairs Board v Auction Alliance,*[1335] the authority of members of the FIC and the LSSA to enter the premises of accountable institutions and seize computer documents without a warrant was declared unconstitutional. Fortunately, the Constitutional Court's decision in *Estate Agency Affairs Board* brings relief also to lawyers.[1336] Before this case, the FIC and the LSSA were authorised to use any computer system when searching

---

[1325]Section 62(1)(a) of the PCMLTFA.

[1326]Section 62(1) of the PCMLTFA.

[1327]Section 62(1)(b) of the PCMLTFA.

[1328]Section 62(1)(c) of the PCMLTFA.

[1329]Section 62(1) of the PCMLTFA.

[1330]The South African position regarding third party access to client records was fully discussed in Section 3.3.4 of this study above.

[1331]See Goredema (2005: 27), Van der Westhuizen (2003: 33) and Henning & Ebersohn (2001: 123). See also Schedule 1 in which FICA lists all the accountable institutions which includes attorneys as defined in the Attorneys Act 53 of 1979.

[1332]See Van Jaarsveld (2011: 490).

[1333]Section 28 and 29 of FICA.

[1334]Section 45B of FICA.

[1335]*Estate Agency Affairs Board v Auction Alliance* 2014 (4) BCLR 373 (CC).

[1336]*Estate Agency Affairs Board v Auction Alliance (Pty) Ltd and Others* [2014] ZACC.

a lawyer's office for data.[1337] Also the lawyer and other persons employed in the law practice were required to assist the FIC's search agents and to furnish them with "any information ... that they may reasonably require".[1338] The FIC had the power to disclose this information to the police.[1339] At least South African lawyers now receive the same protection against warrantless searches of their law offices as their Canadian counterparts.

5.4.4 Comparative Commentary

It is incomprehensible that lawyers' offices could be raided by third parties to acquire evidence against the clients of lawyers, without a duly authorised warrant. Unfortunately, this was precisely the effect that the Canadian and South African statutes envisaged before the offending sections of the statutes were invalidated. Attorney-client confidentiality and legal professional privilege are two of the major pillars of the legal profession. Lawyers are in a unique position of trust, precisely because of the nature of their professions. Lawyers on a daily basis have to deal with information that possibly could incriminate their clients and they are not supposed to divulge it to anyone.

Third party access to client records is not dealt with in a specific statute in the US, as it was in the PCMLTFA in Canada and FICA in South Africa. In the US, attorney-client confidentiality is covered in the ABA Model Rule 1.6 and in the Fourth Amendment which prohibits warrantless searches. In Canada, this was the crux of the constitutional challenge against the provisions of the PCMLTFA. The question was: why lawyers' offices should be used as archives for the prosecution? The Canadian Supreme Court correctly declared Sections 62 to 64 of the PCMLTFA unconstitutional and the Constitutional Court in South Africa likewise declared Section 45B of FICA unconstitutional. In South Africa, lawyers were quiet on this issue and it was left to an estate agent to bring an application to have Section 45B of FICA declared unconstitutional. Ironically, Section 45B has been in operation since the amendment of FICA in 2008. So, for a period of seven years, warrantless searches of the offices of accountable institutions, including the offices of lawyers, were authorised by legislation. The South African legal profession is fortunate that the FIC and members of the LSSA did not act in accordance with Section 45B during this period.

[1337]Section 45B(2)(d) of FICA.

[1338]Section 45B(3) of FICA.

[1339]Section 45B(5) of FICA.

It will be a sad day when lawyers provide evidence and testify against their clients for the prosecution. At least there is some solace for South African attorneys in that the declaration of unconstitutionality of warrantless searches of law offices is one area where they do not come off worse than their US and Canadian counterparts.

6

CONCLUSION AND RECOMMENDATIONS

6.1 Introduction

Lawyers in South Africa are more or less in the same position as their US and Canadian counterparts as far as third party access to client records goes. However, they are in a much more precarious position as regards STRs, CTRs and tainted fees. Whilst it is understandable that the South African legislature had to attempt to curb crime and ensure that lawyers do not facilitate money laundering, FICA and POCA entail near catastrophic consequences for lawyers in the criminalisation of the receipt of tainted fees, and of the failure to submit STRs and CTRs.[1340]

No justification for such criminalisation emerges from the jurisprudence in the US and in Canada. Hence, this chapter investigates the provisions of UN Conventions, EU Directives and FATF Standards in a final attempt to search for authority for the provisions of POCA and FICA.

6.2 The Criminalisation of Tainted Fees

It will be recalled that in both the US and Canada the payment of legal fees with suspected tainted funds is not regarded as a crime. The US has inserted an exemption from prosecution clause in the MLCA for lawyers should they be paid with tainted money. The purpose of this insertion was to guarantee an accused person's right to legal representation. Canada's Criminal Code allows

[1340]In terms of Sections 3 and 8 of POCA and Sections 1, 52 and 53 of FICA.

for the release of funds for legal expenses when an application for forfeiture is made. The topic of tainted fees, however, did not receive the same amount of attention in Canada as it did in the US.

The United Nations Conventions and the EU Directives are silent as to whether the acceptance of tainted fees is to be regarded as a crime. Under the CoE Money Laundering Convention of 1990, it was adjudged incorrect to assume that lawyers should be prosecuted for accepting tainted fees, while the notion that lawyers should be prosecuted for being paid with tainted fees was deemed a misinterpretation.[1341] The international consensus was that it should never be a crime to hire a lawyer or for a lawyer to accept such fees. It was never the intention to criminalise the representation of an accused charged with one of the money laundering predicate crimes. The Explanatory Report to the Convention confirms that certain interpretations which might have raised human rights and civil liberties concerns were invalid.

It was envisaged that an exemption from prosecution would be granted to lawyers who defend clients accused of money laundering. The EU ML Directives were aimed at rooting out corruption in the financial sectors and extend to lawyers when they participate in such corruption by assisting clients in the preparation and execution of financial transactions and in real estate deals.[1342] The Directives never were intended to cover all criminal matters and, according to Gilmore, never were intended as blanket coverage of all activities conducted by lawyers.[1343]

Furthermore, Article 14 of the Charter of the African Union does not contain anything relating to tainted fees and refers only to the right to a fair trial. The FATF is also quiet regarding the tainted fees issue. There is thus no authority in the UN Conventions, the EU ML Directives, the Charter of the African Union, or in the FATF Standards to justify that the receipt of tainted fees for legal representation should be regarded as a crime.

Unfortunately for South African lawyers, there is no exemption from prosecution for attorneys as there is in the US.[1344] In South Africa, attorneys

[1341]The Convention on Laundering, Search and Seizure and Confiscation of the Proceeds of Crime. See also the 1990 Explanatory Report to the Convention on Laundering, Search, Seizure and Confiscation of the Proceeds of Crime Para 33. See § 2.3.1 for a detailed discussion of this issue.

[1342]Article 2a(5) of the 2001 EU ML Directive. See discussion in §2.3.2.2 of this study.

[1343]Gilmore (2011: 231). Recital 16 of the 2001 EU ML Directive. See discusion in §2.3.2.2 of this study.

[1344]Gaetke & Welling (1992: 1168).

could face exemplary prosecution at the behest of the National Prosecuting Authority.[1345] It is, in fact, only a person charged with a money laundering or related offence under POCA and FICA whose right to legal representation is affected, and not that of any other accused person. Lawyers who represent an accused person charged with a money laundering or related offence thus are being treated differently from those who represent other accused persons.

Consider, for example, that X intentionally and unlawfully kills Y, with no one witnessing the incident. Although X does not dispute having committed the offence and admits as much to his lawyer, he instructs his lawyer that he wants to plead not guilty. X's view is that there are no witnesses who observed the killing and the state will be unable to link him to the murder. X is presumed innocent and is entitled to his fair trial rights under Section 35(3) of the South African Constitution. While counsel may not argue that X did not commit the offence, he may argue that the state has not proved that X is guilty beyond a reasonable doubt and that there are not sufficient guarantees in the evidence of the state to warrant a conviction.[1346] In this hypothetical, X is entitled to legal representation, and a lawyer will assist him to enforce his right to silence, his right to be presumed innocent and the privilege against self-incrimination. There is no penalty for X's lawyer, although he was at all times aware of X's factual guilt. If a defence lawyer, however, suspects that money paid as fees is tainted, he commits a crime. Why then is it permissible for a lawyer to represent an accused person who has admitted guilt to a very serious crime, but not for a lawyer to represent an accused person charged with money laundering and be paid money which allegedly stems from the money laundering offence in issue? This contradiction amounts to a persecution of lawyers who represent money launderers.

The argument is not that lawyers should be exempted from prosecution because they are a special breed. If they transgress the law they should be punished and if they are launderers themselves they should be prosecuted to the full extent of the law.[1347] If they allow their trust accounts to be used as a vehicle to clean money they must face the consequences of their conduct.[1348] Similarly, if they assist their clients in schemes aimed at defrauding the tax

---

[1345]See Hawkey (2011: 9).

[1346]Freedman (1966: 1471).

[1347]*S v Hattingh*–unreported, Bloemfontein Regional Court and *Pillay & Others v S* 2004 (1) All SA 61 (SCA).

[1348]*United States v Foster* 835 F.Supp. 360 (1993).

authorities or to launder dirty money, they must be prosecuted.[1349] However, it should not be a crime merely to accept tainted funds as legal fees, if the payment is to give effect to an accused person's right to legal representation. In such a case, an exemption from prosecution for lawyers should be granted.

A lawyer should be allowed to charge a fee which is compatible with his expertise and with the complexity of the case. The Law Societies have broad guidelines on fees that lawyers may charge, and a client who is aggrieved by too high a fee charged by his lawyer, may have the bill of costs taxed by the Law Society or by the courts. Similarly, if the prosecution alleges that a higher than normal fee was charged by lawyer perhaps as a means to launder money, such an account can be taxed. If it is found that a lawyer has overcharged the client, the lawyer could be ordered to refund the excess and he will be penalised also. If it is found that an excessive fee was asked with the sole intention of cleaning the money, then the lawyer should be charged. However, a lawyer should not face criminal charges merely for accepting tainted fees. It is submitted that South Africa should adopt the American approach and exempt lawyers from prosecution for the receipt of tainted fees where the right to legal representation is affected. Such an exemption undoubtedly will vindicate the right to legal representation.[1350]

The criminalisation of tainted fees also may infringe a lawyer's right to exercise his profession.[1351] It may prompt young law graduates not to become criminal lawyers. Established and experienced lawyers could be forced also to look for alternative spheres of legal practice to earn a living. If no exemption from prosecution is allowed for criminal defence lawyers, it is quite possible that they could treat a certain category of accused persons as untouchables. However, while trying to avoid prosecution, criminal defence practitioners still must earn a living and fulfil their constitutional duty to provide legal representation to clients. It is the possibility of prosecution and conviction for accepting tainted fees that constitutes the most dangerous predicament for lawyers.

It is submitted that both POCA and FICA should be amended to exempt lawyers from prosecution if they are paid with contaminated funds. An

---

[1349] *United States v Mcquire* 79 F 3d 1396 (5th Cir.1996) and *United States v Foster* 835 F. Supp.360 (1993).

[1350] The right to legal representation is entrenched in Section 35(2) and 35(3) of the Constitution of 1996.

[1351] See detailed discussion of this issue in §4.4 of this study.

exemption clause similar to that contained in the MLCA should be inserted into FICA and POCA. Surely, combating crime ought not to have the effect of infringing rights. It is submitted that in declaring tainted fees a crime, the South African legislature failed to find the balance between combating lawyer-facilitated money laundering, on the one hand, and the right to legal representation and the right to exercise a profession, on the other hand.

6.3 Transaction Reporting: STRs and CTRs

The South African legislature, in its wisdom, used FICA to make it compulsory for lawyers to submit STRs and CTRs in respect of client activities and to criminalise non-submission. If a lawyer, in his dealings with a client, suspects that the client is busy with suspicious and unusual transactions and he fails to report such suspicions, he commits a crime. This goes against the established objective of legal professional privilege and attorney-client confidentiality to keep certain client information confidential.

Clients tend to expect that what they tell a lawyer in confidence will stay with him and will not be broadcast anywhere and to anyone else. In the comparative study of the US and Canada, no helpful lessons were learnt and no justification could be found for making the filing of STRs compulsory for lawyers and for criminalising non-compliance. US lawyers formed part of the FATF's construction of the RBA and always were opposed to compulsory STRs for lawyers. The ABA resolutions do not make it compulsory for lawyers to file STRs and the Good Practices Guidance provides assistance to attorneys on how to deal with this issue.

In Canada, the FLSC had no problem approaching the courts to obtain an interdict against STRs being required from their lawyers. It not only succeeded in court, but also convinced the legislature to amend the PCMLTFA so that STRs are not compulsory for lawyers.

The United Nations Conventions and the EU Directives likewise do not make it compulsory to submit STRs. The EU Directives require the filing of STRs only when there is no link to judicial proceedings,[1352] in three specific instances: when legal advice provided has the effect that the lawyer is taking part in money laundering; when the lawyer is providing advice for money laundering; and when the lawyer knows that the client is seeking advice

[1352]Recital 17 of the 2001 EU ML Directive.

for money laundering purposes. The submission of an STR to a FIU is not compulsory but can be made to a Law Society, as a self-regulating body.[1353] There is, however, no indication that a failure to submit an STR should be regarded as a crime. Article 14 of Charter of the African Union confirms that an accused person has a right to a fair trial, but, as with the FATF Standards it is silent regarding an STR requirement for lawyers and the criminalisation of non-submission. No authority can be extracted from the UN Conventions, the EU ML Directives, the Charter of the African Union or the FATF Standards to justify compulsory STRs for lawyers and to criminalise non-compliance.

Sadly, South African lawyers are saddled with the possibility of being prosecuted for failure to file an STR with the FIC. It is recommended that FICA be amended to remove the compulsion for lawyers to submit STRs and to decriminalise non-submission.

The non-submission of CTRs is not regarded as a crime anywhere else except in South Africa. The argument that lawyers should be alert not to accept large amounts of cash has merit. However, the failure to submit a report for accepting cash above a designated threshold should not be a crime. It is suggested that South Africa follow the FLSC's No-Cash Rule.[1354] This rule requires each Law Society to implement regulations which preclude lawyers from receiving cash amounts of more than $7 500.[1355] The adoption of the No-Cash Rule effectively rendered it unnecessary for lawyers in Canada to report cash transactions involving $10 000 or more to any government institution.[1356] In Canada, a transgression of this No-Cash Rule will result in disciplinary sanction from the appropriate Law Society.

A No-Cash Rule for South Africa, sponsored by the LSSA, will circumvent the obligation to report a client in terms of Section 28 of FICA. It is suggested that such a rule will be easy for the LSSA to monitor. Every legal practice must undergo an annual audit by an independent chartered accountant. The report template of the auditor can be amended slightly to require him to report whether any cash payments in excess of, say, R20 000 were made in respect of a single matter. A transgression of this rule should result in disciplinary

[1353] Article 34(2) of the 2015 EU ML Directive.

[1354] See Paton (2010: 181), Priestley (2009: 17) and Terry (2010: 42).

[1355] See Gallant (2013: 11), Woolley (2013: 2), Paton (2010: 181), Terry (2010: 42), McDonald (2010: 145), Priestley (2009: 17) and Lawrence & van Houten (2013: 1).

[1356] See Gallant (2009: 215), Gallant (2013: 11), Paton (2010: 181), McDonald (2010: 145), Woolley (2013: 2) and Priestley (2009: 17).

sanction from the LSSA. Such a rule will decriminalise the receipt of cash payments less than R20 000 in respect of a single matter.

6.4 Third Party Access to Client Records

Before the case of *Estate Agency Affairs Board v Auction Alliance,* the FIC had virtually unrestrained access to client records in the possession of lawyers. In both Canada and South Africa this intrusion was sorted out with constitutional challenges. However, whereas the Canadian lawyers challenged the constitutionality of the PCMLTFA, in South Africa it was left to an estate agent. The effect of the judgment is that lawyers' offices should not be used as archives for the prosecution. For a period of seven years (from 2008 to 2015) warrantless searches of law offices were possible in South Africa. The South African legal profession was just fortunate that the FIC and the LSSA did not exploit this possibility.

6.5 Concluding Remarks

Why the South African legal profession failed to defend itself against the assault represented by the provisions of POCA and FICA remains a mystery. Perhaps it was lulled into complacency because no one as yet has been prosecuted for the non-submission of STRs and CTRs and for accepting tainted fees.[1357] However, if the proposed amendments to POCA and FICA are not made, it could come to pass that a lawyer finds himself as an accused person in court without legal representation.

6.6 Recommendations

6.6.1 Amendment to POCA: Tainted Fees

It is recommended that Sections 2, 4, 5 and 6 of POCA be amended to exempt attorneys from prosecution in the event of their fees being paid with tarnished funds.

[1357]This position will change with the proseution of attorney Anthony Broadway in *S v Wei & Others*, pending case before the Western Cape High Court.

A new Section 2 of POCA could read as follows (with the proposed amendment indicated in bold and underlined):

Any person who
(a) (i) receives or retains any property derived, directly or indirectly, from a pattern of racketeering activity; and
(ii) knows or ought reasonably to have known that such property is so derived; and
(iii) uses or invests, directly or indirectly, any part of such property in acquisition of any interest in, or the establishment or operation or activities of, any enterprise;
(b) (i) receives or retains any property, directly or indirectly, on behalf of any enterprise; and
(ii) knows or ought reasonably to have known that such property derived or is derived from or through a pattern of racketeering activity;
(c) (i) uses or invests any property, directly or indirectly, on behalf of any enterprise or in acquisition of any interest in, or the establishment or operation or activities of any enterprise; and
(ii) knows or ought reasonably to have known that such property derived or is derived from or through a pattern of racketeering activity;
(d) acquires or maintains, directly or indirectly, any interest in or control of any enterprise through a pattern of racketeering activity;
(e) whilst managing or employed by or associated with any enterprise, conducts or participates in the conduct, directly or indirectly, of such enterprise's affairs through a pattern of racketeering activity;
(f) manages the operation or activities of an enterprise and who knows or ought reasonably to have known that any person, whilst employed by or associated with that enterprise, conducts or participates in the conduct, directly or indirectly, of such enterprise's affairs through a pattern of racketeering activity; or
(g) conspires or attempts to violate any of the provisions of paragraphs (a), (b), (c), (d), (e) or (f), within the Republic or elsewhere,

shall be guilty of an offence, **<u>but the term "person" does not include members of the legal profession acting to fulfil their responsibilities to give effect to the right to legal representation as guaranteed by the Constitution of the Republic of South Africa, 1996.</u>**

A new Section 4 of POCA could read as follows (with the proposed amendment indicated in bold and underlined):

> Any person who knows or ought reasonably to have known that property is or forms part of the proceeds of unlawful activities and
> (a) enters into any agreement or engages in any arrangement or transaction with anyone in connection with that property, whether such agreement, arrangement or transaction is legally enforceable or not; or
> (b) performs any other act in connection with such property, whether it is performed independently or in concert with any other person, which has or is likely to have the effect
> (i) of concealing or disguising the nature, source, location, disposition or movement of the said property or the ownership thereof or any interest which anyone may have in respect thereof;
> (ii) of enabling or assisting any person who has committed or commits an offence, whether in the Republic or elsewhere—
> (aa) to avoid prosecution; or
> (bb) to remove or diminish any property acquired directly, or indirectly, as a result of the commission of an offence,

shall be guilty of an offence, **<u>but the term "person" does not include members of the legal profession acting to fulfil their responsibilities to give effect to the right to legal representation as guaranteed by the Constitution of the Republic of South Africa, 1996</u>.**

A new Section 5 of POCA could read as follows (with the proposed amendment indicated in bold and underlined):

Any person who knows or ought reasonably to have known that another person has obtained the proceeds of unlawful activities, and who enters into any agreement with anyone or engages in any arrangement or transaction whereby

> (a) the retention or the control by or on behalf of the said other person of the proceeds of unlawful activities is facilitated; or
> (b) the said proceeds of unlawful activities are used to make funds available to the said other person or to acquire property on his or her behalf or to benefit him or her in any other way,

shall be guilty of an offence, **<u>but the term "person" does not include members of the legal profession acting to fulfil their responsibilities to give effect to the right to legal representation as guaranteed by the Constitution of the Republic of South Africa, 1996</u>.**

A new Section 6 of POCA could read as follows (with the proposed amendment indicated in bold and underlined):

Any person who

> (a) acquires;
> (b) uses; or
> (c) has possession of,

property and who knows or ought reasonably to have known that it is or forms part of the proceeds of unlawful activities of another person, shall be guilty of an offence, **<u>but the term "person" does not include members of the legal profession acting to fulfil their responsibilities to give effect to the right to legal representation as guaranteed by the Constitution of the Republic of South Africa, 1996</u>.**

6.6.2 Amendment to FICA: Tainted Fees

It is recommended that the definition of "money laundering" in Section 1(1) of FICA be amended to exempt members of the legal profession from prosecution in the event of their being paid tainted fees for legal representation.

A new definition of "money laundering" in Section 1(1) of FICA could read as follows (with the proposed amendment indicated in bold and underlined):

> an activity which has or is likely to have the effect of concealing or disguising the nature, source, location, disposition or movement of the proceeds of unlawful activities or any interest which anyone has in such proceeds, **<u>but the term "activity" does not include the conduct of members of the legal profession acting to fulfil their</u>**

> **<u>responsibilities to give effect to the right to legal representation as guaranteed by the Constitution of the Republic of South Africa, 1996</u>.**

6.6.3 Amendment to FICA: CTRs

Currently, Section 51 of FICA criminalises the failure by lawyers to submit CTRs to the FIC, in the following terms:

> An accountable institution or reporting institution that fails, within the prescribed period, to report to the Centre the prescribed information in respect of a cash transaction in accordance with section 28, is guilty of an offence.

It is recommended that Section 51 of FICA be deleted in order to decriminalise the non-submission of CTRS.

6.6.4 Amendment to FICA re STRs

It is recommended that Section 29 be amended to exempt attorneys from submitting STRs. A new Section 29 of FICA could read as follows (with the proposed amendment indicated in bold and underlined):

> (1) A person who carries on a business or is in charge of or manages a business or who is employed by a business and who knows or ought reasonably to have known or suspected that-
> (a) the business has received or is about to receive the proceeds of unlawful activities or property which is connected to an offence relating to the financing of terrorist and related activities;
> (b) a transaction or series of transactions to which the business is a party
> (i) facilitated or is likely to facilitate the transfer of the proceeds of unlawful activities or property which is connected to an offence relating to the financing of terrorist and related activities;
> (ii) has no apparent business or lawful purpose;
> (iii) is conducted for the purpose of avoiding giving rise to a reporting duty under this Act;

(iv) may be relevant to the investigation of an evasion or attempted evasion of a duty to pay any tax, duty or levy imposed by legislation administered by the Commissioner for the South African Revenue Service; or

(v) relates to an offence relating to the financing of terrorist and related activities; or

(c) the business has been used or is about to be used in any way for money laundering purposes or to facilitate the commission of an offence relating to the financing of terrorist and related activities, must, within the prescribed period after the knowledge was acquired or the suspicion arose, report to the Centre the grounds for the knowledge or suspicion and the prescribed particulars concerning the transaction or series of transactions.]

(2) A person who carries on a business or is in charge of or manages a business or who is employed by a business and who knows or suspects that a transaction or a series of transactions about which enquiries are made, may, if that transaction or those transactions had been concluded, have caused any of the consequences referred to in subsection (1) (a), (b) or (c), must, within the prescribed period after the knowledge was acquired or the suspicion arose, report to the Centre the grounds for the knowledge or suspicion and the prescribed particulars concerning the transaction or series of transactions.

(3) No person who made or must make a report in terms of this section may disclose that fact or any information regarding the contents of any such report to any other person, including the person in respect of whom the report is or must be made, otherwise than-

(a) within the scope of the powers and duties of that person in terms of any legislation;

(b) for the purpose of carrying out the provisions of this Act;

(c) for the purpose of legal proceedings, including any proceedings before a judge in chambers; or

(d) in terms of an order of court.

(4) No person who knows or suspects that a report has been or is to be made in terms of this section may disclose that knowledge or suspicion or any information regarding the contents or

suspected contents of any such report to any other person, including the person in respect of whom the report is or is to be made, otherwise than

(a) within the scope of that person's powers and duties in terms of any legislation;
(b) for the purpose of carrying out the provisions of this Act;
(c) for the purpose of legal proceedings, including any proceedings before a judge in chambers; or
(d) in terms of an order of court.

(5) The term "person" referred to in this Section does not include members of the legal profession acting to fulfil their responsibilities to give effect to the right to legal representation as guaranteed by the Constitution of the Republic of South Africa, 1996.

6.6.5 No-Cash Rule for LSSA

It is recommended that the LSSA adopt wholesale the Canadian No-Cash Rule, suitably modified for South African conditions. The transgression of this rule should result in disciplinary sanction from the LSSA.

A South African No-Cash Rule, annexed verbatim from the Canadian No-Cash Rule, should read as follows:

1. A lawyer shall not receive or accept from a person, cash in an aggregate amount of R20 000 or more South Africa Rand (R) in respect of any one client matter or transaction.
2. For the purposes of this rule, when a lawyer receives or accepts cash in a foreign currency from a person the lawyer shall be deemed to have received or accepted the cash converted into South Africa Rand (R) at
   (a) the official conversion rate of the Reserve Bank of South Africa for the foreign currency as published in the Reserve Bank of South Africa daily noon rates that is in effect at the time the lawyer receives or accepts the cash, or
   (b) If the day on which the lawyer receives or accepts cash is a holiday, the official conversion rate of the reserve bank of South Africa in effect on the most recent business day preceding the day on which the lawyer receives or accepts the cash.

3. Paragraph 1 applies when a lawyer engages on behalf of a client or gives instructions on behalf of a client in respect of the following activities:
   (a) receiving or paying funds;
   (b) purchasing or selling securities, real properties or business assets or entities;
   (c) transferring funds by any means.
4. Despite paragraph 3, paragraph 1 does not apply when the lawyer receives cash
   (a) from a financial institution or public body,
   (b) from a peace officer, law enforcement agency or other agent of the State acting in his or her official capacity,
   (c) pursuant to a court order, or to pay a fine or penalty.

REFERENCES

Primary Sources

International Instruments

The International Covenant on Civil and Political Rights, 1966.

United Nations Comprehensive Outline in UN International Conference on Drug Abuse and Illicit Drug Trafficking, 1987.

United Nations Convention against Illicit Traffic in Narcotic Drugs and Psychotropic Substances, 1988.

Commentary on the United Nations Convention against Illicit Traffic in Narcotic Drugs and Psychotropic Substances 1988, CN.7/590, 1988.

United Nations Convention against Corruption, 2003.

The Protocol to Prevent, Suppress and Punish Trafficking in Persons, Especially Women and Children.

The Protocol against the Smuggling of Migrants by Land, Sea and Air.

The Protocol against the Illicit Manufacturing of and Trafficking in Firearms, their Parts and Components and Ammunition.

Convention for the Protection of Human Rights and Fundamental Freedoms.

Regional Instruments

The European Convention on Human Rights and Fundamental Freedoms, 1950.

Recommendation No. R80 (10) adopted by the Committee of Ministers on 27 June 1980.

Council of Europe Convention on Laundering, Search, Seizure and Confiscation of the Proceeds from Crime, 1990.

Explanatory Report to the Convention on Laundering, Search, Seizure and Confiscation of the Proceeds from Crime, 1990.

The Council Directive 91/308/EEC (1991 EU ML Directive).

The Council Directive 2001/97/EC (2001 EU ML Directive).

The Council Directive 2005/97/EC (2005 EM ML Directive).
Proposed Fourth 2015 EU ML Directive.
Council of Europe Convention on Laundering, Search, Seizure and Confiscation of the Proceeds from Crime and on the Financing of Terrorism, 2005.
American Convention on Human Rights, 1969.
African Charter on Human and People's Rights, 1987.
African Union Convention on Preventing and Combating Corruption, 2003.

Legislation

United States of America

United States Constitution.
Bank Secrecy Act, 1970.
Continuing Criminal Enterprise Statute, 1970.
Comprehensive Forfeiture Act, 1984.
Currency and Foreign Transactions Reporting Act, 1970.
Internal Revenue Code, 1986.
Money Laundering Control Act, 1986.
Racketeering Influenced and Corrupt Organizations Act, 1970.
Uniting and Strengthening America by Providing Appropriate Tools Required to Intercept and Obstruct Terrorism Act, 2001.

Canada

The Canadian Charter of Rights and Freedoms.
Controlled Drugs and Substances Act, 1996.
Criminal Code, 1985.
Proceeds of Crime (Money Laundering) Act, 1991.
Proceeds of Crime (Money Laundering) and Terrorist Financing Act, 2001.
Canada Gazette Part II, Extra Vol 137, No 2 Sor/2003=102 March 2003 Regulations amending certain Regulations made under PCMLTFA, 2003.
Proceeds of Crime (Money Laundering) and Terrorist Financing Act, 2006.

South Africa

Attorneys Act 53 of 1979.
Bank Act 94 of 1990.
Constitution of the Republic of South Africa of 1996.
Criminal Procedure Act 51 of 1977.
Criminal Law Amendment Act 105 of 1997.
Currency and Exchanges Act 9 of 1933.
Customs and Excise Act 91 of 1964.
Deeds Registries Act 47 of 1937.

Estate Agency Affairs Act 112 of 1976.
Financial Intelligence Centre Act 38 of 2001.
Financial Intelligence Centre Amendment Act 11 of 2008.
Financial Institutions (Protection of Funds) Act 28 of 2001.
Legal Practice Act 28 of 2014.
Prevention of Organised Crime Act 121 of 1998.
Protection of Constitutional Democracy against Terrorism and Related Activities Act 33 of 2004.
Marine Living Resources Act 18 of 1998.

Case Law

Europe

R v Griffiths [2006] All ER (D) 19.
ECJ C305/05 *Ordre des barreaux francophones et germanophone et al V Conseil des Ministries,* Judgment 26 June 2007.

United States of America

California Bankers Association v Shultz-416 US 21 (1974).
Caplin & Drysdale, Chartered 837 F.2d 637, 645 (4th Cir. 1988).
In re Special September 1978 Grand Jury, 640 F.2d 49, 62-63 (7th Cir.1980).
Katz v United States 389 US 347,353 (1967).
Kyllo v US 533 US 27 (2001)190 f3D 1041.
Laska v United States 82 F.2d 672, 677 (CA10 1936).
Miranda v Arizona 384 US 436 (1966).
Ratzlaf v United States 510 US 135 (1994).
United States v Abbel 271 F.3d 1286 (11th Cir.2001).
United States v Anzalone 766 F. 2d. 676. 682 (1st Cir 1989).
United States v Arditti 955F, 2d331 (5th CIR.1992).
United States v Blackman 72 F. 3d 1418 (9th Cir.1995).
United States v Cook 745 F. 2d 1311, 1315 (10th Cir 1984).
United States v Elso 422 F.3d 1305 (11th Cir.2005).
United States v Foster 835 F.Supp. 360 (1993).
United States v. Gertner 873 F. Supp. 729 (D. Mass. 1995).
United States v Goldberger & Dubin PC 935 f2d 501, 504 (2dcir 1991).
United States v Leventhal 961 F.2d 936(11th Cir.1992).
United States v Mcquire 79 F 3d 1396 (5th Cir.1996).
United Sates v Miller 425 US 435 (1976).
United States v Monsanto 491 US 600 (1989).
United States v Puerto 730 F. 2d 627, 633 (11th Cir 1984).
United States v Reed 167 F.3d 984 (6th Cir. 1999).
United States v Rosenstein 474 F.2d 705, 715 (2d Cir.1973).

United States v Ross 190 F.3d 446 (6th Cir. 1999).
United States v Saccoccia 58 f.3d 754, (1st Cir. 1995).
United States v Santos, 128 S.Ct. 2020 (2008).
United States v Thompson 603 F 2d. 1202, 1203-1204 (5th Cir 1979).
United States v Tobon-Builles 706F2d. 1092, 1101 (11th Cir 1983).
United States v Varbei 780 F.2d 758, 762 (9th Cir 1986).
United States v Velez, Kuehne and Ochoa US District Court, Southern District of Florida, Miami Division, Case No. 05-2-770-CR-COOKE.
United States v Velez F.3d 875 (11th Cir. 2009).
Wheat v United States 486 US 153, 159, 108 S.Ct. 1692, 100 L.Ed.2d 140 (1988).
United States v $4,255,625.39.et seq, 551 F.Supp.314, SD Fla 1982.
United States v $814,254,76, 51 f.3rd 207(9th Cir.1995).

Canada

Canada (Attorney General) v Federation of Law Societies of Canada 2015 SCC 7.
Federation of Law Societies of Canada v Canada 2011 (BCSC) 1270.
Federation of Law Societies of Canada v Canada 2013 (BCCA) 147.
Giles v Canada (1991) 63 C.C.C. (3d) 18.
Lavallee, Rackel & Heintz v Canada [2002] 3 SCR 209.
Law Society of British Columbia v Canada 2001 (BCSC) 1593.
Law Society of British Columbia v Canada 2002 BCCA 49.
Maranda v Richer 2003 SCC 67 (CanLII) [2003] 3 S.C.R. 193.
R v Allen [2004] O.J. No. 3423 (S.C.J.) (QL).
R v Appleby (2009) NLCA 6 (CanLII).
R v Battista [2008] O.J. No. 3053 (S.C.J.) (QL).
R v Bedi [2004] O.J. No. 5825 (S.C.J.)(QL).
R v Clymore (1992) 74 C.C.C. (3d) 217 (B.C.S.C.).
R v Comrie [2007] O.J. No. 4502 (S.C.J.) (QL).
R v Gader [2001] S.J. No. 105 (Q.B.)(QL).
R v Gagnon (1993) 80 C.C.C. (3d).
R v Galas (1990) 57 C.C.C. (3d) 353.
R v Gaudreu (1994) 4628 (SK CA).
R v Kalenuik 2004 Can LII 19299(ONSC).
R v Lortie (1985) 21 C.C.C. (3d) 436.
R v Morra (1992) 77 C.C.C. (3d) 380 (Ont. C t.Gen. Div.).
R v Murray 2004 (SKQD).
R v Murtaza & Murtaza, 2011 ONSC [36].
R v Pawlyk (1991) 72 Man. R. (2d) 1.
R v Ro [2006] O.J. No. 3347 (S.C.J.) (QL).
R v Rowbotham (1987), 41 C.C.C. (3d) 1 (Ont. C.A.).
R v Chen [1995] O.J. 4846 (Ont. Gen. Div.).
R v Cheng [2011] O.J. No. 3415 (S.C.J.)(QL).
R v Felix [1993] B.C.J. No. 1870, B.C.S.C.

R v Sterling 1992 1704 (BC SC).
Wilson v R (1991) 68 CCC (3d) (569).

South Africa

A Company and Two Others v The Commissioner for the South African Revenue Services Western Cape High Court, Case No 16360/2013 [2014] ZAWCHC 33.
Alfred Crompton Amusement Machines Ltd v Commissioner of Excise and Customs 1972 (2) All ER 353 (CA).
Auction Alliance (Pty) Ltd v Estate Agency Affairs Board and Others [2013] ZAWCHC 105.
DPP v Aerobe and Others 2000(1) SACR 366 (N).
Estate Agency Affairs Board v Auction Alliance 2014 (4) BCLR 373 (CC).
Euroshipping of Monrovia v Minister of Agricultural Economics and Marketing and Others 1979 (1) SA 637(C).
Fraser v Absa Bank 2007 (3) BCLR 219 (CC).
Gaertner and Others v Minister of Finance and Others [2013] ZAWCHC 54.
Giovagnoli v Di Meo 1960 (3) SA (N).
Harksen v Attorney General Cape and Others 1999 (1) SA 718 (C).
Hirschowitz Flionis v Bartlett and Another 2006 (3) SA 575 (SCA).
Legal Aid Board v Msila and Others 1997 92 BCLR 229 €.
Magajane v Chairperson, North West Gambling Board [2006] ZACC 8.
Minister of Safety and Security v Bennet and Others 2009 (2) SACR 17 (SCA).
Mohamed v President of the Republic of South Africa 2001 (2) SA 1145 (CPD).
National Director of Public Prosecutions v Cole and others 2004 (3) ALL SA 765 (W).
National Director of Public Prosecutions v Elran 2013 (4) BCLR 379 (CC).
NDPP v Geyser 2008 ZASZC and NDPP v Vermaak 2008 (1) SACR 157 (SCA).
NDPP v Macasa 2000 (1) SACR 287 TKH.
Pillay & others v S 2004 (1) All SA 61 (SCA).
Roestof v Cliffe Dekker Hofmeyr Inc (34306/2010) [2011] ZAGPPHC 219 (2012).
S v Boesman 1990 (2) SACR 389 (E).
S v Cornelius and Another 2008 1 SACR 96 C.
S v Du Toit and Others 2005 2 SACR 411.
S v Hattingh, Unreported, Bloemfontein Regional Court, Case Number 17/518/10.
S v Khanyile 1988 (3) SA 795 (N).
S v Lwane 1966 (2) SA 433 (A).
S v Makwanyane 1995 (6) BCLR 665 (CC).
S v Mabaso and Another 1990 (3) SA 185 (A).
S v McKenna 1998 (1) SACR 106 (C).
S v Moos 1998 (1) SACR 372 (C).
S v Mushimba 1977 (2) SA 829 (A).
S v Nkata 1990 (4) SA 250 (A).
S v Price 2003 (2) SACR 551 (SCA).
S v Radebe, S v Mbonanai 1988 (1) SA 191 (T).

S v Rossouw, unreported, case number: B1679/09, SHD163/09, Wynberg Regional Court.
S v Rudman; S v Johnson; S v Xaso; Xaso v Van Wyk 1989 (3) SA 368 (E).
S v Safatsa 1988 (1) SA 868 (A).
S v Tandwa 2008 (1) SACR 613 (SCA).
S v Vermaas, S v Du Plessis 1995 (2) SACR 125 (CC).
S v Wei & Others, pending case before the Western Cape High Court.
S v Zimu and Others case No CC 106/1977.
Savoi and Others v National Director of Public Prosecutions and Another [2014] ZACC 5.
Thint Pty Ltd v National Director of Public Prosecutions and Others, Zuma and Another v National Director of Public Prosecutions and Others [2008] ZACC 13.
Van der Heever v Die Meester 1997 (3) SA 93 (T).

Secondary Sources

Books, Chapters in Books and Journal Articles

Allen KN (1997) "Turning Lawyers into Witnesses: Does Forced Client Disclosure Breach the Attorney-Client Privilege?" *Suffolk University Law Review* 795-824.
Babu RR (2006) "The United Nations Convention against Corruption: A Critical Overview" *Asian African Legal Consultative Organization New Dehli* 1-32.
Beare M (1992) "Efforts to Combat Money Laundering in Canada" *Common Wealth Law Bulletin October* 1436-1457.
Bell RE (1999) "Prosecuting the Money Launderers Who Act for Organised Crime" 3(2) *Journal of Money Laundering Control* 104-112.
Bell RE (2002) "The Prosecution of Lawyers for Money Laundering Offences" 6(1) *Journal of Money Laundering Control* 17-26.
Bellengere *et al*, (2013) *The Law of Evidence in South Africa (Basic Principles)* Oxford: University Press.
Bester B (2002) "Negotiating the Financial Intelligence Centre Act" July *De Rebus* 29.
Brickey K (1986) "Forfeiture of Attorneys' Fees: The Impact of Rico and CCE Forfeitures on the Right to Counsel" 72(3) *Virginia Law Review* 493-542.
Brickey K (1988) "Tainted Assets and the Right to Counsel- the Money Laundering Conundrum" 66 *Washington University Law Quarterly* 47-66.
Brucker T M (1997) "Money Laundering and the client: How can I be retained without becoming a party to an offence?" 55(5) *The Advocate* 679-692.
Bugliosi V (2001) *The Betrayal of America: How the Supreme Court Undermined the Constitution and Chose our President* New York: Thunder's Mouth Press.
Bussenius A (2004) "Money Laundering by Defence Counsel-The Decision of the Federal Constitutional Court" 9 *German Law Journal* 1045-1055.
Carr I & Goldby M (2011) "The UN Anti-corruption convention and money laundering", available at: http://ssrn.com/abstract=1409628 1-25.
Carter TS, Carter SS, Candidate JD & Claridge NE (2008) "The Impact of Anti-

Terrorism Legislation on Charities in Canada: The Need for Balance 6(III) *International Journal of Civil Society Law* 42-74.

Cameron E (1997) "Rights, Constitutionalism and the Rule of the Law" 114 *South African Law Journal* 504-510.

Castilla M (2012) "Client Confidentiality and the External Regulation of the Legal Profession: Reporting Requirements in the United States and United Kingdom" *Cardozo Pub. Law Policy & Ethics* 321-355.

Christensen H (2006) "Application to Lawyers of Current Anti-Money Laundering Rules Adopted by the Financial Action Task Force on Money Laundering (FATF) and the United States Government: Recommendations of Good Practices for ACTEC Fellows" *ACTEC Journal* 302-317.

Cole RJV (2011) "The Right to Legal Representation and Equality before the Law in Criminal Proceedings in Botswana" *Stellenbosch Law Review* 94-111.

Cummings LP & Stephnowsky PT (2011) "My Brother's Keeper: An Empirical Study of Attorney Facilitation of Money Laundering through Commercial Transactions" *Journal of the Professional Lawyer* 1-36.

Currie I & De Waal J (2013) *The Bill of Rights Handbook* 4 ed Juta.

De Klerk *et al* (2006) *Clinical Law in South Africa* 2 ed Lexis Nexis.

De Koker L (2003) "Money Laundering in South Africa" in Goredema C (ed) *Profiling Money Laundering in Eastern and Southern Africa*" ISS Monograph Series 90 Pretoria 83-121.

De Koker L (2004) "Client Identification and Money Laundering Control: Perspectives on the Financial Intelligence Centre Act 38 of 2002" *TSAR* 715-746.

Dendy M (2006) "Watching your back: A guide to FICA and POCA" *De Rebus* 33.

Doyle C (2012) "Money Laundering: An Abridged Overview of 18 USC 1956 and Related Federal Criminal Law" *Congressional Research Service* 1-6).

Durrieu R (2013) *Rethinking Money Laundering & Financing of Terrorism in International Law towards a new global order* Brill Nijhof

Eilman S (2004) "Weighing and Implementing the Right to Counsel" 121(2) *South African Law Journal* 318-338.

Freedman W (2012) "Constitutional Aspects" 16(1) *South African Journal of Criminal Justice* 445-466.

Gaetke E & Welling S (1992) "Money Laundering and Lawyers" 43 *Syracuse Law Review* 1165-1245.

Gallant M (2009) "Uncertainties Collide: Lawyers and Money Laundering, Terrorist Financing Regulations" 16(3) *Journal of Economic Crimes* 210-219.

Gallant M (2013) "Lawyers and Money Laundering Regulation: Testing the Limits of the Secrecy in Canada" 8 *Paper delivered at the 3rd Global Conference on Transparency Research HEC Paris* 1-18.

Gilmore W (2011) *Dirty Money: the Evolution of International Measures to Counter Money Laundering and the Finance of Terrorism* 4 ed Strasbourg: Council of Europe

Goredema C (2005) "Measuring Money Laundering in Southern Africa" 14(4) *African Security Review* 27-37.

Gregory R (2003) "The Lawyers' Role: Will Uncle Sam Want You in the Fight against Money Laundering and Terrorism?"72(1) *UMKC Law Review* 23-50.

Hamman AJ & Koen RA (2012) "*Cave Pecuniam*: Lawyers as Launderers" 15(5) *Potchefstroom Electronic Law Journal* 69-100.

Hamman AJ (2013) "Phishing in the World Wide Web Ocean: *Roestof v Cliffe Dekker Hofmeyr Inc*: A case of Cyber laundering through an attorneys trust account" 48 *Law Democracy and Development* 49-63.

Hawkey K (2011) "FICA and jurisdiction over acting judges on the agenda at FSLS AGM" *De Rebus* 9.

Healy NM, Krauland EJ, Shepherd KL, Stinebower C, Fruehauf RL , Barry WP, Wise A, Nance S, El-Sabaawi E & Capeloto T (2009) "US and International Anti-Money Laundering Developments" *The International Lawyer* 795-809.

Henning JJ & Ebersohn GJ (2001) "Insider Trading, Money Laundering and Computer Crime" 33 *Transactions of the Centre for Business Law: Combating Economic Crime* 105-152.

Hill LL (2010) "The Financial Action Task Force Guidance for Legal Professionals: Missed Opportunities to Level the Playing Field" *Journal of the Professional lawyer* 151-172.

Hinterseer K (2000) *Criminal Finance, the Political Economy of Money Laundering in a Comparative Legal Context* The Hague: Kluver Law International

Hinterseer K (1997) "An Economic Analysis of Money Laundering" *Journal of Money Laundering Control* 154-163.

Hugel P & Kelly J (2002) "Internet Gambling, Credit Cards and Money laundering" 6 *Journal of Money Laundering Control* 57-65.

Irvine MR & King DR (1988) "The Money Laundering Control Act of 1986 and the Criminal Defence Lawyer" 19 *Pacific Law Journal* 171-192.

Itsikowitz A (2006) "Legal Professional Privilege/Intermediary Confidentiality: The Challenge for Anti-Money Laundering Measures" in Goredema C (ed) Money Laundering Experiences *Institute for Security Studies* Pretoria 78-79.

Jacobs A (1989) "Indirect Deprivation of the Effective Assistance of Counsel: The Prospective Prosecution of Criminal Defence Attorneys for Money Laundering" 34 *New York Law School Review* 304-348.

Joyce BP (2002) "E-diligence: Money Laundering Risks in the Electronic Arena" 5(2) *Journal of Money Laundering Control* 146-149.

Kazmerski NS (2011) "Applying Anti-Money Laundering and Anti-Terrorist Financing Controls to the United States Legal Profession: A Response to the Senate Permanent Subcommittee Report on the Proceeds of Foreign Corruption" IX(1) *The Dartmouth Law Journal* 78-117.

Kilbourn L (2008) *The ABC of Conveyancing* Juta.

Kirby D (2008) "The European Union's Gatekeeper initiative enlisting lawyers in the fight against money laundering" 37 *Hofstra Law Review* 261-310.

Klaff (2004) "Fica is unconstitutional" *De Rebus* 5.

Kroeker R (1995) "The Legal and Ethical Propriety of Allowing Accused to Use the Proceeds of Crime to Retain Counsel" 53(6) *The Advocate* 865-878.

LAWPRO (2003) "Respecting the Trust in Trust Account" *LAWPRO Magazine Building for Success* 21-23.

Leslie DA (2014) *Legal Principles for Combating Money Laundering* Switzerland: Springer.

Levi M & Reuter (2006) "Money laundering" 34(1) *JSTOR* 289-375.

Lewis E (1982) *Legal Ethics: A Guide to Professional Conduct for South African Attorneys* Durban: Juta.

Macdonald R (2010) "Money Laundering Regulation-What Can be learned from the Canadian Experience?" *Journal of the Professional Lawyer* 143-150.

Madinger J (2012) *Money Laundering: A Guide for Criminal Investigators* New York: CRC Press.

Maisel P (2010) "The Education and Licensing of Attorneys and Advocates in South Africa" 79(2) *The Bar Examiner* 15-30.

McQuoid Mason D (2013) "Access to Justice in South Africa: Are there enough lawyers?" 230 *Oñati Socio-Legal Series* 561-579.

Meadows S (1996) "Implementing the Right to Counsel in Post-Apartheid South Africa" *George Washington Journal of International Law & Economics* 453-502.

Meintjies van der Walt L (2011) *Introduction to South African Law: Fresh Perspectives* Pearson.

Middleton DJ & Levi M (2004) "The Role of Solicitors in Facilitating 'Organized Crime': Situational Crime Opportunities and Their Regulation" *Crime, Law & Social Change* 123-161.

Migala SA (1996) "I.R.C. S 6050I and the Attorney-Client Privilege: The Misplaced Emphasis on incrimination over confidentiality" 2 *University of Illinois Law Review* 509-532.

Millard D & Vergano V (2013) "Hung out to dry? Attorney-client confidentiality and the reporting duties imposed by the Financial Intelligence Centre Act 38 of 2001" 34(3) *Obiter* 389-427.

Mitsilegas V & Gilmore W (2007) "The EU Legislative Framework against Money Laundering and Terrorist Finance: A Critical Analysis in the Light of Evolving Global Standards 56 *International and Comparative Law Quarterly* 119-141.

Mugarura N (2012) *The Global Anti-Money Laundering Regulatory Landscape in Less Developed Countries* Ashgate Publishing Ltd.

Murphy D (2000) "Canada's Anti-Money Laundering Regime" 58 *Resource Material Series 117th International Seminar Visiting Experts' Papers* 286-302.

Murphy D (2004) "Canada's Laws on Money Laundering Proceeds of Crime: The International Context" *Asper Review* 63-84.

Ndzengu NC & Von Bonde JC (2011) "Legal Expenses POCA Clauses: A Loophole to Make Crime Pay?" 24(3) *South African Journal of Criminal Justice* 309-332.

Nel HS (1991) *Jones Conveyancing in South Africa* 4 ed Cape Town: Juta.

Nelson M (2009) "Federal Forfeiture and Money Laundering: Undue Deference to Legal Fictions and the Canadian Crossroads" 41(1) *Miami Inter American Law Review* 43-104.

O'Brien K (2008) "'Stein' OKs the Nixing of Government's Charging Powers" 240(55) *New York Law Journal* 1-2.

Orentlicher D (1999) "Representing Defendants on Charges of Economic Crime: Unethical When Done for a Fee" 48 *Emory Law Journal* 1339-1376.

Palmer R & Crocker A (2012) "The Payment of Trust Account Interest: The Ethical Duties of Attorneys towards their clients, and the Legal Implications of the Legal Practice Bill *Obiter* 345-350.

Paton P (2010) "Cooperation, Co-option or Coercion? The FATF Lawyer Guidance and the Regulation of the Legal Profession" *Journal of the Professional Lawyer* 165-189.

Phillipsohn S (2001) "The Dangers of New Technology Laundering on the Internet" 1 *Journal of Money Laundering Control* 87-95.

Ping HE (2004) "New Trends in Money Laundering -From the Real World to Cyberspace" *Journal of Money Laundering Control* 48-55.

Pitman A (1998) "Money Laundering: A Challenge for Canadian law Enforcement" 41 *Criminal Quarterly Law Review* 238-260.

Podgor ES (2010) "Regulating Lawyers: Same Theme, New Context" *Journal of the Professional Lawyer* 191-220.

Priestley LJ (2009) "Anti-Money Laundering A Potential Problems for Australian Lawyers" *Address to Society of Trust and Estate Practitioners (STEP) Australia – Sydney Branch at Banco Court, Supreme Court of NSW, Queen's Square, Sydney* 17 June 2009 .

Richards J (1999) *Transnational Criminal Organizations, Cybercrime, and Money Laundering* Boca Raton: CRC Press.

Rider BAK (1999) "The limits of the law: An Analysis of the Inter-Relationship of the Criminal and Civil Law in the Control of Money Laundering" 2(3) *Journal of Money Laundering Control* 209-224.

Ryder N (2012) *Money Laundering - An Endless Cycle? A Comparative Analysis of the Anti-Money Laundering Policies in the United States of America, the United Kingdom, Australia and Canada* Oxfordshire: Routledge.

Rudowsky D (1988) "The Right to Counsel under Attack" 136 *University of Pennsylvania Law Review* 1965-1973.

Schneider S (2004) "Money Laundering in Canada: An Analysis of RCMP Cases Centre for the Study of Organized Crime and Corruption" *Nathanson Centre for the Study of Organized Crime and Corruption or York University Toronto, Canada* 1-94.

Schneider S (2006) "Testing the Limits of Solicitor Client Privilege lawyers. Money Laundering, and Suspicious Transaction Reporting" 9(1) *Journal of Money Laundering Control* 27-36.

Schultz J (2007) "The United Nations Convention against Corruption: A Primer for Development Practitioners", available at www.U4.no/themes/uncac/Anti-CorruptionResourceCentrewww.U4.no 1-4.

Schwikkard PJ & Van der Merwe SE (2009) *Principles of Evidence* 3 ed Juta.

Shams H (2004) *Legal Globalisation Money Laundering Law and Other* Cases British Institute of International and Comparative Law.

Shaughnessy P (2002) "The New EU Money-Laundering Directive: Lawyers as

Gatekeepers and Whistle-Blowers" 34(1) *Law and Policy in International Business* 25-44.

Shepherd KL (2002) "USA Patriot Act: Surprising Implications for Transactional Lawyers" *Probate & Property* 26-30.

Shepherd KL (2009) "Guardians at the Gate: The Gatekeeper Initiative and the Risk-Based Approach for Transactional Lawyers" *Real Property, Trust and Estate Law Journal* 608-671.

Shepherd KL (2010) "The Gatekeeper Imitative and the Risk Based Approach to Client Due Diligence: The Imperative for Voluntary Good Practices Guidance for US Lawyers" *Journal of the Professional Lawyer*" 83-141.

Shepherd KL (2012) "The Gatekeeper Initiative and the Risk-Based Approach for Client Due Diligence" 20(4) *The Review of Banking Financial Services* 33-43.

Shuck W (1996) "The Impact of Anti-Money Laundering laws on Attorney Client Confidentiality" 19 *Suffolk Transnational Law Review* 507-522.

Skinnider E (2006) "Defining Organised Crime in Canada–Meeting our obligations under the UN Convention against Transnational Organised Crime and its protocols against trafficking of persons and smuggling of migrants?" *International Centre for Criminal Law Reform and Criminal Justice Policy Vancouver British Columbia* 1-48.

Slater D (2008) "Scales of Justice: The Right to Counsel vs the Need to Bar Tainted Legal Fees" *The Wall Street Journal* 1.

Steytler NC (1996) *Constitutional Criminal Procedure–A Commentary on the Constitution of the Republic of South Africa* Durban: Butterworths.

Sultzer S (1996) "Money laundering: the Scope of the Problem and Attempts to Combat it" 63 *Tennessee Law Review* 143-237.

Tapley T (2004) "Canada's Law on Money Laundering and Proceeds of Crime" *Asper Review of International Business and Trade Law* 35-43.

Terry LS (2010) "An Introduction to the Financial Action Task Force and Its 2008 Lawyer Guidance" *Journal of the Professional Lawyer* 3-67.

Unger B (2007) *The Scale and Impact of Money Laundering* Edward Elgar.

Van der Westhuizen M (2003) "FICA for attorneys" October *De Rebus* 33

Van der Westhuizen M (2004a) "Interpreting Section 29 and the Obligation to Report (Part 1)" April *De Rebus* 37-38.

Van der Westhuizen M (2004b) "Interpreting Section 29 and the Obligation to Report (Part 2)" May *De Rebus* 37-38.

Van der Westhuizen M (2004c) "Attorneys, Privilege and Confidentiality" June *De Rebus* 37.

Van der Westhuizen M (2008) "LSSA urges Parliament to Respect Professional Legal Confidentiality, Independence of the Profession and the Rule of Law in Amending FICA" July *De Rebus* 18.

Van Jaarsveld IL (2004) "Following the Money across Cyber Highways: A Herculean Task or International Challenge? Some Thoughts on Money Laundering on the Internet" *South African Mercantile Law Journal* 685-694.

Van Wyk R (2001) "Current Situations and Countermeasures against Money

Laundering in South Africa" 58(117) *Resource Material Series International Seminar Participants' Paper* 1-9.

Weatherford J (1997) *The History of Money from Sandstone to Cyberspace* New York: Three Rivers Press.

Weinstein AK (1998) "Prosecuting Attorneys for Money Laundering: a New and Questionable Weapon in the War on Crime" 51(1) *Law and Contemporary Problems* 369-386.

Welling SN (1989) "Smurf, Money Laundering and the Federal Criminal Law. The Crime of Structuring Transactions" 41 *Florida Law Review* 287-343.

Winick BJ (1989) "Forfeiture of Attorneys' Fees under RICO and CCE and the Right to Counsel: The Constitutional Dilemma and How to Avoid it" 43(4) *University of Miami Law Review* 765-869.

Woods PF (1989) *The Art and Science of Money Laundering Inside Commerce of The International Traffickers* Boulders Co: Paladin Press

Zeffert DT & Paizes AP (2010) *Essential Evidence* Lexis Nexis.

Zeffert DT & Paizes AP (2009) *The South African Law of Evidence* Lexis Nexis Butterworth

Yasin NM (2004) "Lawyers, Legal Privilege and Money Laundering: the UK and Malaysian Experience" 5(4) *Journal of International Banking Regulation* 364-386.

Unpublished Theses

Burdette M (2010) *Is the Reporting Obligations of Attorneys in terms of Section 29 of the Financial Intelligence Centre Act 38 of 2001 a Myth or Reality?* (unpublished LLM thesis, University of Pretoria).

Krane JA (2010) *Civil Forfeiture and the Canadian Constitution* (unpublished LLM thesis, University of Toronto).

Rose GJ (1995) *Forfeiting Legal Fees with the Proceeds of Crime: The Ability of an accused to pay reasonable fees out of the alleged proceeds of crime* (unpublished LLM thesis, University of British Columbia).

Van der Westhuizen C (2011) *Money Laundering and the impact thereof on selected African countries: a Comparative study* (unpublished LLM thesis, University Pretoria).

Van Jaarsveld IL (2011) *Aspects of money laundering in South Africa* (unpublished LLD thesis, Unisa).

Wilbern C (2008) *Assessing the Opinion of Lawyers of Canadian Money Laundering legislation* unpublished PhD thesis, North Central University).

Reports, Recommendations and Principles

Basel Statement of Principles 1988.

Basel Core Principles for Effective Banking Supervision 1997.

Basel Core Methodology for Effective Banking Supervision 1999.

Basel Client Due Diligence for Banks 2001.

Basel General Guide to Account Opening and Client Identification 2003.

Basel Committee on Banking Supervision.

Egmont Group Statement of Purpose (2001).

The Egmont Group of Financial Intelligence Units, available at www.egmontgroup.org. [Accessed on 26 March 2013].

Financial Action Task Force Recommendations 1990.
Financial Action Task Force Recommendations 1996.
Financial Action Task Force Special Recommendations 2001.
Financial Action Task Force Report on Money Laundering Typologies (2001-2002).
Financial Action Task Force Report Consultation Paper (2002).
Financial Action Task Force Recommendations 2003.
Financial Action Task Force Report on Money Laundering Typologies (2003-2004).
Financial Action Task Force Report Third Mutual Evaluation Report on Anti-Money Laundering and Combating the Financing of Terrorism (2006).
Financial Action Task Force RBA Guidance for Legal Professionals (*Lawyer Guidance*) (2008).
Financial Action Task Force Report International Standards on Combating Money Laundering and the Financing of Terrorism & Proliferation (2012).
Financial Action Task Force Report Money Laundering and Terrorist Financing Vulnerabilities of the Legal Profession (2013).
Financial Action Task Force Report Mutual evaluation report 7.
Financial Action Task Force "About Us", available at http://www.FATF-gafi.org/pages/aboutus/ [Accessed on 25 March 2013].
Financial Action Task Force "Members and Observers", available at
http://www.fatf-gafi.org/countries/s-t/southafrica/[Accessed on 18 June 2012].
Financial Action Task Force FAQ "What is money laundering", available at: http://www.fatf-gafi.org [Accessed 21 February 2014].
Financial Action Task Force "2020 Mandate ", available at http://www.FATF-gafi.org/media/FATF/documents/FINAL%20FATF%20MANDATE%202012-2020.pdf [Accessed on 25 March 2013].
Financial Action Task Force "Mutual Evaluations" available at http://www.FATF-gafi.org/topics/mutualevaluations/documents/mutualvaluationofsouthafrica.html. [Accessed 25 March 2013].
Financial Intelligence Centre Guidance Note 3-4.
Reports from FINTRAC available at
http://www.fintrac-canafe.gc/intro-eng.asp. [Accessed 1 April 2015].
Report from the Commission to the European Parliament and the Council [2012 Commission Report] (11 April 2012).
Department of Finance's June 2005 consultation paper Enhancing Canada's Anti-Money Laundering and Anti-Terrorist Financing Regime Consultation Paper (June 2005).
The FLSC Submission in Response to Finance Canada's Enhancing Canada's Anti-Money Laundering and Anti-Terrorist Financing Regime consultation: (30 September 2005).
Financial Intelligence Centre Consultation Document Relating to the Commencement of Section 31 of the Financial Intelligence Centre Act 38 of 2001 as Amended.
Financial Intelligence Centre Guidance Note 05 on Section 28 of the Financial Intelligence Centre Act, Act 38 of 2001.
Wolfsberg Principles.

Legal Professional Rules
USA
The Voluntary Good Practices Guidance for Lawyers to Detect and Combat Money Laundering and Terrorist Financing (Good Practices Guidance) United States.
ABA Model Rules of Professional Conduct United States.
ABA House of Delegates Resolution 104 of 2003.
ABA House of Delegates Resolution 300 of 2008.
Canada
Canada Chronology, (2003) "Money Laundering Chronology of events" Federation of Law Societies of Canada (FLSC) and the Canadian Bar Association (CBA) (1-18).
Model Rules to Fight Money Laundering and Terrorist Financing.
SOUTH AFRICA
General Council of the Bar of South Africa: Uniform Rules of Professional Conduct.
Law Society of Free State, available at
http://www.fs-law.co.za/content/fica_circ.pdf. [Accessed on 20 August 2014].
Rules of the Cape Law Society.
Rule 70 of the Rules of the Law Society of the Northern Provinces.
List of Internet Sources
Anonymous "Rael-Levitt steps down as CEO of Auction Alliance-Investec-responds to accusations", available at
http://www.myproperty.co.za. [Accessed on 10 September 2014].
"Black market pesos exchange", available at http://money.howstuffworks.com. [Accessed 21 on September 2014].
Broughton T "Amigo Lawyers in Dock", available at http://www.iol.co.za. [Accessed on 25 June 2012].
Chong C "Federation of Law Societies of Canada (FLSC) v Canada: Lawyers exempt from obligation under proceeds of crime law", available at http://www.law.ualberta.ca. [Accessed on 25 June 2013].
Cooley LPP "4th Anti-money Laundering Directive adopted by the European Council … next stop: the European Parliament", available at http://www.lexology.com [Accessed on 2 May 2015]
Gardiner H "SCC to hear lawyers' privilege argument over money laundering law", available at http://www.canadianlawyermag.com [Accessed on 25 June 2014].
Lawrence & van Houten "Anti-Money Laundering and Counter Terrorist Financing Laws Not Applicable to Canadian Lawyers and Law Firms", available at http://www.actec.org [Accessed on 25 June 2014].
Mabanga T & Pile J "Crackdown on Dirty Money", available at http://secure.financialmail.co.za [Accessed on 18 June 2012].
Marrocco & Furniss "Federation Law-Societies-v-Canada-Attorney-General", available at http://www.jonathan-fisher.co.uk [Accesed on 25 June 2014].
Moodley M "The Extent and Security Implications of Money Laundering in South Africa", available at http://repository.up.ac.za [Accessed on 27 June 2012].
"Money laundering", available at http://www.imf.org/external/np/exr/facts/aml.htm [Accessed 10 September 2014].

Oellerman I "DA seeks answers in Intaka case", available at www.news24.com. [Accessed 10 October 2014].

Peters S "Three Amigos' Trial Date Set", available at http://www.iol.co.za. [Accessed on 25 June 2012].

"Relation back", available at. http://www.thefreedictionary.com/relation+back [Accessed on 21 September 2014].

"Richard Nixon", available at http://conservapedia.com/Richard_Nixon [Accessed on 21 February 2014].

"SA joins anti-dirty money body", available at http://www.southafrica.info [Accessed on 18 August 2014].

Schroeder F "Abalone syndicate set to lose millions", available at http://www.iol.co.za [Accessed on 24 August 2014].

Stuurman J "Property Schemer up for Sentencing", available at http://www.publiceyenews.com. [Accessed on 18 June 2012].

Van der Molen "The Fourth EU Anti Money Laundering Directive", available at www.moneytrail.eu [Accessed on 25 March 2013].